Praise for *177 Lovers and Counting: My Life as a Sex Researcher*

"Part uncensored adventure story, part auto-ethnographic research, this genre-bending tale takes you on an honest anthropological journey, complete with erotic stories, historical sidebars, and personal theoretical reflections on concepts we often take for granted, stuff like intimacy, virginity, consent, and monogamy—in short, all the messy elements that make up what we call 'sexuality.' Leanna Wolfe fearlessly shares all her direct participatory experiences—the good and the bad—in stunning cross-cultural portraits of sexuality from around the world—from Thailand to Jamaica to Mexico and more. Undoubtedly, all readers (even conservative folks with slightly less than 177 lovers!) will appreciate Wolfe's underlaying question that continues to puzzle humanity: Why do people partner with one another? Answer: It's complicated."
—**Michael Mena, PhD, founder, "The Social Life of Language" (YouTube); assistant professor, Brooklyn College, The City University of New York**

"This is a surprising and astonishingly honest book by a professional sex researcher. Through the revealing lens of her own life story as a woman, Leanna Wolfe explores the meaning of various beliefs about sexual behavior in wildly different cultures and phases of life. This book exemplifies the classic anthropological method of participant observation, interspersed with the results of carefully constructed surveys on the differences between what informants say and what they do about sexuality, including Wolfe herself. There is much treasure and wisdom here."
—**Pat Shipman, Pennsylvania State University**

"Leanna Wolfe tells the story—fearlessly, absorbingly, and without apology—of a young woman's sexual awakening (her own) and maturation into an uninhibited carnal expert/educator. She travels the world to glean her fascinating perspective, emerging with a well-researched volume of great wisdom and candor."
—**Ray Richmond, journalist, author, and educator**

"The author's fearlessness and honesty about her love life and her sexual journey throughout her life are truly revolutionary and very refreshing. I especially appreciated the author's ability to convey the 'flavor' and reality of each relationship. Her experience as an anthropologist allows her to provide us with an astute analysis of the sexual mores, relationship styles, and trends of the past half-century. A totally unique book and truly a page-turner!"
—**Kathy Labriola, counselor, nurse, and author of *Polyamorous Elders: Aging in Open Relationships***

"*177 Lovers and Counting: My Life as a Sex Researcher* is a riveting exploration of love, relationships, and sexuality seen through the lens of an anthropologist and trained sexologist. This book chronicles the author's personal journey as she studies cultures around the world and navigates through her own experiences with love and relationships.

"The author's unique perspective as an anthropologist allows her to delve deep into the societal constructs that shape our understanding of love and relationships. She challenges traditional norms and expectations, offering a fresh perspective on what it means to form relationships, encouraging readers to explore their own relationships with an open mind.

"*177 Lovers and Counting* is more than just a memoir; it's a thought-provoking examination of love, relationships, and sexuality. It's a must-read for anyone seeking to understand the complexities of love in the modern world.

"From the rituals of remote tribes to the bedrooms of the modern world, the author takes readers on a journey across continents and through time, challenging preconceived notions about what is 'normal' and 'natural.' With a keen eye for detail and a deep understanding of human nature, she offers a fresh perspective on sexuality that is both enlightening and thought-provoking.

"Whether you're a seasoned scholar or a curious reader, *177 Lovers and Counting* promises to broaden your understanding of one of humanity's most fundamental and fascinating aspects. Prepare to have your beliefs questioned, your knowledge expanded, and your horizons broadened in this journey into the heart of sexology."
—Glen W. Olson, author of *Fifty Years of Polyamory in America*

"Leanna's *177 Lovers* is a one of a kind and a generous offering. She honestly shares intimate details of her erotic adventures in many different countries and from a cultural anthropologist's perspective. She offers extensive research, and she has great knowledge to share."
—Annie Sprinkle, PhD, artist and sexologist

177 Lovers and Counting

DIVERSE SEXUALITIES, GENDERS, AND RELATIONSHIPS

Series Editors

*Richard Sprott, California State University,
East Bay and President of APA Division 44*

*Elisabeth Sheff, University of Tennessee,
Chattanooga and Sheff Consulting Group*

The Diverse Sexualities, Genders, and Relationships Series highlights evidence-based approaches to understanding and serving diverse individuals and families whose relational or sexual practices or identities have been marginalized and understudied; reports of emerging empirical research on these topics; and analyses of the latest trends in cultural and societal developments on the status and place of diverse sexualities, genders, and relationships. Books in the series emphasize the intersections of race, culture, age, social class, (dis)ability, and other factors that shape the social locations of relational, sexual, and gender minorities as they intersect with institutions in fields such as education, law, medicine, religion, and public policy.

The books in this series will serve as sound and critical resources for the training and continuing education of professionals directly serving diverse communities in professions such as counseling, marriage and family therapy, social work, healthcare, criminology, human services, and education. They will also be useful for educators teaching undergraduate and graduate level university courses in anthropology, cultural studies, gerontology, psychology, sexuality studies, sociology, and women's and gender studies. Finally, these books will interest educated laypeople who wish to better understand diversity among relational, sexual, and gender minorities.

Titles in Series

Love and Freedom: Transcending Monogamy and Polyamory, by Jorge N. Ferrer
Please Scream Quietly: A Story of Kink, by Julie L. Fennell
The Handbook of Consensual Non-Monogamy: Affirming Mental Health Practice, edited by Michelle D. Vaughan and Theodore R. Burnes
Mental Health Practice With LGBTQ+ Children, Adolescents, and Emerging Adults in Multiple Systems of Care, edited by Cristina L. Magalhães, Richard Sprott, and G. Nic Rider
Polyamorous Elders: Aging in Open Relationships, by Kathy Labriola
177 Lovers and Counting: My Life as a Sex Researcher, by Leanna Wolfe

177 Lovers and Counting

My Life as a Sex Researcher

Leanna Wolfe

Overlooking the Ganges River with an Indian family.
Photo by Kathleen Rosenblatt. Reprinted with permission.

ROWMAN & LITTLEFIELD
Lanham • Boulder • New York • London

Executive Acquisitions Editor: Mark Kerr
Assistant Acquisitions Editor: Sarah Rinehart
Sales and Marketing Inquiries: textbooks@rowman.com

Published by Rowman & Littlefield
An imprint of The Rowman & Littlefield Publishing Group, Inc.
4501 Forbes Boulevard, Suite 200, Lanham, Maryland 20706
www.rowman.com

86-90 Paul Street, London EC2A 4NE

British Library Cataloguing in Publication Information Available

Library of Congress Cataloging-in-Publication Data Available
Names: Wolfe, Leanna, author.
Title: 177 lovers and counting: My life as a sex researcher / Leanna Wolfe.
Other titles: One hundred and seventy-seven lovers and counting
Description: Lanham, Maryland: Rowman & Littlefield, [2024] | Series: Diverse sexualities, genders, and relationships | Includes bibliographical references and index.
Identifiers: LCCN 2023038769 (print) | LCCN 2023038770 (ebook) | ISBN 9781538174661 (cloth) | ISBN 9781538174678 (paperback) | ISBN 9781538174685 (epub)
Subjects: LCSH: Sex. | Interpersonal relations.
Classification: LCC HQ21 .W83 2024 (print) | LCC HQ21 (ebook) | DDC 306.7—dc23/ eng/20230830
LC record available at https://lccn.loc.gov/2023038769
LC ebook record available at https://lccn.loc.gov/2023038770

In memory of my parents, Irwin and Sarah,
who celebrated adventure and free-spirited living.

Contents

Illustrations

Boxes

Tables and Graphs

Coming Out

Ifelt a tremble in my chest; it jerked downwards, causing my knees to shake. It was January 14, 2017, one day before my 64th birthday, and I was about to present my latest research to an annual conference of community college anthropology professors. I noted the eyes of my colleagues who had listened 18 years prior, when I'd first shared my findings from studying polygyny in East Africa. While these conferences largely featured reports on teaching methodologies and updates on the latest fossil discoveries, my research endeavors had largely been embraced. Despite my often-unconventional research methods—as in 1998, when I sought counsel from my East African subjects (for whom polygyny was a standard cultural practice) to resolve my partner's desire to incorporate his new lover into our relationship—these anthropology conferences continued to invite me to present my work. Ultimately, my research in Africa led to my essay "Adding a Co-Wife," which was published in several anthropology journals as well as a 2006 anthropology reader that was assigned to many thousands of anthropology students.

This time, I would be dropping an even bigger bombshell. My trembling continued as I loaded my thumb drive and opened up my latest project, "Changing Perspectives on Sexual Assault" (2017–2019). The previous fall, I had launched an Internet survey that exposed **gender** and generational differences on seduction, **sexual misconduct**, and **rape**. In presenting my findings, I came out to my professional colleagues as a rape victim. The tides were changing. The **#MeToo movement** was about to rumble, and I decided it was time to release myself from those many years of stuffing away my story.

As a part of my presentation, I shared a photo of myself that had been taken the year I was raped. I was 22, with thick brown hair and a long, embroidered dress, and was seated in an old red wooden upholstered chair.

The rape occurred on a remote, rocky promontory of the Acapulco Bay. I'd accepted a "free" motorboat tour when, suddenly, we stopped for a visit to

Photo by Carol Myers. Reprinted with permission.

Note. My mother is on the far right.

Photo courtesy of author (family collection).

a so-called nude beach. I'd landed in a no-way-out-moment when my overweight boat captain tugged off my bikini top and pounced on me. I was truly on my own, having to comply enough to ensure return to end of the bay we'd started from. I survived and followed my dream to become a professor, an anthropologist, and a writer. In the 42 intervening years, I'd kept that violation to myself. Considering the social climate wherein rape victims bore responsibility for provocative dress and behavior, I sensed there was no way to be a professional woman and a rape victim.

I decided to also have my mother come out as a survivor of **sexual assault** by including a family portrait where she, at age 11, was pictured along with her eldest brother, who had begun molesting her when he was 19, the year the photo was taken. She, too, had stuffed her story. It was only in her last years, when suffering from untethered dementia, that she freely spoke of the abuse he had inflicted upon her.

My double coming out—both as the daughter of an abused mother and as a rape victim myself—rattled the room. And then I shared my well-conceived survey that ultimately portended the ways the world of sex, seduction, and consent were changing.

The applause was thunderous. One colleague rushed forward to tell me it was my best presentation ever. It was time to tell my whole story on my terms and in my words.

A Tale of Two Viruses

Ironically, this book occurred due to two viruses: the Covid-19 virus and a computer virus. While its bones had been nesting on my hard drive for several years, it took the removal of nearly all stimulation (via the 2020 Covid-19 lockdown) for me sit at my desk every day and write, rewrite, design, and redesign this book. Once it felt complete, it was ever so hard to find a publisher. My two previous literary agents had passed away, and the publishing industry was nearly dormant. Then a kismet of a computer virus invaded, and folks I hadn't heard from in years received portentous emails from my account. While most of the recipients knew better than to click on the bait, my friend Kathy Labriola emailed me to make sure. We hadn't been in touch for several years. When she asked how I was doing, I wrote, "I am looking for a publisher for my autoethnography on my life as a sex researcher."

She suggested I reach out to our mutual friend Elisabeth Sheff, who had teamed up with Richard Sprout to create a series on sex, gender, and intersectionality for Rowman & Littlefield. Eventually, my manuscript found its way to acquisitions editor Mark Kerr, whose team greenlighted this book for publication.

What Is an Autoethnography?

Anthropologists typically write **ethnographies**, wherein we describe in detail the norms, values, and cultural practices of a tribe, village, people, or nation state. In an **autoethnography** the researcher draws upon their personal experience using an ethnographic lens, both reflecting upon themselves and their relationships with others.

I began work on this book when I decided to address the personal sex history assignment I had invited my Anthropology of Sexuality students to complete. I would remind my students that sex is much more than sexual intercourse—that it includes messages from family and community regarding touch, dress, and all manner of intimacy. As I approached my own sex history, I faced that I had lived my life as a spectator/observer as well as a deep diver. What emerged wasn't simply a *memoir* but, in fact, an *autoethnography*.

Having spent much of my 20s and 30s keeping copious journals as well as ethnographic field notes, I truly had a plethora of source material from which to draw. And being an anthropologist, I was forever filled with nosy cultural questions that I would slyly pepper into the most casual of conversations. Ultimately, I had been conducting a study of myself while studying the sexual, romantic, and relational worlds in my midst!

Research Methods Used by Anthropologists

Participant observation involves embedding oneself in a community, culture, or **subculture** to fully engage as well as reflect upon its cultural practices. While participant observation is often regarded as a method unique to cultural anthropology, social scientists from other disciplines use it as well. Here the researcher is able to access the **emic** (insider) perspective as well as to generate theory toward the **etic** (observer) perspective. In the process of conducting fieldwork, a **key informant** can emerge who is able to function as a cultural translator when they have access to the worldview of their community as well as that of the world outside.

Other social science research methods can include conducting interviews where a list of topics in the form of an **interview schedule** is used to discuss investigational concerns. A **focus group** can be convened to enable cross thought amongst a selected group of informants, engaging subjects in casual conversation (without the formality of a sit-down interview), which can also facilitate access to native concerns and practices. Certainly, the many times I went on "dates for data" fit into this research method! (Interestingly, many of the folks I have interacted with on dating apps readily ask me observer-scientist questions in the vein of "Have you met anyone on this site?") Written questionnaires that are completed by respondents facilitate **survey research,** especially when done online and with large data sets. Certainly, my active participation in **polyamory** and **swinging** enabled me to create questionnaires that were culturally sensitive to these populations.

The key for me in conducting field research has been to **think as an anthropologist**. In the back of my head, I look for larger paradigms to explain why members of cultures (and subcultures) think and behave as they do. Certainly, (as **postmodernism** contends), an engaged researcher impacts the communities they study; thus, value-free ethnography is impossible. While anthropology acknowledges that, at the core, we are all **ethnocentric** (viewing other cultures through the lens of our own), the dream of engaged ethnographic research is to celebrate the diversity of human ways through the goal of **cultural relativism**, wherein we appreciate each culture's unique way.

Ethical Concerns

Considering that much of my research began well before I had this project in mind, I could not offer informed consent agreements to the friends and associates who'd interacted with me. Moreover, anthropologists focus on culture and cultural behaviors. Not being journalists, we are not expected to disclose names and specific locations when we publish our findings.

For those who granted me permission to use your photography, I so appreciate your generosity. Being that disclosing your names would thus associate you with me, not all photo credits are included. As for professional photo citations, I did due diligence to research sources and paid fees as required. If one of your photos was improperly cited, please contact me via my publisher, Rowman & Littlefield, so that corrections can be made in subsequent editions. In cases where subjects could not be contacted, their faces have been blurred to maintain their privacy, and if we cited rights to publish under Creative Commons that was inaccurate, again, please contact me at Rowman & Littlefield so the error can be rectified.

Being that my recall of incidents and activities is mine alone, I only used full names for folks I interacted with professionally. For people who have passed away, I used their actual first names; all others have been referred to by fictional first names. Certainly, my memory of events is mine alone. Folks that I interacted with over the years may well recall what happened differently. My telling of these stories has been to illustrate a topic and/or to explicate social theory and, thus, not a multivoice perspective. It has not been my intention to cause anger or anguish in my recall of events and situations. In this vein I am not publicly thanking anyone who has managed to impact my life adventure. You all know who you are, and I am forever grateful. Your privacy is of the utmost importance.

I am indebted to Elisabeth Sheff for her above-and-beyond participation in my project, beginning with bringing it to Rowman & Littlefield and then serving as a most astute content editor. I would also like to thank Mark Kerr, my acquisition editor, who enthusiastically green-lighted my book for publication, and Lilith Dorko, who provided fantastic editorial expertise when he retired. Sarah Rinehart ably oversaw every step of the production process, and Alden Perkins was a most organized senior production editor.

I would like to thank the below reviewers, whose thoughtful comments and expertise guided our writing and revisions for the development of this book. As always, any errors and omissions are my own:

Mandi Barringer, *University of North Florida*

Debra Borys

James Fleckenstein, *The Earth Moved, LLC*

Clint Gould, *Community College of Philadelphia, professor emeritus*

Gillian Grebler, *Santa Monica College*

David Hersh, *Institute for Advanced Study of Human Sexuality (IASHS)*

Christine Hippert, *University of Wisconsin–La Crosse*

William Jankowiak, *University of Nevada, Las Vegas*

Phyllis Juster

Peta Katz, *University of North Carolina at Charlotte*

David Kaufman

Hilarie Kelly, *University of La Verne*

Elissa Kerhulas, *UCLA*

Kathy Labriola

Robert Logan, *SUNY Alfred*

Kobie Lyons, *UC Berkeley*

Susana Mayer

Emily Prior, *Center for Positive Sexuality*

Deborah Ranniger, *Nation Alliance on Mental Illness (NAMI)*

Chloe Raub, *Tulane University*

Ray Richmond

Ray Schiel

Nili Shamrat, *American Jewish University*

Ed Shorer, *Bowling Green State University*

Robert Ulin, *Rochester Institute of Technology*

Boyd Willat, *UCLA Business*

Many folks supported me through the challenges of this project, including my cousin Alan Garner, my sister Roselyn Mena, and my open-hearted friends Don Byrd, Boyd Willat, Lee Mandell, Jim Herriot, Paula Achter, Debra Borys, Gillian Grebler, and Elayne Heilveil.

I would also like to thank the Independent Writers of Southern California (IWOSC) support group convened by Sylvia Cary, with special thanks extended to the late Lila Silvern and the late Adolpus Ward.

My Life as an Engaged Anthropologist

From a very early age, I developed the ability to become a spectator of my own pain. When I was a toddler, I would hold my breath, processing the moment, before belting out tears. As I grew older, I absorbed the palpable sensations of injustice rather than seeking knee-jerk retribution.

As a young woman coming of age in the midst of **feminism** and the **sexual revolution**, it felt like everything was in flux. My parents' world of secrets and innuendos would not be my world. Being a righteous adolescent, I saw the stridency of feminism, in one moment, as appealing, and in the next moment, as a curious young woman, as ridiculously rigid. I loved exploring the extraordinary. Through travel and the praxis of anthropology, I sought refuge in other ways. I relished putting my personal travails into a larger social, cultural, and historical perspective. Just because my parents' generation publicly embraced marriage in the form of till-death-do-us-part monogamy did not mean that I would. I had anthropology's Human Relations Area File as a respected source for cross-cultural and historical variation.

Anthropology became my calling card. As a young professor, I loved to lecture on cultural variation in sexual practices and partnering patterns. I excitedly told my students how, in the Trobriand Islands of Melanesia, lovers bite off the tips of each other's eyelashes during especially passionate sex, proclaiming, "Forget hickeys; short eyelashes are a true mark of exuberant passion!"

For perspective on heteronormative **monogamy**, I would lecture on the nearly 85% of human cultures that endorse **polygamy**. I would then clarify that the dominant form has been **polygyny**, where husbands have multiple wives, while **polyandry**, where women have more than one husband, is practiced in just 0.05% of all cultures.

After I added sexology to my professional credentials, I began a private counseling practice where I would encourage my clients to look beyond the restrictiveness of their own cultures to find identity and affirmation. With the explosion of gender role distinctions and sexual misconduct becoming a public conversation, the people who sought my counsel were often caught in the intersection of empowered young women and confused young men.

I resonate with the concept of "Yolo" (you only live once), wherein one seizes every opportunity for whatever it has to offer. When getting pregnant didn't come naturally, I spent $30,000 of my hard-earned money on infertility treatments. Unable to conceive, I used my journey as the basis for field research in studying and lecturing on "How the Bough Bends: The Creation of Family, Kinship and Community Amongst Users of Donated Gametes" (2006–2009).

When my home partner got heavily involved with another woman, I went to Africa to find out how traditional women negotiate the intricacies of sharing a husband. Upon my return, I published and lectured on "Adding a Co-Wife" (1998–2006).

This book celebrates how I figured out how to make very drinkable lemonade out of some pretty tart lemons and, ultimately, live in an extraordinary way.

177 Lovers—What's in a Number?

When I began writing this book, I was tight-lipped about the number of lovers I've had. I wanted my story of how I, a shy but curious girl from Palo Alto (well before it became the home of Google and Facebook), became a sexual anthropologist. I wanted to present myself as an average girl who was a young feminist in the midst of the sexual revolution.

Perhaps the first twist of my journey was all the thinking and researching I did before I decided to have sexual intercourse. As a 20-year-old Cal Berkeley student, I feared I was nearly an **outlier** for how long it took me to "go all the way." Then my unending curiosity led me to find out how to reach **orgasm** and how humans everywhere engage the potency of sexual energy.

To test-drive being a cultural anthropologist, in the mid-1970s, I spent eight months traveling through Mexico. I packed in extended stays in remote peasant villages, along with engaging machismo by dating Mexican men. Admittedly, I was dating to gain perspective on the microworld of Berkeley feminism more than to find a husband!

I faced that I was a cultural virgin when I moved to New York City in 1977 to study anthropology at the Graduate Faculty of the New School for Social Research. Quickly, I learned to avert my eyes from the gazes of strangers and to never stand by myself on late-night subway platforms. My interest in sexual ways continued, and I titled my master's thesis "Towards a Cross-Cultural Understanding of Female Sexuality."

When many of my friends were marrying and starting families and with me being the itinerant researcher, I produced *Giving Birth in New York City: A Guide to Childbirth Options* and the documentary film *Changes in Childbirth*.

Moving to Los Angeles in the mid-1980s, I found the stage was set for me to be a spectator-researcher. I began by immersing myself in the singles culture, ultimately publishing *Women Who May Never Marry: The Reasons, Realities, and Opportunities* (1993).

Arriving in my early 30s, I'd slept with about 70 guys. Some were one-night stands (my generation's precursor to today's hookups), some were driven by sheer curiosity about the adventure of sex, others were brief relationships, and four were veritable boyfriends. For the provincial folks I'd first befriended in Southern California, my number was provocatively high.

As I explored sexual undergrounds and engaged the cultural world of polyamory, more of the people who became my friends lived sexually adventurous lives. In 2002 I enrolled in a PhD program at the Institute for Advanced Study of Human Sexuality, producing a dissertation titled "Jealousy and Transformation in Polyamorous Relationships."

Acquiring skills in quantitative sex research, I assessed that the average number of lovers for people who are not part of an alternative lifestyle was between two and four. Those engaged in alternative lifestyles typically averaged between 14 and 20 lifetime partners. Sex workers, meanwhile, may erotically engage many thousands of clients during the course of their careers. See Table I.1.

Table I.1 Context for My Outlier Number of 177 Lovers

	Number of Sexual Partners
Average folks	2–4
Alternative lifestyles	14–20
Sex workers	1000+
Leanna	177

As for how I became an outlier with (about) 177 lovers, I dated to get stories on how single folks negotiated dating as I conducted research for *Women Who May Never Marry: The Reasons, Realities, and Opportunities*; quietly fell for several married men; had an open relationship for 17 years; participated in a bit of swinging; and enjoyed the full-blown adventure of sex whenever I could.

PART I

Beginnings

Photo by Roselyn Mena. Reprinted with permission.

This section spans early memories of my trying to make sense of erotic sensations in myself by reading anthropological monographs, losing my virginity in the thick of the sexual revolution in Berkeley, figuring out orgasm (with guidance from early feminist icons), and placing my experience within the context of the **generation gap** by assessing differences between my parents' culture of privacy and deception with the emergent world of freedom and disclosure. Reflections upon the 1970s Berkeley world in which I came of age; considerations of **lesbian** sexual orientation; and contextualizing of **gay** liberation, **third genders,** and gender identity are addressed.

CHAPTER 1

Erotic Stirrings

I was once a girl who didn't know what sex was. At best I'd been able to surmise that it was highly charged. And certainly, that made me curious. I tried ever so hard to find out as much as I could . . . safely.

As a young teen in the mid-1960s, I sensed that I was supposed to wait. Despite the fact that a sexual revolution was in the making, my waiting (for the right boyfriend, the right setting, and the right moment) was largely personal. I was shy . . . and I liked to watch. I would watch young lovers tickle and tease each other on park benches and make note of every move and every countermove. Sometimes my watching would cause my heart to flutter and my head to spin. Nonetheless, watching was pretty much safe, as was reading.

One of my first ventures into finding out about sex was reading the ethnographies of anthropologist Oscar Lewis. I would bury myself in the local library stacks, looking for his reports on how his female subjects managed their sexualities. Somehow Lewis's vivid descriptions of how Mexican village women regarded their bodies, identities, and emotions satisfied me.

Growing up in largely monocultural, middle-class 1960s Palo Alto, I yearned for access to other ways. When my Girl Scout troop assignment was to bring in bright-colored yardage to make an apron, my 10-year-old self assessed that a poor child would be relegated to bringing in an old sheet. When my troop leader looked over my tattered sheet, she cut her own daughter's pretty yardage in half and informed my mother of what I had done. My mother, having come from a family of seamstresses, was no doubt perturbed at my effort to study the **culture of poverty**!

Oscar Lewis

Oscar Lewis is best known for his vivid depictions of the lives of slum dwellers and his argument that a cross-generational "culture of poverty" transcends national boundaries (Lewis, 1966). contended that cultural similarities occurred because they were "common adaptations to common problems" and that "the culture of poverty is both an adaptation and a reaction of the poor classes to their marginal position in a class-stratified, highly individualistic, capitalistic society." His ethnographies on Mexican peasant life include *Five Families*, *The Children of Sanchez*, and *A Death in the Sanchez Family*.

When I was 15, I had my first opportunity to *feel* something. I was traveling in a camper van to participate in a student exchange program in Navolato, a village in Sinaloa, Mexico. The van broke down in Hermosillo, a lively town in the state of Sonora. During the wait for it to be repaired, Roberto, a slightly older Mexican boy, reached for my hand and took me on a walk. No one had ever before held my hand with that kind of intention. I was a guest in his city and in his country. Rather than wrenching my hand from his and proclaiming I had no interest in being his girlfriend, I spectated the experience. I allowed him to fondle my hand and to guide me around the town *zocalo* (plaza). My head spun. It was all so foreign—being in Mexico and being treated like a *señorita* with some sort of sex appeal.

In that moment I transcended from being a protected, innocent girl to being a young lady. My first menstrual period had arrived the month prior; seemingly, there was no going back. Being that I wasn't a Mexican Catholic, there would be no *quinceañera*-like rite of passage where I would don a white dress, a first pair of high heels, and be presented to my community as a fertile *señorita*. Unlike with the **Muria** tribe of Central India, where young people are trained in the sensual and sexual arts in a playful youth dormitory, my culture did not subscribe to such mentoring. I would have to sort it out for myself.

In 1969 the San Francisco Bay Area was exploding with new cultural ways. There were love-ins, be-ins, and the brave and exploratory **human potential movement**. This movement ushered in sensitivity-training workshops and encounter groups. For me these functioned a bit like a **Muria** *ghotul*, as they revealed the nature of relationship dynamics. At 16 I attended an adult-led encounter group; I sat on the sidelines as participants listened to, challenged, and hugged each other. My heart was pounding, and I was scared and absolutely tongue-tied. Suddenly, Matt, a 17-year-old-boy who had been eyeing me from across the room, came over and began to stroke my hair. My breathing quieted, and the next thing I knew, he'd become my boyfriend.

We were on a walk one evening when he reached over and offered me my first deep kiss. When his pointy tongue jutted into my mouth, I wasn't exactly sure what to make of it. Like when Roberto had reached for my hand in Sonora the year before, my initial response was to spectate the experience. It triggered primal sensations akin to nursing and thumb sucking. I couldn't figure out how this was supposed to be sexually exciting.

The Muria

Verrier Elwin colorfully discusses how the Muria engage adolescent sexual socialization in *The Kingdom of the Young* (1968), which was an abridged version of *The Muria and Their Ghotul* (1947). He romanticizes the practice marriages engaged by tribal peoples in Madhya Pradesh, India, by contrasting their celebration of erotic knowledge with Western cultural prudishness. The Muria youth lived in *ghotuls*, dormitories featuring murals of the anatomy of the clitoris and hands-on guidance in how to properly engage pubescent girls.

I had landed on what anthropologists call a **cultural particularity**: something that is practiced in some cultures but certainly not all cultures. Amongst the Trobriand Islanders of Melanesia, deep kissing is not part of standard erotic practice. The Trobrianders consider it unsavory, while the postcoital nibbling of a lover's eyelashes is regarded as extremely hot.

My father did his best to deflate this first erotic experience by warning that kissing would lead to sex and that I was on a most dangerous path. In the late 1960s, teen sex was considered dangerous not because one might catch a virus as potentially fatal as AIDS or Covid-19 would one day prove to be, but because it could lead to a career-derailing pregnancy or a tarnished reputation. I really wanted to understand what was going on: "How could this weird tongue jabbing lead to my wanting to go any further?"

Then at 17, I took a solo bus trip to visit colleges. Unlike today's parents, who personally accompany their children to visit prospective colleges, my parents simply bought me a Greyhound bus ticket. On the ride down, I met a girl who was a student at UC Santa Barbara. Being that I had applied to go to school there, she invited me to stay with her. When I arrived at the student community of Isla Vista to look for my new friend's apartment, I couldn't find it. I was very much on my own in that it was nearly 30 years before the advent of cell phones!

Distraught, I wandered down to the beach as salty tears rolled out of my eyes. I had a rucksack with some basics as well as my sleeping bag; I figured I'd just camp there. Reuben, a tall late-20s male hippie with a young child, approached me. His blond hair fell to the middle of his back, and he reeked of patchouli oil. He blotted the tears from my eyes and assured me I'd be okay. After chatting for a while, we (he, his child, another woman, and I) had dinner at a little café. I munched on a falafel sandwich and waited for the evening to unfold.

Reuben, who was clearly not a student, did not live in a standard Isla Vista student apartment. He lived in a red barn. Around dusk we all climbed into the barn. The other woman soon left, and his young child fell asleep. I unrolled my sleeping bag in the furthest corner and crawled in, hiking boots and all. Reuben stripped (his was the first erect penis I'd ever seen) and called me over. I told him I'd be okay by myself. He then crawled next to me and began to stroke my hair. Then his tongue explored my ear. My belly filled with anticipation. I'd never before felt such surges; I was both scared and curious.

Cultural Features

Anthropologists codify cultural features in three tiers: *universalities*, *generalities*, and *particularities*. Universalities are found in all cultures and may be unique to humans, such as a long period of infant dependency and year-round sexual receptivity (rather than a mating season). Generalities occur in certain times and places but not in all cultures. An often-cited generality is the nuclear family. While these families predominate in much of the Western world, elsewhere there is much family diversity, including polygamy, extended families, lesbian and gay families, and the Nayar female-headed households of India's Malabar Coast (Kottak, 2011, p. 242).

He told me to relax and assured me that he would be gentle. It was so not my fantasy for how I'd lose my virginity! Eventually, I blurted out that I was a **virgin** and that he needed to leave me alone. I must have been shaking so hard that he eventually returned to his spot in the barn. I stared into the barn ceiling all night, hoping that I'd preserve my virginity if I kept my hiking boots on and stayed awake.

The next morning, I boarded the bus back to my parents' home and did not tell them a word of what had happened. The following fall, I became a student at UC Santa Barbara and Reuben still lived in the barn. Occasionally, I'd see him in the distance, and those surges of anticipation and fear would return. I'd been imprinted with his look and his touch. For many years the men that turned me on the most had long blond hair, blue eyes, and scented themselves with patchouli oil.

CHAPTER 2

My Parents' World/My World

My parents in 1949, the year they met.
Photo courtesy of author (family collection).

My parents and I were very much poster people for the ubiquitous generation gap. Their world was a world of proper public images and secrets,
while mine celebrated honesty and truth telling. My parents told me that
my mother had carefully guarded her virginity until she was 30, when she properly married my father. It was only after my Mom had bequeathed me her journals
(when she was nearly 93) that I found out that she had had lovers in her 20s. When
I questioned her about the virginity story, she explained, "Dad and I decided that it
would set a good standard for you."

For my mother the virgin charade helped hide her troubling adolescence. Beginning at the age of 11, she had been molested by her eldest brother, who was then
19. As she recalled, "He insisted on inserting his finger into my vagina as often as he
could. He would tell me that what he was doing pleased him."

This brother did this to her into her teen years. At least one time, he invited several other young males to join him in the act.

"Loose" women of the 1920s and 1930s.

From File: Marion Martin original 1930s portrait photo.jpg, c. 1930, in Wikimedia Commons (https://commons.wikimedia.org/wiki/File:Marion_Martin_original_1930s_portrait_photo.jpg).

From *Woman modeling dress and hat, half-length portrait, seated,* [online image] by Joseph, c. 1921, Library of Congress Prints and Photographs Division (https://www.loc.gov/pictures/item/89710488/).

From *Woman modeling evening gown,* [online image] by J.A. Migel, Inc., c. 1920, Library of Congress Prints and Photographs Division (https://www.loc.gov/pictures/item/2003678054/).

Her Romanian immigrant parents modeled gender roles of a dominant older husband and a compliant younger wife, providing my mother no inspiration for female independence, let alone resistance. It wasn't until his early 90s (and close to the end of his life) that my uncle placed a call to my mother to apologize for what he had done to her.

My dad did not marry until he was nearly 45, and he'd had lovers, girlfriends, and several fiancées during his bachelor years. My parents habited a culture of double standards, not just between men and women but between different kinds of women. My father explained, "There are *virgins* and there are *whores*."

My parents presented my mother as a proper, marriageable virgin, despite the fact that she didn't actually have such a status. Meanwhile, my Dad had sexually engaged (and arranged abortions for) quite a few "whores." I was duly confused!

One of the things my Dad enjoyed doing was looking over his personal stash of photos of loose (and alluring) women and former girlfriends. He kept the photos in the middle drawer of a multiuse cabinet that also held my parent's blue and white bone china holiday dishes. I was advised to not look at these photos; mostly, I didn't.

When my dad passed away, my mother made me the custodian of this photography collection. Some were purchased transparencies with models posing with their come-hither looks, and others were nicely groomed girls who smiled sweetly into my father's lens. No doubt at least some of them had been his lovers, but it was not for me to know who or when or how.

From File: Young women running over a sand dune on an unidentified beach, ca. 1935 (3841385110).jpg, in Wikimedia Commons (https://commons.wikimedia.org/wiki/File:Young _women_running_over_a_sand_dune_on_an_unidentified _beach,_ca._1935_(3841385110).jpg).

From *Women, half lgth., seated, modeling dress, fur stole, and feathered hat,* [online image] by Joseph, c. 1921, Library of Congress Prints and Photographs Division (https://www.loc.gov/pictures/item /2003662348/).

Beyond his collection of stills, my Dad also had an extensive 16 mm pornography collection. He would screen selections for male friends and relatives in darkened basements at family gatherings and parties. An older cousin once reflected on my dad's bachelor years and my own array of lovers and curiosity about sex: "The apple doesn't fall far from the tree."

Despite my parents' efforts to hide the details of their own sexualities, I viscerally sensed that beneath their careful chats about menstruation and reproduction, there was a burbling tsunami of emotions. While my father would hold me tight and tell me he loved me, my mother was uneasy holding a gaze and generally preferred not to be touched. She was no doubt hurting inside from the abusive misconduct and the culturally prescribed lie of having saved her virginity for marriage, plus all of the effort it must have taken to approximate a perfect 1950s wife and mother.

I became a spectator in response to this emotional turbulence. As a little girl, I held my breath and watched before belting out screams and tears. As a young woman, I gravitated toward **participant observation**, the primary methodology of cultural anthropology. After carefully dipping in for a taste, I would safely distance myself from erotic hurricanes by stepping back to observe, analyze, and generate theory.

When I reflect on parenting styles associated with Ainsworth's attachment theory, I see that as an infant and young child, I was a much-wanted baby and was parented in a very attentive way, meriting secure attachment. I will never know if the abuse that my Mother carried from her pubescent years could have led her to become ambivalent about touch and affection toward me as an adolescent. Ultimately the secure attachment style of my childhood gave way to avoidance and anxiety.

As an adolescent, much more was in play. Post–World War II stay-at-home mothers and gray-flannel-suit homogeneity led to cultural shifts that upended my parent's world of appearances and trust in authority. Their world of secrets and innuendos was being displaced by the human potential movement and a new culture of truth telling. With the sexual revolution abuzz, I readily faced that my mother and father were not in a position to be my confidants and that all they could do was be righteous and, in my 14-year-old estimation, "absolutely wrong!"

Ainsworth Attachment Theory

The concept of attachment styles evolved from psychological research conducted by John Bowlby and Mary Ainsworth in the 1970s. They proposed that attachment styles are established in childhood through the infant-caregiver relationship and that attachment has four key characteristics: proximity maintenance (desire to be physically close), safe haven (return to attachment figure for comfort and safety), secure base (attachment figure serves as a base for childhood exploration), and separation distress (anxiety when the attachment figure is absent). Ainsworth noted three distinct attachment styles: secure, ambivalent-insecure, and avoidant-insecure. Subsequent psychological research has culled out further attachment distinctions, including anxious-ambivalent, dismissive-avoidant, and fearful-avoidant (Bretherton, 1992, p. 759).

CHAPTER 3

Saving It/Losing It

With my parents, when I was 20.
Photo by Roselyn Mena. Reprinted with permission.

During my teen years, I thought endlessly about how, where, and with whom I would lose my virginity. There were no easy answers in that my dear parents blanked out on me, neither offering support nor guidance. All I heard was their mythical story: "Your mother saved her virginity until she married at 30."

Once the sexual revolution rumbled, I knew my mother's "story" would not be my story. I sought advice from a college guidance counselor who I felt was wise

Defining Sex

In the 1970s (and for several decades after), "sex" referred solely to penile-vaginal intercourse. Non-**heterocentric** forms of sexual expression such as **oral sex**, **mutual masturbation**, **BDSM**, **anal play**, and **cybersex** fell outside of common nomenclature. In 1998, when President Bill Clinton claimed that he "did not have sex with that woman" (Baker & Harris, 1998), it was because his generation did not consider oral sex and the vaginal insertion of a cigar to be sex. Ultimately, Clinton's contention expanded American society's limited definition of what sex could be!

and reasonable. He assured me that it would be okay to defy my parents' directives: "You will be fine making the decision on your own; you will know when it's right."

Taking this step of independence was very difficult in that I had not been a rebellious teen. I worried that I would lose my parents' love and support. At 19, in a back room at a summer party, I nearly agreed to do it but then backed out. The guy and I barely knew each other; it was simply an offer to release me from the "virginity burden." The longer I waited, the more significant this cherry-popping act became, causing even semiserious boyfriends to refuse. Despite the burden of waiting so very long, I clung to the idea that it should be loving and romantic.

The next year, at 20, I confidently set forth to make love with my boyfriend of five months, Jerry. He had shoulder-length blondish brown hair and an androgynous presentation. He was patient, sweet, and had soft skin; his sexuality felt manageable. We would be coexplorers. Being a young feminist, it was extremely important to me to be an equal. We mutually decided that I would use a diaphragm for birth control, and he dutifully shared the cost of our contraceptive gel.

Our first time was erotically uninteresting. What mattered to me was that it worked: I didn't rip or bleed or otherwise suffer. No doubt the last several years of **finger-fucking** had contributed to a pain-free penile insertion! Nonetheless, my housemates told me, "You look so different!"

On the outside all that had changed was that I had washed my brown curly mane, and without a detangling conditioner, it had spun into an unruly mess. Soon after, I informed my parents, "Jerry and I are now a couple, and we are going to live together."

My shocked parents then queried, "Have you had sex with him?" I told them I had. They then declared, "You are engaging in a meretricious affair." I then asked, "Are you going to disown me?" They replied, "We will still visit you, but we do not want to see your and Jerry's bedroom."

They met me on a street corner a block from the house Jerry and I had rented for the summer. I coaxed them, "At least come inside the house."

They relented. I then valiantly stood up to them, forcing them to look over our bedroom with the Indian-print "bedspread" draped over our futon floor mattress. I introduced them to Jerry, and they then took both of us out to dinner. My parents' hypocrisy faded as they agreed to treat Jerry as a family member.

That year was 1973, the year *Roe v. Wade* became the law of the land, legalizing abortion in all 50 states. While I would never be indiscriminate about who my lovers would be, I knew that I had an out if an unplanned pregnancy were to occur. Despite that, my periods were occasionally heavy with much cramping, which might have portended a miscarriage, and unlike the 25% of American women who have accessed an abortion during their reproductive years, I never did.

To rally a voter base for his 2016 presidential bid, Donald Trump, who previously had been proabortion, built an alliance with Christian evangelicals promising that he would work to reverse *Roe v. Wade*. He delivered by appointing pro-life Supreme Court judges Neil Gorsuch, Brent Kavanaugh, and Amy Coney Barrett. On June 24, 2022, following the court's upholding of *Dobbs v. Jackson Women's Health Organization*, which prohibited abortions in Mississippi after the 15th week of pregnancy, the right for American women to choose whether or not to abort an unplanned pregnancy ceded to state law. While states including California and New York continued to provide abortions on demand, laws as draconian as banning abortion following fertilization emerged in many central and southern states, including: Oklahoma, Alabama, Arkansas, Indiana, Kentucky, Iowa, Louisiana, Mississippi, Missouri, South Dakota, Tennessee, Texas, and West Virginia.

Despite a 2021 Pew Research study that reported 61% of Americans believe that abortion should be legal in all or most circumstances, conservative legislators tried to limit access to abortion pharmaceuticals and travel to secure an abortion. In August 2022 voters in the otherwise conservative state of Kansas turned out in unprecedented numbers to defeat a bill restricting abortion access. Then the November 2022 midterm elections averted predictions of a Republican "red wave," when unprecedented numbers of young voters turned out to secure abortion rights. Michigan, Vermont, and California enshrined abortion rights into their state constitutions. Kentucky voted down the "protection of human life" that would have further limited the states' six-week trigger law, and Montana decriminalized the health care workers who provide abortions (Yetter, 2022).

Never before had the rights of the unborn (based on a religious belief that the human soul comes into being upon conception) been pitted so soundly against the rights of sexually active women!

Across many times and places, babies have neither been named nor considered persons until their viability was established. In *Death Without Weeping*, anthropologist Nancy Scheper-Hughes chronicled the extraordinarily high infant death rate in the Brazilian village Alto do Cruzeiro. She noted that tears were not shed in that such destinies were part and parcel of ordinary life. A confluence of factors associated with poverty eased mothers who had birthed upwards of 16 babies to accept the improbability of their survival. When death arrived, nameless infants quickly transitioned into heaven-bound angels.

Whether unborn embryonic and fetal cells had the right to life was not a concern during the Middle Ages; rather, abortion was banned because it could be used to conceal **adultery** and other sinful acts of nonmarital sex. Meanwhile, wealthy families, wary of out-of-wedlock sons claiming birthright to resources, depended on abortions to ensure rightful inheritance.

In both colonial America and 19th-century England, abortion was legal prior to the quickening of the fetus (when fifth-month gestational movements begin). The medical literature of that day openly published information on emmenagogic herbs that could bring on a missed menstrual period. It was only Black slave women who had no reproductive freedom, in that their masters restricted their access to abortifacients so as to grow their human chattel.

CHAPTER 4

Orgasm Me-Search/Research

My next goal was to figure out how to "see stars." Jerry and I lived in the thick of early-1970s Berkeley, where feminists were celebrating the clitoral orgasm whilst proclaiming that the vaginal orgasm was a patriarchal myth. This all countered Freud's proposition that mature women experienced vaginal orgasms (presumably without direct clitoral stimulation), while adolescent girls required clitoral stimulation. As a young woman with limited body awareness, I was overwhelmed by this feminist diatribe. I fantasized about escaping to an unfettered Eden with an equally innocent boy and discovering the wonders of sex without any pushy agenda!

Now, many years later, as a professional sexologist, I contend that an orgasm is an orgasm. Whatever triggers it (be it nipple stimulation, anal stimulation, fingering the **G-spot**, pornography, or direct stimulation of the clitoris with a tongue, vibrator, fingertip, or well-positioned pelvic bone) doesn't actually make it physiologically different. All I knew then was that I had not yet "seen stars," and I was determined to figure out how that part worked.

After picking up a jumbo-sized tube of spermicidal gel, my next purchase was Betty Dodson's *Liberating Masturbation*. I tried some of her techniques but was not at all able to wake up my body. In my **feminist women's consciousness-raising group**, I heard about the bathtub water-spigot technique. I lived in a Berkeley group house with one bathroom and eight roommates. Being determined, I locked the bathroom door tightly, positioned my crotch under the bathtub spout, and ran a warm stream of water. Soon a fullness built in my belly, and then my whole body began to tingle and shudder. I got it. I then proclaimed to myself, "I am now on the road to owning my sexuality!"

Next, I took Jerry into the bathroom and had him watch my body engage in this orgasm thing. Following the surefire bathtub technique, I tried my fingers—they sort of worked, but I was more likely to end up with a cramped hand than a warm belly and fluttery extremities.

Some years later, I walked into Good Vibrations, Joani Blank's very first vibrator store on 22nd and Guerrero Streets in San Francisco. The store had private test rooms where buyers could sample the goods. Five vibrators later, I emerged with a very red face and a full smile. She asked, "How were they?" and I noted, "Very effective." Joani giggled, "The rooms are for *testing*, not for *trying*!"

Joani Blank

Joani Blank's small, women-friendly sex shop eventually blossomed into nine retails stores—seven in the San Francisco Bay Area and two in the Boston area. A premier sex educator, she also founded three publishing companies, including Down There Press and Good Releasing, an erotic video production company.

I became quite in awe of orgasm. As a mid-20s anthropology graduate student, I chased down monographs from around the world to find out whether women everywhere were as touched by the power of orgasm as I was. I saw it as a timeless gift that connected us to our ancestors and made several oil paintings of vaginas exploding into sensation-rich orgasm. When I stashed my worldly goods in my parents' garage in preparation for my 1975 footloose trip through Mexico, my parents squirmed uncomfortably at the paintings, causing me to donate them to the Berkeley Feminist Women's Health Center.

I was still confounded by the question, How is it possible for a woman to orgasm through penile-vaginal intercourse?

In 1976 *The Hite Report: A Nationwide Study of Female Sexuality* reported that "70% of women are unable to reach orgasm through intercourse alone" (Hite, 1976).

I was determined to get to the bottom of this puzzle, at least for myself. As I learned more about female versus male anatomy, I saw that the male equivalent of the standard female experience of sexual intercourse would be a light stroking of the testicles with minimal, if any, attention to the corona, the head of the penis.

In 2012 I completed a study, "Orgasm in America: Current Beliefs and Practices" (2012–2013), that found that "more than 75% of people over 36 do not believe that women can reach orgasm without direct clitoral stimulation." These same people reported a very low incidence of males and females being able to

Early Anthropological Studies on Sex

The frankness that my 1970s Berkeley subculture used to make sense of female sexual satisfaction was an anathema in the anthropological literature I'd engaged. In 1932 Bronislaw Malinowski published the *Sexual Lives of Savages in North Western Melanesia* based on his interviews with Trobriand Island men. No parallel studies were done on the female experience.

My cultural concerns about mind-blowing orgasms were not addressed in Margaret Mead's 1928 *Coming of Age in Samoa*. Nonetheless, it was one of the most widely read anthropological reports of the 20th century. Mead rocked the Western world, contrasting Samoan girls' enjoyment of casual sex with the stridency of American cultural ways. In 1983 Derek Freeman published a critique of Mead's work, contending her research was a slur on Samoan morality. Ultimately, Freeman studied Samoan adolescents at a later time and through a vastly different lens than Mead, who was a 24-year-old woman when she conducted her research.

orgasm together, with 2.6% of males and 1.7% of females claiming that it always happens.

My study delved into this disconnect between penile-vaginal intercourse and orgasm with graphs such as this (see Figure 4.1), where nearly half of my respondents reported that coital sex could be satisfying without orgasm.

Nonetheless, the challenge of sexual satisfaction through intercourse alone was a constant topic in my 1970s and 1980s women's support group meetings. Did I ever get there? Yes, I did! Did my personal research ever lead to a surefire formula like the bathtub spigot or Joani Blank's supereffective vibrators? Pretty much!

When I began writing this chapter ten years ago, I reflected, "This grand dream is very intermittently possible." I had settled for the thought that "following a super-explosive (non-intercourse) orgasm, intercourse can be a grounding and emotionally rich experience."

It took until I was in my mid-60s for me to partner with a man who matched me sexually. We could be fully present with each other and explore positions that enabled us to grind my clitoris into his pelvis. Orgasms would tumble through my body as we'd keep each other awake, making love over and over again.

My research on orgasms demonstrated that our bodies and our openness to honest-partner communication do change over time. The youngest men in my study claimed that they and their partners were highly orgasmic, while their female counterparts reported that 59% of the time, they were faking. The biggest fakers in my

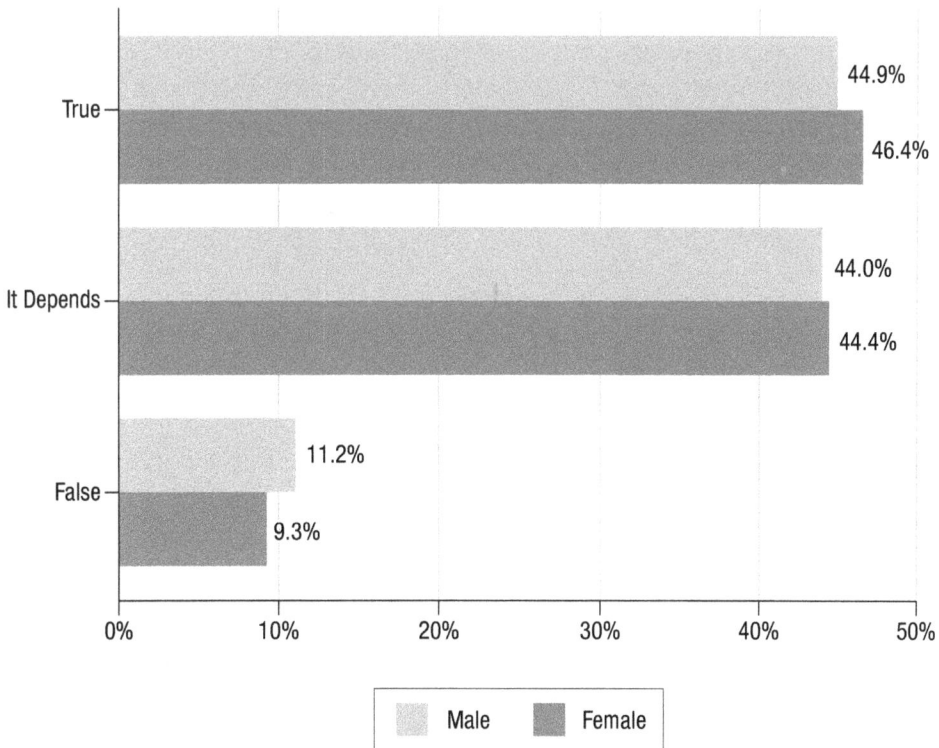

Figure 4.1. **Can Sex Be Satisfying Without Orgasm: True/It Depends/False**

study were those in their middle years (ages 30–35), with over 74% of females and 31% of males disclosing that they were faking their climaxes. No doubt agendas including establishing or sustaining a relationship for childbearing and then raising a young family could take priority over personal (and mutual) sexual satisfaction.

My own personal discovery was that once earlier life cycle agendas faded, including finding "the one," and having parented and quieted my inner chatter, I was able to relax into having better sex and better communication than when I was younger.

CHAPTER 5

Am I Gay?

Feminism in my 1970s Berkeley world merged with lesbian identity and sexuality. Women's bookstores became lesbian women's bookstores and women's cafés became lesbian cafés. I noted that I'd had much deeper conversations with near-soul-sister resonance with several of my (platonic) girlfriends than with any of the guys I was dating. I wondered, Am I gay?

One afternoon, I dropped by the home of Katrina, one of my closest girlfriends. We hadn't seen each other since she had come out as a lesbian. We hugged in a tender, sensual way. I felt her breasts against my breasts. It was sweet and, at the same time, odd. I was used to being the only one with bouncy breasts. Our sameness made me uncomfortable.

My **heterosexual** inclinations felt suffocated by the onslaught of Berkeley's women-identified political and erotic culture. I hoped to dodge it by applying to graduate school in New York City. Soon after deciding on my fall class load, I joined the Women's Anthropology Network, which collected students and professors from all over Manhattan. Much to my chagrin, following the meetings, the group would

Contemplating lesbian culture, 1970s.
Photo by anonymous. Reprinted with permission.

adjourn to a lesbian bar to drink and dance. For a moment I figured it was my destiny and tried to kick up dance energy with a gal who seemed interesting. I couldn't feel a thing and snuck out a side door, vowing to avoid all post-meeting socializing!

Mutual friends hooked me up with a nice Jewish guy, and he took me to meet his mother. She liked me so much, she was ready to plan our wedding and babysit for her future grandchildren! Then he got accepted into an MFA program in Colorado, and suddenly, we were in a long-distance relationship. I flew out to Boulder for a visit.

Meghan, a fellow anthropology graduate student, was doing a field assignment at a museum in Colorado Springs. The guy and I had lost whatever it was that made us feel matched, which led me to spend most of my time with Meghan. We drank tea and stayed up late, talking over everything under the sun. We shared her bed because it was the only bed she had. In the middle of the night, I would semiconsciously roll into her, hoping she would respond. When she didn't, I would innocently roll back to my side. When I returned to New York City, I sent her a letter confessing my attraction to her. She confirmed that she felt the same. About a month later, a large letter arrived. It was an invitation to her and her boyfriend's wedding. I shed half a tear, feeling largely relieved that my future love interests might all be men.

The pull I felt toward engaging the lesbian world of the 1970s was no doubt fueled by the burgeoning movement for gay liberation. At the time openly gay actors, politicians, and even teachers did not exist. Despite that, psychiatry's 1973 *Diagnostic and Statistic Manual of Mental Disorders* (**DSM**) declassified homosexuality as a mental disorder, and it took the 1985 decision of the nation's beloved actor-heartthrob Rock Hudson, who revealed he was dying of AIDS, for mainstream Americans to reconsider its disenfranchisement of gays.

Erotic acts that our Western world considers defining of a gay sexual orientation have had no such imprinting in other times and places. The adolescent male consorts of Greek statesmen grew up to marry wives and became statesmen themselves. Amongst the Simbari and Ettoro tribes of Papua New Guinea, boys would ritually engage in oral sex with older males to access their semen (Herdt, 1999). Ingesting this life-giving substance was believed to cause the formation of adolescent secondary sex characteristics (particularly the emergence of pubic hair and the growth of the penis and testicles). When these boys married heterosexually, their adolescent participation in homoerotic ritual transactions did not in any way impact their heterosexuality.

Across cultures there is much variance in what acts define homosexuality. Regarding contemporary sexual practices, penetrative anal sex is hardly just the domain of **homosexual** men. In my 2012 research project, "Anal Play: Who is Doing It and Why," I found that about half of my heterosexual subjects had engaged in anal play, with the most popular activity being finger insertion (85%) and the second most practiced activity being anal intercourse (78%). The incidence of male-penetrative anal sex is relatively new as a homosexual act; in 1914, German sexologist Magnus Hirschfeld reported that just 8% of gay men engaged in anal intercourse. Then, oral sex, mutual masturbation, and **frottage** were the standard practices. In ancient Greece the youthful consorts of mature statesmen also did not typically engage in penetrative anal sex. Now 80% of gay men engage in anal intercourse, with about half preferring penetration and the other half preferring reception.

In many non-Western cultures, a male who penetrates, be it an anus or a vagina, is regarded as a heterosexual. It is only the men who receive penetration that are considered members of a third gender. Thus, feminine-presenting physiological males, such as the *travesti* of Brazil, the **ladyboys** (*kathoey*) of Thailand, and the *fa'afafine* of Samoa engage in receptive anal eroticism. Their status and proclivities do not engender partnership with similarly inclined men. Partnership is based on gender: feminine-presenting people partner with masculine-presenting people, and genitals do not figure in the matching of partners.

Today, gender identity, which was relatively unexplored when I dipped my toes into the lesbian world, has compelled a massive incorporation of gender pronouns and bathroom usage laws. Transgender celebrities have gained the media spotlight, including Elliot Page, Laverne Cox, and Caitlyn Jenner, generating opportunity and respect. Still, there is a huge disconnect between Hollywood casting director's open-mindedness and middle America's visceral discomfort. This was blatantly confirmed by a 2022 UCLA law school study, which found that transgender-presenting people are four times more likely to be subject to violent victimization including sexual assault, rape, and murder.

Today, the quest for respect that gays and lesbians sought in previous decades is paralleled by the 1.2 million young adults (largely in their teens and 20s) who identify as **nonbinary**. Making up 11% of the **LGBTQIA** population and embracing they/them pronouns, they typically identify with a gender other than their assigned sex. Some, however, claim a third gender or identify with more than one gender. Being nonbinary is not at all the same as being **intersex** (1.7% of humans have intersex traits, while about 0.5% have ambiguous genitals), in that intersex people typically embrace either male or female identities.

Relative to 50 years ago, when erotic acts in and of themselves defined sexual orientation, today we very much live in fluid times regarding sexual and gender expression. This separation between a sexual act and full incorporation of sexual orientation provided me permission to play a bit further with women. Sex parties, ecstatic dance, and polyamorous connections in my 40s to 60s led me to kiss and run playful erotic energy with equally exploratory women. While I found female emotional sensibilities to be decidedly unappealing, I did share some delicious kisses with several gals.

While a younger generation of men and women feel beckoned to play with gender normativity, I find myself decidedly stodgy in feeling and appearing thoroughly female. Clarifying my gender pronoun as she/her feels redundantly laborious, though I absolutely believe all gender variants deserve a seat at the human table! Reflecting back on how feminism was eventually wrangled out of lesbian control, I do wonder if today's courtship with the nonbinary will one day fade.

PART II

Stepping Out Into the World as a Young Woman

Photo by Judith Rubenstein. Reprinted with permission.

This section chronicles two 1970s research adventures. In my early 20s, following my graduation from UC Berkeley, I took my interest in other sexual ways on the road and very personally studied machismo during a six-month solo trip through Mexico. In my mid-20s, I uprooted myself from my culturally familiar digs of the San Francisco Bay Area and moved to New York City to both engage my cultural homeland (being that my parents were native New Yorkers) and enrolled in graduate school at The New School for Social Research. There I trained to be an anthropologist and, along the way, gained exposure to sexualities I'd never before considered.

CHAPTER 6

The Gringa Studies Machismo

The men who became my boyfriends in 1970s Berkeley did their best to distance themselves from anything that reeked of **male chauvinism**. They cultivated an androgynous meekness that complemented the I'll-take-care-of-my-own-orgasm feminists. I sensed I was missing an important piece of the human experience. I wanted to know what it was like to swoon to a dominant, self-assured man. I wanted to feel the fire that Clark Gable kindled in Scarlett O'Hara. Berkeley was devoid of such men and such encounters. Thus, in 1975 at the age of 22, I went to Mexico.

Counter to the androgynous world fomented by American feminism, Mexican culture featured a fiery gender dance between *machismo* and *marianismo*. Macho men were direct—sex with women was not negotiated; it was confidently imposed. *Marianismo*, deriving from the Virgin Mary, positions women as submissive, chaste, good, and morally superior to men. A grand cat and mouse game ensues with testosteronated men imposing their will on compelling yet pure women.

Having just graduated from UC Berkeley, I wanted to test-drive my freshly minted BA in anthropology by doing participant observation in a Mexican village. While it's hardly standard behavior for anthropologists to consort with their subjects, depending on circumstance, opportunity, and personality, participant observation can take many forms. Anthropologist Kenneth Good chronicled his research journey and marriage to an Amazonian tribal woman in his 1997 book, *Into the Heart: One Man's Pursuit of Love and Knowledge Among the Yanomami*. As for myself, my curiosity and passion for deep access to human experience often sidestepped concern with safety and consent. Being a guest visitor in a foreign land, I did not expect to be on a level playing field. When uncomfortable things happened to me, I sucked it up, recorded details in my journal, and moved on. My parents raised me to be an adventuress!

My journey led me to study two very distinct aspects of Mexican culture. In the villages (I lived in several), I was the innocent *señorita* who playfully engaged questions from my hosts centered around the question "¿Por qué no estàs casada?" (Why aren't you married?).

My Berkeley feminist world was about self-actualization. Marrying would have been a "sellout" to becoming an independent, professional woman. As a young anthropologist, I would incorporate the Mexican villagers' reality into how I presented myself by conjuring up a story about an imaginary boyfriend and passionately proclaim, "When I return to home to California he will become my *novio* (sweetheart)."

The story (which calmed me a bit as well) did much to generate an acceptable persona for 1970s Mexican pueblo life. When I wasn't being a virginal *señorita* in a remote village, I was an exploratory *gringa*. Feminism had not yet arrived in Mexico, and *machismo* was king. I was very curious; having sex with Mexican men became my research strategy for understanding the Latin male psyche.

One of the first men I met was Marcos, a gorgeous 28-year-old journalist with light-brown curly hair. We met while I was writing in my journal and sipping iced tea at an outdoor Guadalajara café. I was staying with my girlfriend Minerva and her traditional Mexican family. While Minerva wasn't allowed to go out on unescorted dates, her parents could not stop me, as I was an independent gringa. With Marcos I was flung into the arms of an exciting, superseductive, confidant Latin man and wildly hurled 180 degrees from the strident world of Berkeley feminism!

Marcos first plied me with alcohol at an exclusive nightclub where the women wore skimpy dresses and the dance floor exuded the promise of full-on sex. The ladies' partners were running their fingers everywhere they could. Marcos tried his best to do the same. I was confused. I wanted to participate but felt like a deer overwhelmed by blustery headlights. Sensing my reluctance, he announced he was going to take me to a very special place. We drove up to a lovers' perch that overlooked all of Guadalajara. For a second we made small talk about the pretty view below, and then he expertly thrust his tongue in my mouth. I tried to match his energy and passion.

My brain split off from my body. Upstairs I was this anthropological researcher who was on a mission to understand the erotic world of the Mexican male, while downstairs, my body was barely compliant. I allowed myself to be just compliant enough to learn what the scholar needed to know, while deep inside, I was one terrified *gringa*. I was an unescorted young woman who had never been on such a date before. This was certainly the kind of date Minerva's brothers and parents did all they could to protect her from! I was alone with Marcos, gazing down at the entire city of Guadalajara, with no idea how or where our date would end. Ultimately, Marcos returned me to Minerva's home. He offered plans to get together again. Being on a mission of discovery rather than in search of a husband, I did not show up.

The following week, I traveled to the sleepy fishing village of San Blas. On my second day in town, I met Rafael, a sexy 33-year-old with smooth caramel skin. He invited me to stay with him in his casita, which was next-door to his parents' casa. His parents would nod "*Hola,*" but they never invited me into their well-appointed home. I was simply the *gringa* of the week. No doubt it was a post that had been filled many times before. The walls of Rafael's bedroom were lined with his large collection of Betamax pornography. Having viewed them countless times, he claimed to be a sexual expert.

I was curious what a Mexican sexual expert might know, and so again, I engaged fully in participant observation. Every night and every morning, we fucked for hours—his passion for fucking fascinated me. After my week with Rafael, I felt exhausted by attempting to match his demanding libido. I did have a good time, despite our different worlds and barely matching bodies.

Afterward I traveled to the lively market town of Patzcuaro and then embedded myself on Janitzio Island with a Tarascan Indian family. I'd been told to secure a letter of introduction to give to my host family. A librarian at a state research center agreed to write one for me. While he gathered materials for me to read, he inched up behind me, imposing his desire into the crotch of my jeans. I was startled and confused, thinking, "I didn't come to his office for this! Was this another macho cat and mouse game? Did I really need a letter of introduction?" Ironically, my Tarascan hosts spoke limited Spanish and would have not been able to read such a letter. Being a guest visitor, I had my escape strategy—to politely slip away without acknowledging this discomforting attempt at seduction.

That evening I escaped from the stresses of my high-intensity participant observation project when I met Stephen, an American photographer. We shared dinner, walked around the town plaza, and then snuggled together in his hotel room. We were equals in passion. My body and mind finally relaxed. That evening I wanted all of him—not for research but just because his soft skin felt delicious and we could really talk.

The next morning, we kissed each other goodbye, and I boarded the ferry for Janitzio Island. There I lived for a week with a humble fisherman, his friendly wife, their two shy sons, and all of their hungry pigs. We slept on *petates* (reed mats), and they fed me plenty of delicious fish soup with warm tortillas. It was my first time to live as an anthropologist with a traditional family, and I was in heaven.

A week later, I arrived in the then sleepy fishing village of Zihuatanejo. Guillermo, a classy Mexicano in his late 30s, was loading a huge amount of camera equipment into a little beach *palapa* (cottage) he had just rented. I was stumbling myself awake from an all-night bus ride.

"¿Quieres desayunar con un liquado?" (Would you like a breakfast smoothie?) He had his made with raw eggs; cautious, I accepted one with just bananas and fresh orange juice. He regaled me with stories of being a *National Geographic* photo journalist who documented deep trance peyote ceremonies amongst the Huichol Indians.

After an afternoon of swimming in the ocean, beer, and freshly caught clams that wriggled under heavy squirts of lime juice, he invited me to join him in his *palapa*. I told him about my adventure of sleeping on reed mats with the Tarascan Indian family on the Island of Janitzio. My career was just starting . . . I hoped he could mentor me.

He was a married man who wanted sex; it wasn't like me to say no to such requests. Everything was an adventure or, at least, a cultural learning experience. However someone kissed, cuddled, or fucked was all interesting. Ultimately, Guillermo's mentoring consisted of one suggestion: "Go to Maní, Yucatán."

He had shot photos of the children in the small Mayan village of Maní and noted their playful innocence. He surmised that with my own relative innocence, the town might be a good fit. Despite the fact that I believed he'd be in touch with me forever following our sweet time together, he, being a married man, never reached out to me again.

The next man I met crushed my innocence and nearly drowned my spirit. I choose not to remember his name. After leaving Zihuatanejo, I traveled down the coast to Acapulco, which, even in the mid-1970s, was a bustling place. Its megahotels dotted the edges of a striking aquamarine bay. I'd rented a cheap little room and wandered out to the beach with about 20 dollars' worth of pesos in my pocket.

A heavy-set man driving a small motorboat approached. He offered me a ride out to explore the bay. I told him I had very little money and would be unable to afford his services. He then looked me over and offered to take me out for *gratis* (no charge). In that I'd had a great time with Guillermo and had survived Marcos and Rafael, I must have felt quite invincible.

I boarded the boat and chatted politely. Soon we were out in the middle of the bay, and he told me he'd take me to a special beach that very few people know. Suddenly, we'd docked on a rocky cove with absolutely no one and nothing in sight. He told me to get off of the boat and then began to ply me with rum and Coke. I kept my drink weak, sensing that I'd best stay on full alert. He then announced that we were at a nude beach and said, "*Quite tu traje de baño bikini*" (Take off your bikini).

I did my best to refuse until he began grabbing at the strings of my bra top. I stopped resisting, hoping that we could then return to my humble end of the bay. Viewing the removal of my top as compliance, he pounced on me in such a way that I could not get out from under him. My very worst fears exploded. An ugly, over-weight boar of a man was attempting to penetrate me. I screeched, "*Soy virgen!*" (I am a virgin!).

I did my best to not comply. His ejaculate spilled wherever it did, and then my disheveled body was hauled back into the boat. Being before the days of cell phones, there was no way I could risk staying behind, presuming I could call for help. I was forced to consort with my rapist. In the middle of the bay, he announced, "*Necesito pesos para la petrolina*" (I need cash to pay for the gas).

I offered him the pesos in my purse; he snatched them from my trembling hands and then sped onwards, dumping me in the shallow water near where he'd found me. A fisherman reached out to my bedraggled being and walked me over to my little hotel. The hotel *dueña* (owner) combed out my hair and served me some warm soup. Believing there would be no justice for *gringas* in 1975 Mexico, the next morning, I boarded a northbound bus and, for many years, kept the details of this rape story to myself.

The next day, I landed in the inland town of Guanajuato. There I went to a medical clinic to find out if I was okay. The doctor examined me and prescribed some penicillin. No lab tests were performed. I presume he felt it could kill whatever it was (if there was anything) that I had been exposed to. The doctor, having had a good look at my vulva, seemed relatively unconcerned about my state of health in that immediately after writing my prescription, he asked me out on a date! I shrieked; the relentlessness of *machismo* was unbelievable! I found a long-distance phone center and called my parents. I told my mother about the ugly boar of a man who had so pounced on me that I had to comply. She pleaded, "Leanna, just come home now! You've had enough. We love you and want you to be safe!"

When Maryse Holder's *Give Sorrow Words* was published posthumously in 1979, I pored through it, noting the parallels in our stories. She was also an American feminist and a writer who engaged in risky travel in Mexico in the mid-1970s. The letters she sent to her friend Edith Jones were ultimately organized into a most tender and tragic book. While we were both seeking to resolve the stridency of 1970s American feminism by engaging the raw passion of Mexican men, our approaches differed. She participated in the culture of *machismo* with an honesty and vulnerability that I did not. I was an **autoethnographer** who, at 22, was much more interested in the cultures around me than an inner life. I was forever the spectator who was quick to put on the brakes when she did not feel safe.

To me the thought of returning home with my tail between my legs was so not how I wanted to end my research adventure. While visiting Chapultepec Park in Mexico City, I took a touristic boat ride through Xochimilco as part of my self-imposed healing. There I paid the elderly oarsman in advance and safely enjoyed pretty flowers as we punted along with other sweet boats.

With the 2017 emergence of the #MeToo movement, I began to feel less alone in recalling my own experiences with sexual misconduct. Rape is about power and not about penetration. No matter how seductively a person is dressed, how drunk or stoned they appear, how little they resist, or how vulnerable they may appear, they are not asking to be sexually assaulted. These are rape myths.

Certainly, cultural practices such as being escorted, veiled, and creating gender-specific spaces can offer protection. Nonetheless, each time I accepted offers, I would assess potential positive payoffs versus the possibility of negative consequences. Most of the time I absorbed much of anthropological, if not personal, value! At the end of the day, human erotic behavior is complicated . . . and intercultural erotic behavior is even more so. Being overpowered by a large man on a remote rocky peninsula was wrong . . . very wrong. Like my mother who weathered adolescent sexual abuse at the hands of her brother, I chose to keep the hurt to myself and to forge ahead with my career and my dreams. My choice to stuff my pain and misfortune was what women throughout most of human history have done. Like all my sisters before me, I chose not to live my life as a victim.

Disparities in the Incidence of Rape

There is considerable variation in how rape is defined. In some jurisdictions only male-on-female rape is reported, and many countries do not consider forced sex on a spouse as rape. Victims may choose not to report to maintain privacy, because they believe that attempted penetration is not rape, or because they fear the consequences of conviction. There is a wide disparity between the incidences of rape, rapes that are reported, and rapes that are ultimately prosecuted. According to a United Nations report (Eighth United Nations survey, 2005) compiled from cases reported to the police, across 65 countries, 250,000 rapes are reported annually. Conviction rates are extremely low. The data from the World Population Review (n.d.) on rape statistics note that 70% of women experience physical and/or sexual violence in the course of their lives, less than 40% seek help, and just 10% attempt legal prosecution. In the United States, just 9% of rapes get prosecuted, and only 3% of rapists serve time in prison.

In 1990 resilience training emerged as a protocol for overcoming stress and hurtful events, including sexual assault. Workshops dissect cultural beliefs and practices that have normalized rape culture and offer survivors tools and techniques for rebuilding their lives. Rather than scratching at emotionally bloody scabs and scars, participants are encouraged to strengthen themselves physically, psychologically, and spiritually.

I eventually found my way to Maní, the Yucatán town Guillermo had suggested I visit. I nested there for several months. I assessed it was best that I keep what had happened in Acapulco a secret. I focused on the ins and outs of local textile production, learning how to make hammocks and to embroider *huipiles* (traditional smock-like dresses). I formed lasting friendships with several of the young mothers; wrote copious notes in my field journal; and, to appear purposeful, offered English lessons to the village children.

After my first month in Maní, the tedium of Mayan pueblo life began to get to me, and I took a bus to the Caribbean coast. I stayed with relatives of my friends in Maní in Isla Mujeres and the beginnings of Cancún, which was then just an extension of Playa del Carmen. My host families watched over me; staying with them was very much a continuation of my life in Maní.

One day I decided to visit Tulum, a gorgeous archaeological site on the coast of Quintana Roo. Having no *Manileños* to stay with, I found a cheap hotel. It was the first time in over a month that I could stretch out on a clean bed; in Maní as well as amongst the coastal Manileños, I'd been sleeping in well-worn hammocks. I took a shower and then spread myself out on the bed to masturbate. I thought about Betty Dodson's suggestions in *Liberating Masturbation* and took some time to appreciate my still, beautiful body and to focus on my breathing. As my breathing intensified and I began to quietly moan, I heard a man excitedly hissing. I looked up and noted that the walls to my very cheap room did not extend to the ceiling. A janitor was looking down at me. I shrieked. He began banging at my door. I screamed, "¡Quítate!" (Get out!).

Being a young anthropologist in Maní.
Photo by anonymous. Reprinted with permission.

I quickly threw on some clothes, ran down to the reception desk, and reported that the janitor was peering into my room while I was dressing. The receptionist would not refund my money for a very odd-sounding incident; I felt too mortified to admit that the janitor had witnessed me touching my vulva and had attempted to dive in.

While Betty Dodson and all of the feminists of North America might have argued that I had a God-given right to masturbate in privacy, back in Tulum in 1976, there was no courtroom in which to duke it out between my weirdly enlightened culture and Mexico's then endemic *machismo*. Fearing for my safety, I repacked my bag and rented a room in the town's other hotel, where the guest rooms had floor-to-ceiling walls. Wrapping myself tightly in all of the sheets and blankets, I breathed a huge sigh of relief when morning came.

Not in my 1970s wildest dreams would I have imagined the emergence of **consent training** or the #MeToo movement. The self-defense classes I enrolled in following the rape were designed to build confidence to effectively negotiate physical aggression. The thought that a partner might ask permission before imposing a kiss, a hug, or a bit of groping was unheard of. I essentially viewed seduction as a cat-and-mouse game that was edgy, potentially exciting, and possibly dangerous. I did not consider the world around me to be safe. I expected to hear catcalls and aggressive whistling when walking by a construction site. I learned to act as if I heard nothing and to keep walking. I distrusted compliments from all strangers. I had little idea of what I wanted for myself sexually; I was largely skilled at saying no. Moreover, I expected my ardent boyfriends to convert my "No" into "Maybe" and that "Maybe" into a quiet, little "Yes" (Farrell, 1986). I had no experience in using words to describe what I wanted.

CHAPTER 7

Discoveries and Dalliances in Late 1970s New York City

In the fall of 1977, I entered a master's in anthropology program at the graduate faculty of the New School for Social Research in Manhattan. With classes meeting in the evenings, my days were free for work and community research. I volunteered with a Lower East Side oral history project, offered a workshop on **cultural imperialism** at a progressive community center, and studied feminist/**Marxist anthropology** and **political economy**. One summer I worked with young people in central Brooklyn. I taught them interviewing and oral history techniques, ultimately creating *Flatbush From the Youth Perspective: Histories, Research and Stories of Afro-American and Caribbean Youth*. Pacifica Radio personality Dennis Bernstein, who was then a WBAI radio producer, created a lovely feature profiling the students and the book.

When I arrived in New York City, I was a cultural virgin. One night, while waiting for the subway at Astor Place, I found myself alone on the platform about ten feet away from a man who was staring into me while furiously stroking his cock. I ran toward the stairs and waited on the landing with my ears trained on the rumble of the next train. As a distant rumble sounded, I ran down the stairs only to discover it wasn't my train. The guy was right there where I left him, with his pants still open. I charged up the stairs again, my heart pounding with chest-gripping fear. Eventually my train arrived; once home, my head would not stop spinning. As I became a more seasoned straphanger, I learned to avoid empty platforms by inching toward groups of strangers or staying near the station agent and only heading downstairs when I was absolutely sure a train was on its way. In that taxis were well beyond my graduate-student budget, my other strategy for avoiding these uncomfortable encounters was to stay over wherever my late-night forays ended.

One night Juan, a Dominican grad student, invited me over for dinner. He shared a small apartment with his identical twin brother, Carlos. We got stoned and talked about philosophy and the human condition for hours and hours. At about 2:00 a.m., I asked, "Can I sleep over?"

Being that they were identical twins, I was equally attracted to both of them. Nonetheless, Juan made sure that I slept with him and not his brother. Eventually, the chatter transitioned into kissing and quietly turning each other on while equally interesting Carlos snored away.

The following year, I met Tom, a short, intense Italian American with curly auburn hair. He sported a newly minted PhD in anthropology from Columbia University and had a wild, unruly side that readily matched mine. We first met at the dawn of 1979 at a crowded New Year's Eve party on the Upper West Side. Despite the fact that I had arrived with a date, Tom and I flagrantly flung ourselves across the dance floor. We then chatted about his soon-to-be-published book based on his dissertation fieldwork. I slipped Tom my phone number, advising him not to call right away, in that I was leaving for California the next day. Meanwhile, my date was decidedly perturbed that Tom and I were so drawn to each other.

Several weeks later, I attended an anthropology seminar at Columbia University featuring Richard Lee's work on hunter-gatherer cultural and economic practices. Tom was in attendance. I could not get my eyes off of him. As the crowd dispersed, I approached him. He grinned, "Of course I remember you! But I was reluctant to call—your situation sounded complicated."

He wrote his number on a scrap of paper. The next week, I invited him over for dinner. He spoke about the fieldwork he had done in the slums of Naples. I was captivated. Like me, he was drawn to the gritty underworld and had the capacity to go deep to capture every nuance. After dinner we walked ten blocks over to his place. He lived in a studio apartment furnished with a small dining table, a couple of chairs, and two single beds. We were in no particular rush to make love and agreed that whatever the attraction was between us, we'd give it time.

For our second date, we arranged to see *Norma Rae* at a Greenwich Village movie theater. The movie was about to start, and he had not arrived. I went in, presuming he would join me. My experience was that he stood me up. His experience was that I stood him up in that I was not in front of the movie theater when he showed up five minutes later. He waited outside the movie theater for an additional half hour, went to a bar to get a drink, and then returned to the movie theater to catch me when I exited. He didn't see me, and I didn't see him. At 10:00 p.m. we boarded different trains back to our homes in Park Slope.

The next day I called to find out what happened. We both accused each other of inappropriate behavior! I was apparently "more interested in seeing the whole movie than in getting together." And he wasn't "a mind reader" who knew to enter the theater and grab the seat I was saving for him. If we'd only had cell phones, this would not have happened! Sadly, it was some 20 years before I would get my first flip phone. We finished patching things up that afternoon at a romantic café in Little Italy.

Our next date was a dinner party with several editors from Knopf Publishing. I downed two gin and tonics and did my best to converse with one of the well-heeled editors about my commitment to social change and activist anthropology. Tom and I were seated next to each other; his fingers were exploring whatever they could discreetly access below the tablecloth. As I munched a mouthful of rich chocolate cake, he whispered, "Let's get out of here."

I smiled, "Yes."

Outside in the blustery February cold, we shared a deliciously long kiss. My body shuddered all over. We snuggled close on the subway back to his place. He offered me some sweet apricot juice, and we resumed kissing, and then he playfully threw me onto one of the beds. I wanted him and I was scared. We matched and we didn't. I liked his rough masculinity and the way he confidently removed my clothes. I was too anxious to orgasm together or even admit that I had faked a shudder and a moan.

Afterward he crawled into the second bed across the room. I was freezing and barely slept, knowing he was nearby but not snuggled into me. As we saw more of each other, we started having amazing sex. He was funny, confident, and full of passion. I was no longer anxious—I would spill my thoughts all over the room, and he would track each one of them. We'd talk about doing engaged fieldwork, authenticity, and postmodernism and scheme about revolutionizing the **lumpen proletariat**. I would then lie back and bellow, "Oh my god . . . oh my god!"

We couldn't get enough of each other. His unbridled passion and my curiosity with the edgy and extraordinary unleashed a potent connection. I became completely captivated. In his presence all I could do was tremble and beg for more: more heady conversation, more of his Italian cooking, the red wine, and—yes—more, much more sex. Sometimes he'd slap me on the butt or pin me down onto the bed; I had no idea why it worked or why I liked it. At the time, I was clueless that any of this behavior had a name or a subculture attached to it.

Ultimately, our dating relationship was short-lived. Tom had recently divorced, having fled a working-class Long Island suburb for an erotically exciting life in New York City. His capacity for intimacy was limited. He absolutely refused to share a bed, contending, "Such an act is extremely sacred . . . it would take me a couple of years to feel that sort of bond! The ascetic scholars of the Middle Ages knew better than to share their beds!"

Bisexuality was on both of our minds. While my encounters with women were rich emotionally and slightly erotic, his explorations with men were decidedly intense as he engaged post-Stonewall, pre-AIDS gay New York. Being that I could not tolerate his refusal to engage in postcoital snuggling, we migrated to Wednesday-night visits, where we'd engage in no-holds-barred conversation and the wildest sex I'd ever known. We'd snort potent fumes from a small bottle that would raise our heart rates, producing an intensity I'd never imagined. Afterward I'd somehow pull myself together, and he'd walk me home.

My erotic life began to impact my scholastic interests. I volunteered to be a guest editor for the sexuality issue of *Heresies*, a feminist arts magazine, and I poured much passion into my master's thesis, "Towards a Cross-Cultural Understanding of Female Sexuality." I was so overcome by the orgasms I was experiencing that I wondered if women in other times and places were equally moved. I noted that male anthropologists who reported on sexual behaviors had little access to women's stories and sensations; I sought to create a sexual anthropology that celebrated the female experience.

Feminist anthropologists had begun to challenge the "**man the hunter**" hypothesis, countering with "**woman the gatherer.**" I readily embraced the idea that women's labor and skill sets were important factors in the evolution of early modern humans and that cooperation fostered by hunting was certainly not just a male characteristic. The likelihood that women invented horticulture, cooking, and the rich gossip of multifaceted group living fueled my appetite for a feminist anthropology.

I started dating Sean, a political organizer I'd met over the phone. I had placed a call to NYPIRG (the New York Public Interest Research Group) for assistance in research methodologies for a school project. I was referred to Sean, who was not only helpful but very engaging. When he told me he would prepare a packet of materials for me to review, I offered to drop by his office so we could meet in person. At the time, he was living with a girlfriend and presented himself as unavailable for a more personal connection. He was tall and blond with sparkling blue eyes, slightly crooked teeth, and a delightful mix of quirky, passionate, and adorable. Like me, he very much wanted to make the world a better place.

One weekend his girlfriend went out of town, and he invited me to see *Peppermint Soda* at a Midtown movie theater. Afterward we walked in the rain along the southern edge of Central Park and then ducked into a café for hot chocolate. As he disentangled from his girlfriend, we began to spend more time together. Ours became a full-bodied relationship, where we'd go backpacking in the Ramapo Torne, the Grand Canyon, and the High Sierras; get to know each other's families; share a home; and raise several cats.

Sean had grown up in a small Ohio town in an austere Missouri Synod Lutheran community. He, too, was seeking a life apart from the world of his parents. Considering the divide between their world and his early-1980s New York City world, he, on Christmas morning, would peruse the religion section of the *New York Times* and note the services he might have attended. After a lazy morning of giggles, lots of sweet sex, and the deepest emotional connection, he would call them with his faux sermon and choir report.

Soon after Sean and I began living together, it became clear that I wouldn't be able to hang without my Tom fix. And thus I became polyamorous—some 12 years before the word *polyamory* (the consensual engagement of multiple partners) was coined. While Sean was a wonderful guy who I absolutely respected, every Wednesday, I'd find my way over to Tom's apartment for delicious pasta, **poppers,** and to completely lose my head and shriek it all out. I'd arrive home with a gooey diaphragm gently leaking the night's pleasures into my panties and curl up quietly on my side of the bed. While part of me wanted to take a shower and wash Tom away, I dutifully followed the diaphragm instructions and left it in for the prescribed post-sex six hours. Tom, with his two single beds and disdain for postcoital cuddling, had no interest in displacing Sean. While Tom and Sean certainly knew about each other—and Tom would drop by for the parties Sean and I hosted—the disconnect I'd feel sleeping on my side of the bed with the dripping diaphragm was excruciatingly private.

Thinking back, the intersection of our lives where Tom would pound into me and I'd grab all of him might have saved both of us. His sexual explorations ultimately led him to contracting AIDS; he passed away in 1995, having lived an exhilarating but truncated life.

I cried hard when a mutual friend recalled how he would gloat over our potent connection. Ah, if I could have weathered the two separate beds and thus averted his deadly HIV infection! I remain grateful to him for kindling in me a high standard for passion and playful kink.

Rayna Rapp, one of my graduate school professors, invited me to research the nascent home birth and midwifery movements in New York City. Brigitte Jordan's *Birth in Four Cultures* (1978) had just been published, which exposed how, relative to Holland and the Yucatán (where I had witnessed a quiet and simple hammock-based home birth), the medical industrial complex had begun to co-opt childbirth in North America. Women were being hooked up to fetal monitors, and C-section rates were skyrocketing. As the American story unfolded, I sensed that an applied anthropological approach would be in order and began to research a book that would celebrate the empathic synergy between an awake and aware birthing mother and her midwife.

Sean arranged for NYPIRG to publish the book *Giving Birth in New York City: A Guide to Childbirth Options* (1981). We put together both an advisory board to ensure the book's accuracy and a base of community support; we then worked together on the book's design and layout. Sean organized the press campaign, which included coverage in the *New York Times, New York Magazine*, and an appearance on *Apple Polishers*, a TV show featuring good work done by New Yorkers. To keep up with all the press we received, I would hand distribute copies to bookstores all over Manhattan and Brooklyn.

Following the success of the book, I made *Changes in Childbirth* (1986), an award-winning documentary film, which featured many of the 1980s players in New York City's natural-birth movement. Like the days I'd spectated sex as a teen virgin, in my 20s, I'd become a childbirth expert without ever having birthed a child. From a purely chronological perspective, the early 1980s (when I was 28) would have been an ideal time to have had my own children in that I'd finished my MA in anthropology and Sean and I had begun to live together.

After graduate school it was a challenge to find sustainable employment. I worked for a semester teaching at several New Jersey colleges—the commute was overwhelming with subways, carpools, trains, and a bit of hitchhiking (where the police would pick me up, admonishing me to not hitchhike)! On the days I wasn't teaching, I worked as a Spanish bilingual/bicultural research assistant for a social services study in East Brooklyn. When these assignments ended, I worked as an employment counselor for a Manhattan technical school and then was offered an impossibly tedious assignment at the New York State Department of Labor. One day the paper shredder broke, and my supervisor assigned me to be a human paper shredder. I tore two pieces of paper in half and then quit on the spot. I paced around Central Park that afternoon, determined to never again accept menial work!

I never found my way to becoming a wife and a biological mother. I worried that having children would derail Sean from his demanding career as an activist and political organizer. I admired his impassioned speeches and gave lip service to the causes he embraced. Still, I wished that he could work fewer hours, limit the size of his book collection, and make a bit more money. One of my close male friends suggested that I trick Sean into getting me pregnant in that it could lead us to good things like marriage and family. I was way too scared (and perhaps had too much integrity) to pull off such a manipulation.

In 1982 Sean and I left New York City and moved to Berkeley, my cultural hometown. I focused on being a documentary filmmaker, and Sean continued his political activism. We lived in a white-picket-fenced house where we might have raised a young family. Instead, we rented out the second bedroom to a series of roommates, and my restlessness led me to scrutinize our once-lovely sexual connection. I flew back to New York City to attend a friend's wedding and wallowed in a couple of nights of supercharged sex with Tom. I returned to Berkeley in a dither.

I tried to get Sean to slap my butt and pin me to the bed the way Tom did. It didn't work. Sean was no Tom; there was nothing that could be done about it. Our erotic appetites could not line up. Without the buffer of children, we were really stuck.

We felt powerless to rekindle the excitement of the attraction phase of romantic love, when our brains had been afire with **dopamine** and **norepinephrine**. Our brain chemistries had long since converted to the attachment phase, generating oxytocin and vasopressin, the snuggle hormones. I did not know that relationships go through cycles and that deepened passion could ignite new layers of intimacy and excitement. All I knew was that we could no longer access our early-in-love attraction-phase madness when we'd make out between sips of fresh squeezed orange juice under the table of Oggi's, our favorite Soho café; snuggle tight on roundtrip Staten Island ferry rides; and kiss under the moonlight on the Lower Manhattan rooftop of Sean's office.

I had an affair with a successful San Francisco attorney named Ron. My dopamine receptors fired up, and I would fantasize over the wonderful life I might have with him. The affair was short-lived. Afterward Sean and I saw a relationship counselor, who was unable to help us through our impasse. I implored Sean, "At least get mad at me for getting so smitten over Ron!" He couldn't. His focus was on changing the world, and I was too much trouble. My crazed dopamine receptors were out of gas. The madness of feeling "in love" again had overtaken my brain, and I reluctantly left an otherwise wonderful human being.

Romantic Love Hormones

Anthropologist Helen Fisher began discussing the phases of romantic love in her 1994 essay, "The Nature of Romantic Love." She proposed that the four phases of romantic love (lust, attraction, attachment, and detachment) and their concomitant hormones (testosterone, dopamine/norepinephrine, oxytocin/vasopressin) function as a **serial monogamy**, human-mating strategy. Humans can readily lust after a variety of potential partners but, ultimately, become smitten with just one (at a time). This intense focus on "the one" is fueled by elevated levels of dopamine and norepinephrine, which characterize the attraction phase of romantic love. After about 18 months, if the relationship is still viable, the attachment phase ensues, wherein a more enduring set of hormones (oxytocin and vasopressin) are produced. Lovers that cannot tolerate the loss of attraction-phase hormones may break up, causing a new cycle to begin with their next partner. Fisher observed a four-year itch following the attachment phase for couples that had not produced children (or another form of triangulation). They might then cut their losses and move onto a reproductively more viable pairing.

American Perspectives on Romantic Love

French Anthropologist Clotaire Rapaille (2006) reflected on the American adolescent obsession with romantic love's attraction phase, which he contrasted with the French for the attachment phase's level-headed acceptance of a mature, enduring love. Americans love movie scripts where a couple stumbles over droplets of attraction and finally gets to be with their special "one." Their favorite love songs feature lines like "The first time I ever saw your face" (Roberta Flack) and "At last my love has come along" (Etta James). They love the post-journey triumph; their cultural mythology is bereft of ways to savor sweet, quiet times.

American couples spend countless amounts of time and money in therapists' offices and marriage restoration retreats to recapture that long-gone dopamine-laden spark. The Masters and Johnson Institute's couples' workshops report that a sad 15% of couples recover and retain that spark the following year. Largely practical things keep American couples together, like raising a family; running a business; or, for later-life couples, companionship and caretaking. While there are erotic tricks and communication strategies that can jump-start an emotionally and erotically flattened relationship, enduring partnership is fundamentally survival-based.

PART III

Adult Sex Education

Traditionally, human cultures provided emerging adolescents with hands-on sex education. In that my culture did not (and I was intent on learning everything I could), my chapter "Learning About Sex" follows my anthropological reading alongside the learning I accessed by volunteering with the Los Angeles Sex Information and Helpline, engaging **More University**, and exploring American tantric sex practices, G-spot massage, and **female ejaculation**. In "Forays Into Alternative Sexualities," I employ my novice inquisitiveness to explore the worlds of BDSM and swinging.

CHAPTER 8

Learning About Sex

Growing up, I never managed to walk into my parents' room while they were having sex—I knew they were affectionate but could not picture what that looked like. The first time I witnessed sexual intercourse was walking in on my freshman college roommate, Akiko, and her boyfriend Richie on the bunk bed above mine. Akiko would giddily proclaim, "We're fucking!"

I would distance myself from their moment, sensing that whatever they were doing was not for me. At best I was a slightly curious and somewhat tolerant spectator. I noted the activity and waited patiently for their pounding and giggling to end so the bed would stabilize and I could get some sleep.

My meager adult sex education was a far cry from how the girls in the freewheeling Polynesian Island of Mangaia were schooled in the erotic arts (Marshall, 1971). Teaching young girls how to achieve orgasm (and become multiorgasmic) was a community project, with instructions provided by older women and tutelage offered by skilled male partners.

I readily became overwhelmed by my college boyfriends' knowledge about how to stimulate my body: my nipples, earlobes, the back of my neck, and even the backs of my knees prickled excitedly when touched! Intense erotic sensation scared me. My escape fantasy was to be on a desert island with a very cute and equally inexperienced boy so we might figure it out together . . . I forged ahead, and by 22, I'd had more than the American average of two-to-four lifetime partners, and by 25, I'd surpassed the 10-to-14 lifetime partner median found in the surveys I eventually designed as a sexological researcher.

As a young woman, I discovered that, for me, sex was largely the culmination of deep (and seductive) conversation. The synergy of mind and soul and the pounding of my heart compelled hugging and touching and all of the rest. I sought access to the essence of the men who became my lovers. To me, none of my partners, no matter how brief the relationship, was ever casual. It was never indiscriminate; each time, there was a potent seduction and sincere interest.

The day after I graduated from UC Berkeley, one of my favorite professors seduced me. Being that I was no longer a student and he was no longer my professor, it was technically legal. At the same time, we were not on equal footing. He was nearly 20 years my senior and partook in a sexuality I knew nothing about. He growled and shrieked, while I remained quiet and quizzical. While I knew about orgasm, whatever he was doing with all of the pounding, yelling, and sweating was beyond me. As a student, I'd felt like he was a mentor, but as a barely adult college graduate, I was quite confused. I didn't want to say no, but my body wasn't saying yes. While I certainly wasn't coerced, the dynamic of him having been my favorite professor made me decidedly uncomfortable.

Despite the shared body of knowledge that the feminist women's health movement developed (including the 1971 publication of *Our Bodies, Ourselves*), I sensed that feminism was pretty prudish when it came to sexual learning. Sexual intercourse was portrayed as a patriarchal ruse, with feminist literature expounding on "The Myth of the Vaginal Orgasm."

As lesbian separatists steered the women's movement toward their own passions and proclivities, being a heterosexual with a tinge of bi-curiosity, I felt left in the dust. Solace arrived through the 1972 publication of *The Joy of Sex*; the sheer variety of coyly drawn positions awakened my curiosity. I hoped to find a partner who would be game to try them all! Largely, I read about sexual educations in other times and places, especially the inner worlds of shared partners, ideologies, and practices.

I was captivated by the idea of erotic training as I discovered details of the 19th-century Oneida community's 500-person group marriage in upstate New York. According to the dictates of self-styled preacher John Humphrey Noyes, monogamous partnering was banned, as was partner dancing (circle dancing was practiced, as were group projects like quilting bees). To prevent pregnancy, *coitus reservatus* was implemented (which required men to engage in nonejaculatory orgasm). Considering the previous century's travails with uncontrolled pregnancy and perilous childbirth mortality rates, this was considered an excellent innovation.

In that training was needed to effectively practice *coitus reservatus*, postmenopausal women were assigned the task of initiating (i.e., training) the adolescent boys. When the community decided to reproduce, the ascending fellowship, comprised of the community's older male leaders, created the **stirpiculture breeding program**, declaring that they would be the inseminators of the next generation. This decision, understandably, did not sit well with the male age-mates of the community's fertile females. Once word of the practice leaked out, child abuse accusations were hurled, and the Oneidans were forced to disband.

I savored William and Jean Crocker's ethnography, *The Canela: Bonding Through Kinship, Ritual and Sex*. Details of the Amazonian Canela tribe group sex festivals were disclosed, wherein women would joyfully make love to a series of age-mates. The tribal community knew (and discussed) each other's proclivities, such as wetness, speed, and intensity. The thought of a world where members might engage in such intimate conversation very much intrigued me.

I also admired the survival logic behind the Canela's practice of **partible paternity**. Here deep community bonds would be generated resulting from the belief (not informed by cell biology!) that a pregnant woman's multiple lovers would each pass on personal qualities to her in-utero fetus. Once born, these lovers would then function as protectors, providers, and teachers throughout the child's life.[1]

When I got my hands on *Human Sexual Behavior: Variations in the Ethnographic Spectrum*, a 1971 collection by Donald Marshall and Robert Suggs, I pored

---

1. For more information and photos of the Canela tribe, see Siasi/Sesai. (2012). *Canela Apanyekrá*. Povos Indígenas No Brasil. https://pib.socioambiental.org/en/Povo:Canela_Apanyekrá

The Myth of the Vaginal Orgasm

"The Myth of the Vaginal Orgasm" was first published in 1970 in the feminist journal *Notes From the Second Year*. It gained traction as a seminal text and was republished as a freestanding book/pamphlet. It argued that contemporary understandings of female pleasure were an inaccurate product of a male-dominated society—that the clitoris (best accessed through direct stimulation) was the source of female pleasure and not penile-vaginal intercourse. The essay contended that "women have been defined sexually in terms of what pleases men . . . we are fed the myth of the liberated woman and her vaginal orgasm—an orgasm which in fact does not exist" (Koedt, 1970). It referenced Freud's contention that the clitoral orgasm is adolescent and that mature women transfer the source of orgasm to the vagina. It went on to propose that women who report vaginal orgasm either misunderstand their own anatomies or are faking orgasm to fit into male-defined notions of sexual normalcy. Portentously, it warned that men might become "sexually expendable" once the clitoris alone becomes recognized as the female center of pleasure . . . thus making heterosexuality an option, leading women to prefer the companionship and sexuality of other women (Koedt, 1970).

First Publication of *The Myth of the Vaginal Orgasm*.

Oneida Community, circa 1850.
Photo courtesy of the Oneida Community Mansion House. Reprinted with permission.

through Marshall's account of sex education on the South Pacific island of Mangaia. There adolescent boys are provided hands-on instruction by older women to ensure they learn a variety of positions focusing on how to pleasure women. Older women taught girls how to masturbate to orgasm; girls might also learn orgasmic techniques from their well-schooled male partners. A boy who failed to bring a girl to orgasm could get a bad reputation; a girl who had been so failed would readily seek a better-skilled consort, never once considering herself to be inorgasmic!

In the late 1980s, I became a volunteer for the Los Angeles Sex Information Helpline. Via weekend workshops I was invited into a shared body of knowledge and language that could facilitate deeper emotional and sensual communication. I was trained to answer helpline callers' questions about how to bring a woman to orgasm, how to perform **fellatio** and **cunnilingus**, and how to apply lube for comfortable anal sex. While I had not actually engaged these activities with any level of personal confidence, being the one to offer such guidance was thrilling.

In the early 1990s, I began to attend Mark Groups, which functioned as a recruiting arm for More University's hands-on human sexuality workshops. I traveled to More University's hub in the San Francisco area, hoping to access something akin to the world of the Canela. I attended a party hosted at one of the "Morehouses" and met Doug and his wife, Lynn. Lynn encouraged me to dance and flirt with Doug. According to More ideology, the excitement he generated with me would then be received by her to ultimately expand pleasure and intensity in their relationship.

What might otherwise cause jealousy was converted into turn-on. I really wanted to have a "do-date" with Doug, but because I wasn't a screened member of More University, I was considered off-limits. (The only way I could test-drive his fingers was to turn over my bank account, submit to a series of STD tests, and wait for six months.) Being more committed to anthropology than to joining a cultish group, I instead tempted him to make out with me in a backyard nook. He kissed well . . . I did want more—no doubt my appetite for such data was quite voracious!

I then wrote an essay detailing my exploration of the culture of More University, which I sent to Lynn and Doug. It found its way to the organization's public relations department, and suddenly, all hell broke loose. My unorthodox research methods were challenged, and I was admonished to not publish my paper in that I had not acquired my data through proper channels. Being that Lynn and Doug were not spokespeople for the organization, I'd seemingly engaged them for my own purposes, and my findings relative to the public image the university had for itself were decidedly at odds. While I believed I had uncovered the truth—that More University was a publicity-wary sex cult that charged exorbitant fees for hands-on training in **expanded orgasm**—I, lacking a legal team, stuffed the story into the nether reaches of my hard drive.

Meanwhile, my social-erotic community in Los Angeles had begun to grow. I participated in a workshop where I was required to practice touch technologies with class members. Armed with boxes of latex gloves, lube, condoms, and dental dams, we engendered a grand group conversation. Our group was instructed to follow a training cycle wherein we'd first show appreciation for what a partner was doing, correct their technique, compliment them on how much better they had become, offer more microcorrections with many more compliments, and then, ultimately, moan in appreciation! My favorite moment was when two decidedly heterosexual men were instructed to demonstrate how to deep kiss using plastic wrap as protection. I could not stop giggling about that kiss!

Love and intimacy coach Mare Simone invited me to one of her first tantric *pujas* to experience the raising of erotic energy with one partner after another, with

More University

More University was the brainchild of Victor Baranco, a charismatic used-appliance salesman. Beginning in 1968 Baranco sought to conduct social research on pleasurable group living via an erotic-pleasure-oriented curriculum. Doctoral degrees (lacking standard accreditation) were granted until 1997. The More philosophy was that women have large sexual appetites that men must learn how to satisfy; once satisfied, a woman will enthusiastically pleasure her man. The process prescribed to satisfy a woman was the "do-date." Here the upper right quadrant of a woman's clitoris would be lightly stroked with a single finger. This activity was practiced amongst all of the safe-sex-bonded members of the residential Morehouses. It might lead to orgasm, but there was no expectation that it had to, and intercourse was not expected to follow. Today More University functions online as Lafayette Morehouse (http://www.lafayettemorehouse.com/).

One Taste

In 2001 Nicole Daedone founded One Taste, which adapted the "do-date" into the practice of **orgasmic meditation (OM)**. A San Francisco State University graduate in gender communications, she engaged in More University training in the 1990s. Daedone assessed that the upper left quadrant of the clitoris was the prescribed spot for gentle stroking; the process was considered an end in and of itself, with no orgasmic splash (climax) desired or expected. One Taste also offered live-in as well as external workshops and trainings. While More University do-dates were reciprocal, with women hand pleasuring men, One Taste was wary of providing training for the pleasuring of men by women. Like More University, very high fees were charged for demonstration-based classes. The goal of orgasmic meditation (delivered by males to females) was to train the male to focus fully on the woman and her response. As a woman's excitement built, the man (and all others in the room) were encouraged to connect with her body's vibrations.

the goal of shared group enlightenment rather than simply a couple of orgasms with one partner. I got horribly dizzy and nauseous—the experience of engaging so many different men (whom I barely knew) must have been viscerally revolting. Thinking that maybe it was a male-energy problem, Mare invited me to a women's-only fire-breath orgasm workshop. Here ten women laid on their backs with their heads in the center of her small living room and hyperventilated in unison. The more I tried to match the group's ferocity, the dizzier I got. The vision was beyond sweet, but the execution still turned my stomach.

By the mid-1990s, the conversation in my erotic community became focused on the G-spot and the possibilities of female ejaculation. My lover at the time knew how to finger mine just perfectly. While our partnership was short-lived, he'd awakened my appetite! Soon after I was invited to a screening of a female ejaculation film. I could not believe my eyes—it looked like a waterfall was splashing out of the actress. I wondered if it was special effects or if a mere mortal such as I could have such an experience. To conduct primary research on this possibility, my partner and I developed a cycle wherein we'd rotate between oral sex, G-spot massage, and full-on intercourse. The G-spot massage would eventually produce bed-wetting ejaculations, which we'd then follow with more intercourse, which enabled my body to calm down and bask in gorgeous waves of afterglow.

The Clitoral System

In 2005 Australian urologist Helen O'Connell, through dissection research, assessed that the clitoris is ten times larger than was previously believed (being that 90% of its structure is internal). This discovery would then incorporate the G-spot as part of the system as well as explain why women who have been subjected to a clitoridectomy (where the head is surgically removed) can still be orgasmic.

The G-Spot and Female Ejaculation

Sexologist Beverly Whipple named the G-spot for Ernst Gräfenberg, a German physician who first noted the erotic zone on the anterior wall of the vagina adjacent to the urethra. In 1982 Whipple authored *The G-Spot and Other Recent Discoveries About Human Sexuality*, wherein her research on postcoital vaginal fluid was discussed. Though initially this ejaculate was believed to be urine, Whipple's analysis determined that it was, in fact, a milky prostate enzyme that is produced by the Skene's gland. Even today the existence of the G-spot is widely contested: some scientists contend that it is an extension of the clitoris, while others believe it is a distinct part of the vagina. When a woman squirts copious amounts of fluid, the substance expelled through the urethral opening contains a bit of skene's gland ejaculate mixed with odorless, watered-down urine.

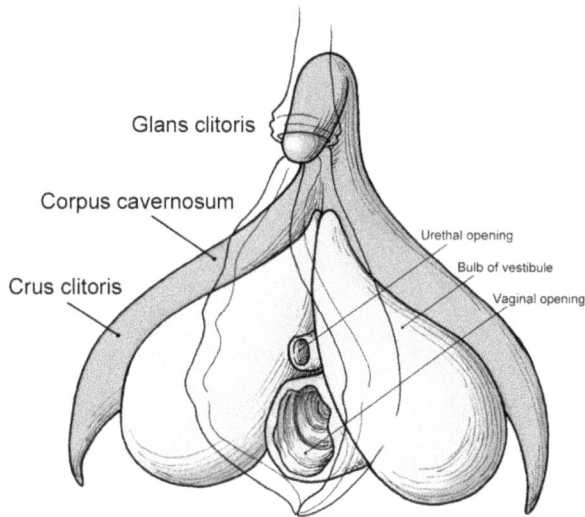

Glans clitoris

Corpus cavernosum

Crus clitoris

Urethal opening

Bulb of vestibule

Vaginal opening

The full clitoris.
Image by Amphis, 2007. (https://commons.wikimedia.org/wiki/File:-Clitoris_anatomy_unlabeled.jpg).

As sex education and research as well as pornography began to habit the Internet, all the experiential research I did in my 20s and 30s became available at the swipe of a mouse. Upon reflection, I saw that my methods and curiosity had taken me on an amazing journey!

CHAPTER 9

Forays Into Alternative Sexualities

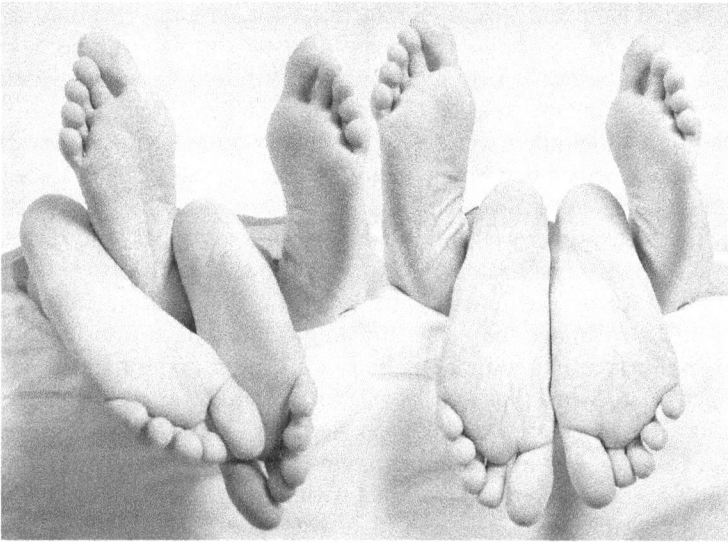

Image © SeanShot/E+/Getty Images.

I came of age in 1970s Berkeley, where no one in my world practiced strict monogamy. Soon after I'd had sex with my first lover, Jerry, I became curious about what other guys were like, noting, "How else might I find out about my erotic potential unless I conduct primary research?"

In New York during the late 1970s and early 1980s, I continued to have open relationships. My partner Sean and I had an understanding that experimenting and exploring with other people was completely acceptable. On Wednesday nights I'd see my wild lover Tom to offset the relatively vanilla sex I was having at home.

Tracking BDSM

Soon after I arrived in Los Angeles in 1986, I tracked down the BDSM scene, hoping to land a sexually exciting relationship. The first group I found was Threshold, a social club that offered introductory and educational meetings as well as dungeon parties. I went to an introductory meeting, which met in a nondescript room with rows of metal folding chairs.

An extroverted guy named Bill waved a ping pong paddle to call the group to order. The paddle was then passed around the room as each attendee whacked it in the air and introduced themselves. That week I had placed a personals ad in the *LA Weekly* requesting an adventurous partner who might want to date an anthropologist. Greg, an archaeologist who was well-seasoned in alternative lifestyles, was seated several rows in front and had just read my ad. Once my turn came to wave the paddle in the air and say something about myself, Greg became quite certain I was the writer of the ad he had just read. Following the meeting, he approached me, "Are you the anthropologist who wrote that ad?" I nodded, "Yeah, that's me."

We laughed at the coincidence of him being able to meet up with the writer of the intriguing ad so very quickly! We immediately started dating . . . and experimenting. We tried light bondage, spanking, and then, we went to a dungeon party.

When we walked in, I saw Stan, a guy I knew through another social circle, chained to a table. He was surrounded by several onlookers and was being mercilessly whipped by someone wearing a black hood. When I lunged toward the table to save him (in that the others were doing absolutely nothing), I was quickly ushered away. I was then informed that Stan was involved in a *consensual act* and that he had a safe word he could use if the whipping became too much for him. In this unique subculture, there were microspecific vocabularies that were used to define consent. A **masochist** could freely yell and scream, but the scene would continue until the agreed-upon safe word was uttered or the **sadist** was done with their performance.

I continued to wander the party and found more hard-to-believe consensual behavior. There was a man with a gag ball in his mouth who handed me a paddle and motioned me to whack his butt. A stark-naked guy was locked up in a cage. A woman hung from a ceiling hook received electric shocks via a wireless device that controlled a ball that was lodged in her vagina. Following each intervaginal shock, her whole body jerked, and the room filled with her screams.

While all I wanted was to be held down by a partner's hands and lightly spanked (which was barely the purview of Threshold), I became very curious about the psychology of dominance and submission. There were **dominatrices, submissives,** and **switches** (people who enjoyed playing both ends of the spectrum). *Prodoms* were paid professionals whom submissives hired to expertly meet their needs. Submissives, who enjoyed controlling the vagaries of a scene, "topped from the bottom." I figured that since I wanted to experience all aspects of this fascinating world, I must be either be a switch or a submissive, who likes topping from the bottom!

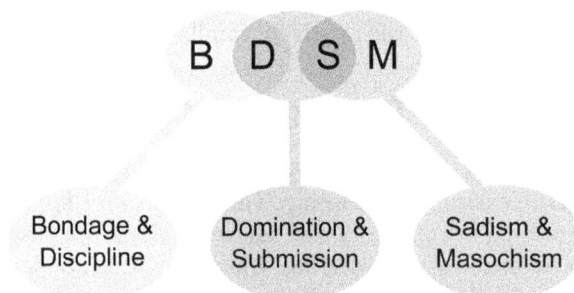

From "File: BDSM acronym.svg," 2012, in Wikimedia Commons. (https://commons.wikimedia.org/wiki/File:BDSM_acronym.svg). CC-BY SA 3.0.

BDSM

BDSM communities generally welcome anyone with a nonnormative streak, including cross-dressers, body modification enthusiasts, animal role-players, and rubber enthusiasts. Sensual experience may be accessed by a variety of means including pinching, biting, scratching, whipping, erotic spanking, handcuffs, ropes, and chains. Practitioners are primarily concerned with power, humiliation, and pleasure toward the pursuit of intense psychological emotions. Couples engaging in consensual BDSM have been shown (via hormonal measures) to have reduced stress and increased emotional bonding. Pleasurable experiences depend upon both the top's (sadist's) competence and the bottom's (masochist's) physical and mental state, as well as their engaging a shared mindset.

I was very curious about members who engaged in increasingly risky activities. I wanted to know about the guy who arranged to be whipped from a 30-story-high balcony with no railing and the people who had their chests threaded with pectoral hooks and were hung from a line until they nearly lost consciousness. As I came to understand, **aftercare** was an essential part of the culture, where, following a dramatic scene, the submissive would be wrapped in blankets and held lovingly as blasts of adrenaline dissipated.

The theater of exhibitionism interested me as well. While I relished giving lectures—getting my audience to laugh at my jokes and receiving enthusiastic applause—I was clueless about why the dungeon attendees wanted to be watched. Eventually, I surmised that these sensation-rich scenes could be intensified by having others bear witness. While this quest for sensation did not typically engage the genitals, the goal appeared to be a transcendence that parallels the *petit mort* (little death) of orgasm.

Popularizations of BDSM

The 2011 publication of *Fifty Shades of Grey*, followed by *Fifty Shades Darker* (2012) and *Fifty Shades Freed* (2012), brought BDSM into mainstream American conversation. While the books were critically slammed, they were nonetheless page-turners for women seeking affirmation for the pleasures of sexual submission. While traditional feminism was suspicious of anything that reeked of violence against women, the popularization of sexy consensual dominance and submission proved to be a game-changing hit. The books and later the films (2015, 2017, and 2021) affirmed an expansion of America's sexual palate.

In 2022 Netflix premiered British luxury interior designer Melanie Rose's *How to Build a Sex Room*. Here all sorts of couples (as well as a polyamorous family and a gal looking to enjoy her single life) are provided makeovers for their spare rooms, basements, and vans. Rose breezily proposes kink-inspired paraphernalia, such as sex swings, bondage beds, crosses, floggers, handcuffs, and butt plugs, inviting further expansion of the American erotic appetite.

The Swing Scene

Greg wanted to take me to a swing club. While I'd kept a cool, anthropological distance at the dungeon party, he encouraged me to participate at Marina Del Rey's exclusive swing club, Sea Breeze. When we arrived, Greg handed the host $30, and suddenly, I was surrounded by swingers! Lingerie that would be typically reserved for the privacy of one's own bedroom was boldly paraded. Breasts spilled out of ill-fitting bra tops, and everyone was super friendly. The club had a living room area where attendees helped themselves to a macaroni and cheese casserole, Caesar salad, potato chips, and soda. There was a Jacuzzi at one end of the space as well as a series of small rooms for private activities and several large rooms for orgy enthusiasts.

We did swaps with two couples, wherein we split off from each other and went to private rooms. Greg had full-on intercourse with the women (whom he was clearly attracted to). I tried kissing the guys I swapped Greg for, and I felt my body repulsively cringe. I was not attracted to either of them. Kissing them was like chewing on regurgitated sandpaper, and I vowed I would never again erotically engage someone I was not interested in. (I remain in awe of the sex workers of the world who are able to make their livings providing touch and attention to clients of all sizes, shapes, and smells.)

Overwhelmed, I told Greg I wasn't going to participate in any more swaps. He then chatted with a sassy-looking single woman with dark roots peering from her dyed-blond hair and a mélange of purple and turquoise eye shadow. We all three soaked in the club's bubbly Jacuzzi. Suddenly, he began to have intercourse with her

Research on Swinging

In the pre-AIDS 1970s, many participatory sociologists studied swinging. Conventions afforded the opportunity to both present and share research as well as to play (e.g., swing). One of the most highly regarded books from the time (published in 1978) was *The Gilmartin Report* by psychologist Brian Gilmartin. Funded by a National Science Foundation grant, he codified swingers into three different types: egotistical (avoided emotional involvement), recreational (emphasized social aspects of swinging), and interpersonal (built close personal relationships with fellow swingers).

Anthropologist Gilbert Bartell published *Group Sex: A Scientist's Eyewitness Report on the American Way of Swinging* in 1971. He and his wife Ann devoted three years to interacting with a cohort of 20 couples by placing ads in swingers magazines and attending parties. Decidedly against engaging in sexual activity with their subjects, Bartell and his wife disrobed and carried drinks at parties, obfuscating the limits of their participation. Terry Gould, a Canadian journalist, published *The Lifestyle: A Look at the Erotic Rites of Swingers* in 1999. His book followed many of the key players and made sense of the culture in a way the previous decade of sociologists had not. Like the Bartell's, he, too, never stepped into the fray. His findings were so respected that the Lifestyles Organization invited him to deliver the keynote address at their 1999 convention.

right in front of me. After witnessing him penetrate her, I completely lost interest in him as a partner and refused to ever see him again. It took me a full six years to revisit the swing scene.

The year was 1992, and I was the host of KIEV Radio's interview talk show, *Intimate Matters*. My guests were members of alternative sexual and gender lifestyles who would be interviewed by me, an open-minded and curious anthropologist. Robert McGinley, the president of Lifestyles, a national swing club, agreed to a guest interview. Afterward he offered me a press pass to attend the organization's next convention, which would be in Los Angeles. I sat in on workshops, wandered the exhibit halls, and lingered at the play parties. At these parties couples might engage in threesomes, participate in group sex in an orgy room, or engage in a full swap with another couple (as Greg and I had done). Sometimes a woman would "pull a train" and have intercourse with a series of men, one after another.

Viscerally, I didn't understand any of it. The idea of engaging in full intercourse without a "proper" seduction was not part of my sexual scripting. I noted to myself, "I need to look into my lover's eyes, share secrets, and feel a connection!" Even the one-night stands that were emblematic of the 1970s' sexual revolution were, to me, potential beginnings. I easily became heartbroken when a one-night-stand lover that I liked failed to call.

The women who happily engaged in swinging subscribed to a different script and presumably had different emotional wiring than I did. I wanted to understand how it worked—and how they processed it all. Following the 1992 Lifestyles Convention, I became friends with a group of people in Los Angeles who hosted sex parties. I made it my project to interview as many women as I could. I joined a women's support group, which included women who attended these parties, to better understand their culture and their psyches. Apparently, these women were both secure in their marriages and accessed an endorphin surge following an evening of serial lovers.

The lack of personal connection confused me. Many of the men at these parties gazed into the distance as they engaged one willing woman after another. One woman confided that in the context of swinging, she would only have sex with men she didn't feel particularly attracted to so as to maintain the integrity of her marriage. Heterosexual swingers very much embrace female bisexuality, permitting women to freely access female–female eroticism in the context of their play parties.

Being a rebel at heart, I managed to break many of the swinger "rules." At one party my boyfriend saw me exchange phone numbers with an attractive man and chastised me for not respecting that man's wife and marriage. By 2001 I felt that I'd figured out enough that I gave a professional presentation to the Lifestyles Convention in Las Vegas, titled "Why Women Swing." Following my presentation, Chuck and his lover Helen approached me. Rather than sticking to standard swinger protocol and agreeing to meet them for dinner and then a partner swap, I accepted the dinner and refused the swap. Everyone at the dinner sensed Chuck and I were intensely well matched. I wanted more time to really get to know him.

Ultimately, he and I did generate a deep intellectual and erotic connection that was rich and messy in every way possible. At a subsequent Lifestyles Convention, Chuck and I offered a presentation on how swingers manage jealousy-provoking situations, such as witnessing their partner getting lost in lovemaking with someone else. Recalling how I immediately dropped Greg after witnessing him penetrate that sassy single woman with the exotic eye shadow, I sought theories and practices that could counter my primal wiring. I arrived at several. One was that party-based trysts functioned as titillation, enabling committed couples to access elevated endorphin levels. Another was that once a couple returned to each other, the adrenaline-spiked mini threat of possibly losing their connection could convert into a relieved and loving embrace. Finally, a couple could bond with a "tribe" of fellow swingers; engaging each other erotically would further intensify intertribal and communal bonding and, potentially, group transcendence.

Several years later, I confided to my boyfriend Michel about how difficult it was for me to have sex with a stranger. He created a scenario where he arranged an encounter with a man I found attractive. He then offered the guy details on the things I liked and even demonstrated how to best touch me. Afterward I felt that this encounter with a stranger was only enjoyable because of Michel's participation. The following week, I ran into the guy and felt extremely awkward. We had experienced something with each other's bodies that was quite disconnected from the world of relationships and personal connection. While I remained attracted to him, without Michel to act as go-between, I felt completely tongue-tied.

I did continue to attend sex parties, but still found sex with anyone other than my partner to be uncomfortable and did my best to avoid it. If anything veered toward intimacy with a stranger, I would slip away, start new conversations, and disappear into other rooms and spaces. If I ran into an ex whom I still had feelings for, I found having sex with him in the context of a party could be delightful. It was akin to a "hall pass" back to the time when we were a connected couple. Being that we were in the context of no-strings-attached swinging, following the encounter, he and I could go our separate ways, recalling the glow of who we once had been.

Many years later, I connected with Doug, who had a substantial box of BDSM toys. The submissive in me was up for all of it, and then one morning, I woke up and didn't want any of it. Whatever it was that intrigued me about the scene and its glorious intensity had all whooshed away. Out of the bedroom, I didn't want his "guidance" or even his opinions. As for my community of friends who enjoy sex parties, I never stopped endorsing their appetite for personal liberation. And to this day, I would never turn down an intriguing opportunity for edgy sex research!

PART IV

Rethinking Marriage

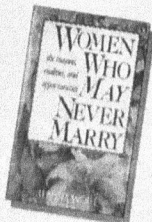

Reprinted courtesy of Southern California News Group / Pasadena Star-News.

My training in anthropology fueled my questioning of my parents' notions of till-death-do-us-part heterosexual monogamy. I devoured reports of other ways and ultimately devoted much of my career to the exploration of alternative-marriage patterns and perspectives. This section features my investigation of late-1980s Southern California singles culture. Arriving at 33 and newly single (Sean and I had broken up and abandoned that white-picket-fenced house), I made it my personal research project to uncover the "odd" rules of Los Angeles's gender and dating culture.

CHAPTER 10

Researching Singles Culture in Los Angeles

I came to Los Angeles in 1986 to work on a documentary film on the Great Peace March. At 33 I saw myself as a dyed-in-the-wool Berkeley-feminist documentary filmmaker with progressive politics and no interest in participating in the superficiality of La-La-Land. A West Hollywood production company was housing the film project. After a couple of days, my assignment ended, and Dean, one of the company producers, asked me to lunch.

Dean had just completed an award-winning HBO documentary on teen athletes and was fishing for a new project; he invited me to propose ideas. I offered him a list of 55 stories and projects, including the social dynamics of swinging, the geographic trajectories of Hispanic immigrants, and how lesbian feminists co-opted the women's movement. He picked one of them: my previous year's dilemma following the affair with Ron, the well-heeled San Francisco attorney who personified the yuppie 1980s world of material success, versus patching up the relationship with Sean, who was a selfless 1970s-style political activist.

Julia (the character with my dilemma) respects Sean's commitment to making the world a better place but finds herself dazzled by the pricey dinner dates and personal attention that Ron offers. We called the project "Between Times." Over the next three months, Dean and I spent countless hours at his office and on weekends at his apartment developing dialogue between the three characters. While I wasn't being paid, I was fed in that Dean was able to bill development costs, which included working with me, an expert on my recent romantic dilemma.

It felt special to be spending so much time with Dean. While we were not lovers, we had very much engaged each other's romantic psyches by our generating intense and passionate dialogue. Being that we saw each other constantly, he would invite me to screenings at the Directors and Writers Guilds. I was bursting with excitement over thoughts of Kevin Costner playing Ron and William Hurt playing Sean for my soon-to-hit-the-silver-screen script. The script was optioned for a year by Bay Area film producer Woody Clark. After the option expired, I continued trying to sell it and then eventually gave up.

During those heady no-income days, I stayed on my cousin Bob's boat in Marina Del Rey and couch surfed with friends. Eventually, I rented a bedroom with a skinny single bed for $90 per month from Jenny, the mother of one of my college roommates. Jenny worked in catering. Following her late-night gigs, she'd drink cheap wine until sunrise, puke in a bucket for hours, and then cry apologetically the rest of the day. I decided to join Al-Anon to better deal with my home situation.

After a couple of meetings, I faced that Jenny was not a family member and that I could put an end to my situation by simply moving out.

I found an apartment share with Darleen, a bright businesswoman, in the north end of Santa Monica. I had to come up with $450 per month for rent, as well as a deposit, and I had to purchase a chest of drawers and a queen-sized futon. My first round of Hollywood dreaming abruptly ended! In that I had exhausted my small savings writing the spec script with Dean, Sean, who still called every weekend, offered to lend me money. He had been awarded a hefty financial aid package at Harvard and was happy to share some of it with me. My parents, whose home was paid off, were clueless about the current rental market. They offered me $50; I couldn't break it to them that, in fact, I needed $1000.

Dean got a deal to produce a documentary for Lifetime television on the challenges of finding childcare. He hired me to be a research assistant and do a scratch track for the voice-over. I became part of the Hollywood gig economy in that I had several months of paid work. Next, I worked as an event planner and video editor for the Empowerment Project, a documentary film production company that was based in a private home in Venice. When work there was spotty, I signed on with a temp agency to do secretarial work. Every morning I would jog along the Palisades Park cliffs that overlook Santa Monica Bay, shower off the mélange of salty air and sweat, and await a call. The temp work was dreary; all I was doing was running in place to make rent and buy tortillas, cheese, and salad greens.

Mutual friends introduced me to a fellow anthropologist who was teaching at Cal State University, Long Beach. She introduced me to the department chair, who then hired me to be a part-time adjunct professor. Two years later, I was offered a two-semester, full-time assignment at Southwest College in South Central Los Angeles. While I found teaching anthropology to be far more satisfying than secretarial work, my dream was to be a seminal thinker, a writer, and a film producer.

Despite the fact that Sean called on Sunday mornings and I kept a picture of him on my bedstand, I decided to at least try to date. I was very suspicious of anyone who wasn't a political activist or a serious academic. The actors I met disturbed me; I couldn't understand how someone could put so much energy into making entertainment.

Yet the activists I met felt too familiar. As a way to learn more about Los Angeles, I decided to date guys in the creative arts—several who proved to be extraordinarily self-absorbed. One, a UCLA film school graduate, had devoted over 10 years to screenwriting but had yet to sell a script. To him all of his scripts were alive—if I were going to be his girlfriend, I had to believe in them as much as he did!

To engage my new world, I tried to shed my Berkeley feminist "uniform" of baggy jeans, light blue work shirts, and hiking boots. A couple of my new friends encouraged me to purchase cleavage-enhancing bras, skimpy tops, tight jeans, makeup, and heels. It felt awkward—showing skin, walking with confidence, and overtly presenting as a sex object. Yet I wanted to get inside of this culture—to feel how it ticked and how it worked!

The push-up bras dug into my ribs; coupled with tight jeans, I could barely breathe. The mascara would make my contact lenses drip messy black tears, and eating with lipstick made food taste horrible. I was so uneasy dressing sexy; the hotter I looked, the more I was driven to lead with my brain. I felt like such a confederate! The moment I'd return home, I'd tear off all the uncomfortable clothes, wash my face, and put on my softest sweats. This dissonance led to my new research project: Los Angeles's dating and singles culture.

The scene was so very different from what I'd seen in my previous ten years in the Bay Area and in New York City. There I dated men I'd met in grad school or while working in movements to overthrow every bit of the liberation-squelching establishment. Many of the Southern Californians I met struck me as provincial. Few had traveled to far-off places like Maní, Yucatán, and lived amongst the natives. Most of the women were quite aghast at my willingness to participate in sexual activities to learn about unique cultural practices. I quickly surmised that my journey was far from theirs. I tried to not roll my eyes when they'd tell me that, altogether, they'd had sex with four different guys (which my later sexological research did record as the norm).

Many of these women claimed they wanted to get married; they hoped to make themselves into the kind of woman a man might like. To better understand late-1980s **singles culture**, I participated in every way I could. I attended singles lectures, mixers, and dances (volunteering to work the events I could ill afford) and placed personals ads in local papers and magazines. (Internet dating apps didn't yet exist and phone dating was in its infancy.)

I had a multipurpose quest. While I very much missed having a partner, if I couldn't get back with Sean or find someone better matched, I'd shift into a dating and singles researcher. My research strategy included befriending several women who I'd encouraged to call in "reports" on their dating escapades. I'd engage them in the best girl talk, noting the virtues and challenges of their dates. Suddenly, my favorite mode of conversation, where women gleefully generate practical social theory, was elevated from a guilty pleasure to a research strategy!

My new friend Leesa intrigued me. She would hold out sexually on men she believed had marriage potential while engaging in wild affairs with those who were decidedly hot. We were both running personals ads in the *LA Weekly* and would compare notes on our respondents, who were often the same men. I'd gain added insight on her and her strategies by going out with her dates and quizzing them about her. One of them was too busy to personally meet either of us, but he indulged in endless hours of phone chat. He would send her expensive gifts, while all I got was data (which I did appreciate).

Los Angeles's late-1980s dating scene was a perplexing cat-and-mouse chase. Women would attempt to play coy, and men would pay for the meal, implying (perhaps) that they could afford a traditional marriage and all of the incumbent expenses. I managed to eat a lot of dinners and lunches and weekend brunches. One of my *LA Weekly* phone-linked ads netted 80 responses in 30 hours. As a committed dating researcher, I scheduled each of my respondents in half-hour slots to meet for coffee at Venice's Rose Café. While several interested me personally, I queried the rest on their dating experiences. A couple were even game to fill me in on their own quests for Ms. Right when I told them I was conducting anthropological research.

One of these blind dates managed to show up twice. First, he'd responded to one of my *LA Weekly* ads. We'd enjoyed dinner and then retired to his place, made love, and then mutually surmised we weren't a match. I thought he was overly smitten with New Age beliefs and practices, while no doubt, he'd found me to be too much of a hard-ass scientist. About a year later, we found each other on one of the new phone-dating lines. He sounded good; not realizing we'd already slept together, we met again. Politely, we sat down for a drink, caught up on the last year, and allowed each other to quietly slip away.

Noting that we both had remained relatively single for an entire year, I began to wonder whether *singles culture* was a culture in and of itself, rather than a *transitional status*. Despite the energy some singles were expending trying to meet and marry "the one," I assessed that, ultimately, it was not socially, economically, or erotically necessary to marry in order to be a fulfilled person. Moreover, independent singles were generating what I saw as **extended families of choice**. Such families would help each other in times of need and generate such celebrations as "Friendsgiving."

In search of theory, I began to attend relationship psychologist Pat Allen's standing-room-only lectures in Westwood. She advised that relationships require one party to play the dominant role and a counterpart to engage the receptive role. Noting feminism's impact on gender dynamics, she advised professional women to take off their business suits and transform themselves into submissive sex kittens. While I concurred with her observation that heterosexual relationships gain traction via a masculine–feminine gender dance, I doubted such directives would fly for late-1980s America. When challenged on her **retro-feminist** prescription, she would retort, "A dominant woman can partner with a submissive man!"

As an anthropologist, I surmised that a gender-role revolution was about to explode and that Pat Allen's quick fix was a dubious solution. More women were attending college, as well as securing professional identities and well-paid employment, while increasing numbers of men were losing their footing as protectors, providers, and even inseminators.

My observations and gender-role research led to my 1993 book, *Women Who May Never Marry: The Reasons, Realities, and Opportunities*. I hoped to offer a salient perspective on the loosening of marriage and the ensuing gender flip, wherein by the second decade of the 21st century, women would be the primary breadwinners in 40% of committed couples.

I thought about my new girlfriends who went through the motions of trying to meet a Mr. Right rather than facing the fact that they enjoy their independence and did not want anyone telling them what to do and how to live. I saw this unaddressed ambivalence in their continuously finding imperfections in the men they'd meet, thus accessing more years to be single and free.

To me, American marriage was in the midst of a shakedown. The divorce rate was hovering at 50%, young people were marrying later than ever, and over a third of babies were being born to financially independent "**single mothers by choice**."

Initially, I tried to sell *Women Who May Never Marry* as a movie of the week. Several production companies expressed interest, and I began to videotape interviews with 1980s relationship experts and social observers, including Warren Farrell, Barbara Ehrenreich, and Pepper Schwartz. I confided in a girlfriend about my frustration in trying to sell the project, and she suggested I make the project into a book. She introduced me to Mike Hamilburg, a Beverly Hills literary agent. He generously guided me through developing a book proposal and introduced me to several New York editors, including the absolutely delightful Judith Regan. These introductions did not pan out.

With a fire in my belly, I picked up *Writers Market* and mailed three-page descriptions of my book project to over 100 publishers. The rejection letters piled in. Then two editors expressed an interest. I invited Hamilburg to handle the bidding. I signed a contract with Longstreet Press in Atlanta, received a $5,000 advance, and wrote like a madwoman. I would turn off the phone ringer, mute the answering machine, and write. I would wake up and write, eat, take a walk, and then write some more. In the evening I'd munch a quick dinner and return to writing. When I needed more data, I'd call up my girlfriends and query them about their latest dating escapades. I would mail finished chapters to my editor. We would then have long chats on how to fix odd phrasing and rethink some of my ideas. In September 1993 the book was declared done. In November it began to arrive in bookstores.

For an unknown writer, *Women Who May Never Marry: The Reasons, Realities, and Opportunities* received substantial media attention. I was featured on three nationwide and seven regional television shows, articles about the book appeared in over 100 newspapers, and I was interviewed on nearly 100 drive time radio shows. My first book signing was scheduled at Santa Monica's Midnight Special Bookstore. The week before, an *LA Times* reporter had contacted the store in search of a story. My book (and I) became the story. A photo shoot was arranged on the beach with me wearing a tight black lace top and a flowy skirt that blew in the ocean breeze. A full-page story emerged. The line to enter the bookstore snaked onto Third Street Promenade. I shivered at the realization that I had become a little bit famous!

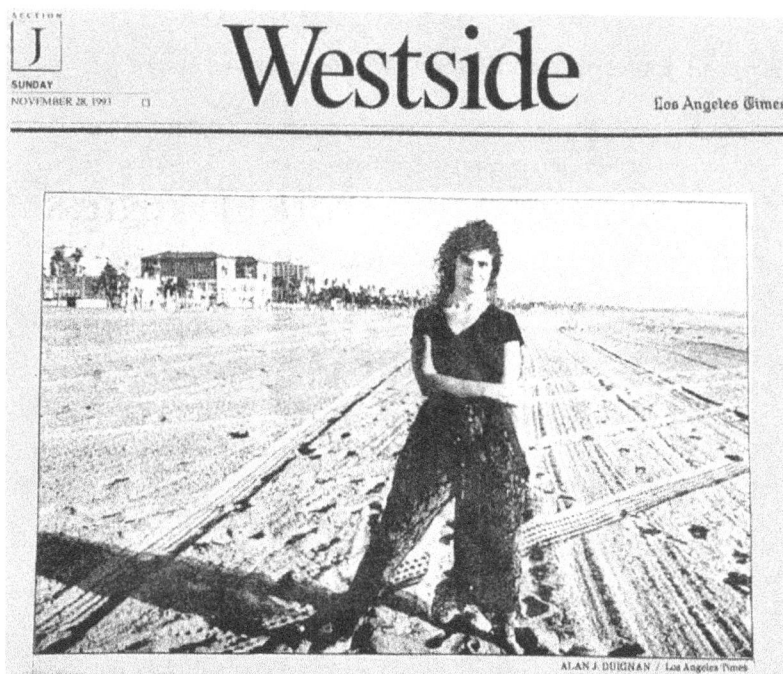

Westside section of the *Los Angeles Times* on November 28, 1993.

From A. J. Duignan, 1993, *Los Angeles Times*: Westside, section J., copyright 1993, by *Los Angeles Times*. Reprinted with permission.

For the first six months, several mornings a week, I would set my alarm for 4:30 AM to be interviewed on East Coast morning drive time radio. In the spring of 1995, I was flown to New York City to appear on a popular talk show, *The Phil Donahue Show*. A limousine met me at JFK and took me to a well-appointed hotel suite. The next morning, another limousine appeared, and I was taken to the show studio at Rockefeller Plaza. Once seated, words rolled out of me. I knew the smart, savvy tone of the show's guests and piped in, "I basically believe in **Me-search**, where you research the things that are interesting to you. . . . Women were putting energy into making themselves extraordinary rather than living through men—they had very high standards for what a partner had to be like."

Donahue then asked in his incredulous, playful way, "They were looking to meet a man to marry?" I continued, "The more I looked at what they were doing, the more I found that they weren't getting married."

When I was invited to speak at a women's issues conference in Washington, DC, a media coordinator arranged an interview with a *USA Today* reporter. The article, which was then syndicated to 80 Gannett newspapers, celebrated my book's premise: that women do not need marriage to be self-realized, successful, or happy.

After 18 months of being chased by the media, I grew tired of the singular interviews. There was so much more in the book, but journalists only asked about why growing numbers of women had no need for the things traditional marriage provided. I couldn't sustain a one-trick-pony media presence and returned to teaching anthropology. For several years I assigned (and taught every word) of *Women Who May Never Marry* to my Gender, Sex, and Culture students.

Excerpt from *Women Who May Never Marry*

Marriage means different things in different cultures. Likewise, women who aren't married can be accorded different statuses depending on the value and availability of marriage. In Jamaica, 98% of the population is unmarried. Marriage is seen as an expensive ritual that most folks cannot afford. Nonetheless, Jamaicans fall in love, live with their sweethearts and raise families together.

Much of what allows a woman the freedom to consider not marrying or fully rejecting marriage is the awareness that she can survive just fine without a husband. Traditional hunter-gatherers such as the !Kung of Africa's Kalahari Desert, have no private property to entice a prospective wife or to pass on to heirs. Thus a young woman may feel no compulsion to work things out with her husband to better survive. Some !Kung women report that they have lovers in every neighboring band because these alliances better meet their needs for food and sleeping spots when visiting. (Wolfe, 1993, p. 18)

PART V

Engaging Polygamy and Polyamory

When I was a graduate student in New York, an acquaintance informed me that she was living with two men who were both her lovers. I was both intrigued and repulsed. I didn't think the kind of men that I liked (independent and artsy) would ever tolerate in-home competition. This incredulity led to my own exploration of multiple-partner sexualities. I quickly became captivated by open relationships along with their post-1990s incarnation, polyamory. To put this all in context, I explored polygamy in East Africa in 1998 and then in Papua New Guinea in 2001. I attended my first **Burning Man** Festival in 1998—it proved to be a potent place to both engage and study polyamory. Altogether, I participated in 10 Burning Man festivals, making PolyParadise my home camp.

CHAPTER 11

Researching Polygamy in East Africa and Papua New Guinea

In 1993 I met Jon, who was an artist, a guitar player, and the father of Xiomara, his beautiful nine-year-old daughter. I had been trying to focus on being single to more authentically write *Women Who May Never Marry*. He nonetheless persisted; eventually, we became a couple and shared a home, and I became Xiomara's stepmother. I came to love Jon's touch and his way. We became a little family, going to Disneyland and seeing movies like *Toy Story*. Xiomara and I would have swimming contests and roll down hills together. She was still young enough to be obedient and appreciative and had not yet begun to roll her eyes at the weird behaviors of adults. She would earnestly ask my permission for things, such as asking, "Can I eat this piece of candy before we have dinner?"

When *Women Who May Never Marry* was published, I was suddenly treated like the darling of parties and events. Jon had a hard time of it. Everyone was paying attention to me; he felt like an unacknowledged plus-one. I lacked empathy for his attention deficit and angrily snapped, "Why don't you find yourself an additional girlfriend?"

Jon needed a constancy of attention I was incapable of providing. I wallowed in the rush of media attention and exotic adventures and proved to be a poor companion for his home-based lifestyle. While I'd gobble up the Southern-style comfort foods he'd make, like biscuits and gravy, chicken-fried steak, and lumpy mashed potatoes, I had little appetite for domestic life.

To me, my house was where I wrote. On my own, cooking consisted of salads, omelets, stir-fries, and quesadillas. Yet Jon and I generated an interdependency. My own father, who had fixed everything for me, was nearing the end of his life; Jon ably stepped in and repaired things in my parents' home as well as ensured that my computer had the latest software and was virus-free. He came to love my finicky Russian blue cat, Poppy, and eventually, we adopted additional cats and a couple of dogs. Noting that the world of the new better held my interest, he'd claim, "You are always one foot out the door!"

Briefly a Polyamorous Triad

Four years into our reasonably good relationship, I was blindsided when Jon got involved with a woman named Violet. While, years before, I had suggested that he "find an additional girlfriend," I did not believe he actually would. Adding insult to injury, he'd begun seeing her for several months before I was informed. Considering we both had a history of multiple-partner relationships, I figured we could work it out.

We really did our best. We created a schedule wherein each of our **dyads** (he and her, he and I, and she and I) had date nights; then on the weekends, we all shared a bed together. They were smitten with each other, while she and I would never have chosen to spend private time together. I experienced her as an attention-seeking drama queen who sulked and sobbed on my date nights with him and would generate endless excuses for why he had to abandon me in the middle of the night and drive over to comfort her.

When he first began to openly spend the night with her, I would shiver all night and fear the house was about to be broken into. Eventually, I grew to enjoy the freedom of time off from him. I could live a double life; on the nights when Jon was not home, I'd go to parties and events and meet new guys. After a couple of months, our triad crumbled when Violet and I mutually decided to break it off, declaring, "We're just not that into each other."

While Violet and Jon were becoming a true-blue item, I felt increasingly out in the cold. It was so unlike how Sean and I had handled additional lovers. Then we were decidedly primary partners, while my visits with Tom were a bit of delectable frosting. Violet sought full recognition of her place in Jon's life and expected to talk to him many times a day and see him every other night. I was furious. I so wished she had other things to do than disrupt my home relationship. Meanwhile, they contended, "You are attempting to be a puppet master in telling us how to behave!"

I desperately needed a break from Jon's and Violet's smitten gazes. I decided to take a really long trip to Africa. Being that Africa has a long-standing tradition of polygyny (where one husband is shared by multiple wives), I hoped to gain insight into how partner sharing is done.

Polygyny Field Research in Africa

Arriving in Nairobi in 1998, I treated every safari guide, home-stay host, and random person as a potential source of insight on how women share a husband. The Africans I met were incredulous that I, an American, believed that they would have answers for me. They'd point out, "In your country divorce is common because, in America, women go to college and have careers. They can afford to leave their husbands!"

Nonetheless, I persisted and was ultimately offered valuable (though not necessarily applicable) insights. A Kenyan grandmother who had begun sharing her husband 10 years into her marriage explained, "The first couple of years were difficult, but eventually I adjusted to having a **co-wife**." Being that her co-wife was unable to conceive children of her own, she became a valued family member, working in the fields and co-mothering the children. My struggles with sharing Jon with Violet

What Is Polygamy?

Polygamy refers to multiple-partner marriage, as opposed to **monogamy,** which is a one-partner marriage. There are two forms of polygamy: **polygyny** and **polyandry**. Polygyny is a marriage wherein multiple wives share a single husband; this is by far the most common form, with 84.5% of world cultures practicing it. Polyandry is practiced by just .5% of world cultures and refers to the unique marital configuration where multiple husbands share a single wife. This is seen amongst the Nyimba of Tibet, where brothers share a wife. Despite the preponderance of cultures that permit multiple-partner marriages, just one-third of the world's population lives in such a cultural context. Within these communities just 20% of men can afford to maintain multiple-partner households.

Mormons belonging to the Fundamentalist Church of Jesus Christ of Latter-Day Saints (FLDS) refer to their practice as polygamy despite the fact that the form they practice is, in fact, polygyny. Their practice is sustained by the notion of **celestial marriage**, wherein a man gains a higher place in the afterlife when he has multiple wives and many children in that spousal and parent-child relationships are believed to continue into perpetuity. The Muslim Quran prescribes that a man may marry up to four wives if and when he can establish that he can afford to care for them as well as the resulting children. Today less than 1% of Muslim men have multiple wives (Kramer, 2020).

gained a universal feel, as I learned how people 10 time zones away encountered parallel problems. There was one wife who was so enraged by her co-wife's entertaining their husband on nights that were not hers that she attacked her with cooking pots. The fight then escalated to kitchen knives, and the two of them ended up in the hospital.

For Africans, polygyny is an expression of elevated status for men who can afford to maintain additional wives and the many children that might be created. In that my visit coincided with the media frenzy surrounding President Bill Clinton's affair with White House intern Monica Lewinsky, the Africans I met weighed in, saying,

> It's absurd that Clinton, who is clearly a wealthy and prestigious man, is being shunned for courting a woman who ought to become a second wife. A man such as the American president certainly deserves to have additional progeny! The president's wife, Hillary, might be barren due to her advanced age, surely that girl Monica would be able to produce a good son for the president.

In Africa, polygyny functions to maintain and expand **patrilineages** (male family lines). If a man passes away, one of his brothers would step in and marry his wife (or wives). Ultimately, wives and their progeny belong to their husband's family line. Likewise, if a wife passes away, one of her sisters or cousins would be brought in to replace her in the marriage. In that a **bride price** (often the gift of cattle) had been negotiated between the husband's family and the wife's family, a lifelong alliance would need to be maintained.

The business/exchange aspect of African polygyny very much eclipses American polyamory's relatively lightweight quest for an expansive "tribe" of compatible lovers. The African approach is very practical. A man cannot abandon his wife (as in an American-style divorce) in that she and their progeny would need his support. While a husband might view his newest wife as his sexual favorite, ultimately, all of his wives retain status (and financial support) by continuing in their marriage to him.

While divorce in America separates children from their fathers, polygyny in Africa expands family alliances. In that polyamory is more directly about love, passion, and eroticism, in many ways, it habits a different sphere. Still, long-standing polyamorous triads and **intimate networks** can potentially become financially interdependent and face similar issues.

Interpersonally, what happened to me in Africa was very different than what happened in Mexico. I took my six-month research trip through Mexico when I was 22, while I went to East Africa when I was 45. The Africans addressed me as "Madame," and I was largely regarded as a post-reproductive professional woman. Occasionally, a polygamous man would blush and giggle while speculating about the benefits his family might access if he were to marry me: "While my other wives can cook and work in the fields, you would be able to bring in cash in that you are a professor and a writer!"

These calculations felt neither romantic nor erotic, revealing the no-nonsense considerations that African families make in negotiating marriage. Likewise, in the

The Many Forms of Polyamory

As polyamory, the consensual engagement of multiple romantic and sexual partners, has evolved in the Western world, new terms have emerged. Largely, these terms function to distinguish between those who seek to generate extended-family connections amongst themselves and their partners' lovers, as in **kitchen table polyamory**; those who seek to give priority to a primary partnership or marriage, as in **hierarchical polyamory**, where additional lovers are regarded as *secondary*, *tertiary*, or *comets* (long-distance with intermittent visits); and those who practice **solo polyamory**. Solo polyamorists do not have the goal of cohabiting with their romantic partners, contending that their primary relationship is with themselves.

Parallel polyamory acknowledges the existence of **metamours** (one's partner's other partners), but details are not disclosed and socializing is not expected. *Garden party* or *birthday party polyamory* describes the dynamic where metamours only see one another at their shared partner's special event (e.g., a birthday party). **Triads,** or *throuples*, are three-person relationships; they may be *V-triads*, where the *hinge lover* is the only one who is sexually intimate with each of the others. Triads may practice **polyfidelity** by only engaging each other sexually and romantically. Finally, there is **relationship anarchy** that recognizes no particular set of rules or hierarchies; romance isn't assumed to be more important or life affirming than one's friendships. At the end of the day, relationship anarchy is much more a life philosophy than a relationship structure.

villages, hefty bride price negotiations spurred anxious banter about very young girls being offered up for marriage to much older husbands. The manipulations of the wealth-seeking parents would be weighed against the suffering a young bride might endure.

While African men largely ignored my sexuality, I was forever regarded as a potential source of money and First World connections. Children would befriend me, hoping I could arrange for them to study in America; when I traveled with African villagers in tow, buying them food and beverages became my unspoken responsibility. As a guest in the private homes of Africans, I was expected to gift them baskets of fruits and vegetables, and whenever a colorfully dressed Maasai tribesperson appeared, I of course paid for the opportunity to photograph them.

Apart from all the relational gifting, beggars, pickpockets, and scam artists were all on my tail. Moreover, Nairobi, my East African home base, was fittingly nicknamed Nairobbery. While my African hosts did their best to protect me, the moment I was left alone, I would be quickly targeted, noting that no matter how you engage Africa, you pay. If I were to book a fully escorted, pricey safari, then a tour company, and their ancillary workers would profit, being that I was a solo adventuress, I was either providing my (protective) hosts with gifts, being grabbed at by pickpockets, or more subtly robbed by scammers.

There was only one instance during my time in East Africa that a "beach boy" approached me with a sexual agenda. It happened along the gorgeous Mombasa shoreline, an exotic beach destination on Kenya's east coast. Being that Mombasa largely attracts Northern European tourists, the guy who tried to pick me up was skilled in ferreting out women who might be seeking an erotic adventure. By chatting him up, I gathered that such adventures begin with indirect payments. If I'd been game, I would have purchased meals, little gifts, and either snuck him into my hotel room or rendezvoused in the dark of night at a secluded, palm-studded beach cove. Then at the end of my stay, I would have given him a substantial tip.

Due to the African focus on the financial and alliance-building aspects of marriage, expressions of romantic love can inhabit the back burner. This became dramatically clear during my Valentine's Day visit to Uganda. I was staying with a family in Kampala, the capital city, and I asked them: "Do you exchange Valentine's gifts?"

They laughed, explaining,

> That wouldn't be a very African thing to do. We Africans consider public displays of affection between mature husbands and wives to be improper. Only adolescents would purchase romantic flowers or chocolates. To us, such gifts would be unnecessary. The youth who do this are surely being influenced by Western capitalist marketing!

When I arrived in Amsterdam, following my stay in Africa, the starkness of Africa's lack of such displays hit me hard. There, in the midst of the buzzy Schiphol airport, couples were engaged in long, very public kisses and embraces. My body shuddered, sensing how long it had been since I had been touched. I managed to remedy that lacking when my Amsterdam host invited me to share his bed. In a way it seemed very sudden . . . and, in another way, my skin had begun to feel near prickly from the supreme lack of touch I'd weathered in Africa.

Thinking over my stay in Africa, I saw that anxiety over HIV-AIDs coupled with the serious financial negotiations that were part and parcel of patrilineal marriage all contributed to my being literally untouched. There was just one moment where something sweet, sensual, and then ultimately amusing occurred. I was staying on Rusinga Island at the edge of Lake Victoria, and my hosts instructed me to join the other women for bathing. I walked down to the shore and gingerly removed my clothes; then one of the women sweetly poured some water over my feet. I smiled deep inside, sensing I'd finally accessed the intimate world of Africa's co-wives. Suddenly, a boatload of the village men paddled right into the women's secluded cove to personally look over my very foreign body. I'd been assured the cove was a private women's area, but then I quickly faced the fact that no such rules apply for a strange-looking woman with very white skin and pink nipples!

The moments of wandering around markets where nothing looked edible, taking taxis that required the driver to push start them, and having curious children run over to touch my skin (to see if it might rub off) enabled me to see life through a hugely expanded lens. Beyond being able to witness traditional polygamy in action, Africa had whetted my appetite for the exotic and the otherworldly.

Papua New Guinea Beckons!

Three years later, in 2001, I pursued perhaps the most down-under experience of my life. I found my way to several traditional Highland villages in Papua New Guinea. When I was growing up, the most exotic-looking *National Geographic* photography had featured people from that inimitable Melanesian island. Having been isolated from world trade until the 1930s, the island had fostered hundreds of unique cultural practices amongst its many isolated tribes. There were cargo cults in which believers imitated everything the Christian missionaries, the first Whites they'd ever seen, did. Observing these "magical" practices work for the White missionaries, the islanders diligently replicated these "spells," hoping to gain fortunes for themselves. They would sit at desks, scribble little markings on paper, and wait for airdrops of useful cargo.

Papua New Guinea was also the homeland of **kuru**, the deadly prion disease (akin to mad cow) contracted by eating the brains of a dead loved one, a ritual practice amongst the Fore tribe's women. As a sexual anthropologist, I'd been intrigued by the initiation rites practiced by the Ettoro and Simbari tribes: preadolescent boy-on-adult-male **fellatio** was performed to enable the ingestion of sperm so that secondary sex characteristics (growth of the testicles, the penis, and pubic hair) would emerge.

I began to sense the otherworldliness of Papua New Guinea as I waited to board a small plane from Cairns, Australia, to Port Moresby. In front of me were a group of stocky caramel-skinned women who reeked of campfire smoke and sweat. I kept a distance, noting that soon enough, that scent would be my scent. Then as we were seated, these travelers from another century required hands-on assistance with their seat belts. Next, the flight attendants made an announcement that was clearly directed to them, warning that no chewing (and spitting) of betel nut would be allowed on the flight. As I soon came to know, betel nut is a mild intoxicant that requires a chew-spit action, creating little patches of red sputum on the paths and streets of the island.

While in Papua New Guinea, I stayed in the villages of the Enga and Huli tribes and attended several *singsings*, which are a cross between county fairs, powwows, and strut-your-stuff dance contests. The attire at the *singsings* often featured bare-breasted ceremonial dress. In getting ready, the women would unabashedly remove their bras and then cover their bouncy breasts with oil to make them shine. Despite the fact that Western tourists were keen on photographing every little bounce, the Papuans themselves did not regard their costuming as sexy nor provocative.

I would absorb information from my hosts about sex and gender as I munched on sweet potatoes (their every-meal staple) during lazy afternoon chats. Like in Africa, polygyny is commonly practiced in New Guinea. My Papuan informants explained that they really don't experience the kind of jealousy I witnessed in Africa. Being that the genders live in separate houses, issues of favorite wives monopolizing their husband's sleeping nights do not occur. The genders sleep in separate houses due to intense fears of menstrual blood pollution, which is believed to be debilitating for men, and sperm pollution, which could destroy a woman who wandered into the men's quarters. These beliefs and their incumbent fears have kept many Papuans close to their home villages; seeking medical care at a regional health center was regarded as risky in that menstruating nurses could be damaging to tribal men. When I was allowed inside of the men's house, which no doubt was well-stained with nocturnal emissions, I asked, "Why is it safe for me to step foot in here?"

They explained, "Because you are so white and so foreign, you are immune to the spirits that can destroy Papuan ladies." The villagers regarded me as a culturally naïve visiting dignitary. I was valuable to them in that I had cash. Moreover, their reputations were at stake in keeping me safe. If anything untoward were to happen,

With my Huli tribe hosts in Papua New Guinea (2001).
Photo courtesy of author.

the whole world could find out, and no more visitors with cash-lined pockets would ever visit again. I slept in a hut with several other women, who watched me like a hawk. If I had to go pee in the middle of the night, they'd spring to action, making sure I didn't stumble on my way to the outhouse.

I treasured those quiet moments in the villages when I felt like we were all one people, regardless of language, culture, and appearance. These people who had never worn shoes in their lives (the calluses on their feet were as thick as the soles of hiking boots) and who were clueless about the techno vagaries of modern life agreed to share their sexual secrets with me, disclosing where sex happens (since their houses are gender segregated): "Private moments are shared in the late afternoons in our sweet potato gardens."

At the end of my stay, I spent several days at a tourist hotel in the Highland town of Mt. Hagen. There one of the guides chatted with me about what I'd seen during my monthlong stay in Papua New Guinea. When I admitted I hadn't been to the coast, paddled down the Sepik River, or gone scuba diving, he contended that my trip had been a near-total loss. When I thought about the fascinating conversations I'd had discussing menstrual blood and semen pollution and the specifics of where pollution-wary Papuans make love, I sensed that the ways I'd accessed cultural secrets about sex, gender, and intimacy made me the big winner.

CHAPTER 12

Researching Sex, Drugs, and Polyamory at Burning Man

Burning Man.
Photo by Jim Herriot, 2002. Reprinted with permission.

Unlike some research venues in which I'd traveled halfway around the globe and visited a single time, I've journeyed to the inimitable Burning Man Festival in Northern Nevada's Black Rock Desert 10 times. Despite the hardships of damning dust storms, which can bring on whiteouts so intense that one can barely see objects (and people) even a foot away, and air so smoky and gravelly that respiratory infections become the norm year after year, I could not resist.

During the last week of August and culminating on Labor Day, Black Rock City becomes the most interesting place on earth. Artists from around the world gather to perform, enchant, and connect. Attracting upwards of 90,000 attendees, five square miles of dusty desert **playa** become the third-largest city in Nevada (just behind Reno) with an axiom like Las Vegas: "Whatever happens at Black Rock City, stays at Black Rock City."

History and Context of Burning Man

While humans throughout history have created festivals to mark harvests, religious days, and connect with others, Burning Man holds much significance in the sphere of utopian dreaming. Its biggest competitor is India's Kumbh Mela, which generates a temporary city that is a thousand times bigger than Burning Man, attracting nearly 100 million attendees. Both festivals compel community connection through belief in a higher purpose as well as nurturing of personal expression. Carnival in Rio de Janeiro, Mardi Gras in New Orleans, and Mexico's Day of the Dead also attract crowds seeking community through artistic expression.

Burning Man began with a group of friends who gathered at San Francisco's Baker Beach to celebrate the summer solstice with a bonfire. On June 22, 1986, two members of the group, Larry Harvey and Jerry James, burned an 8-foot effigy of a man. The event was billed as a form of radical self-expression associated with the Cacophony Society. As the event grew in popularity, it was relocated to the Black Rock Desert in Northern Nevada. Initially, there were no rules other than "No guns in central camp," and "Don't interfere with anyone's immediate experience."

In 1991 the man was outfitted with neon lights, and a legal permit was secured through the Bureau of Land Management (BLM). Attendance grew from 20 in 1991 to 100 in the following two years. As the population grew, tickets were sold online, and rules and restrictions were added, including limiting speed limits to 5 mph, imposing safety standards on art cars and requiring that art only be burned on approved burn platforms. While 80,000 folks attended the festival in 2019, Covid-19 shut it down in 2020. A renegade festival emerged in 2021, which drew 20,000 participants. In 2022 the festival reemerged with nearly 90,000 attendees; sadly, about 20% of the attendees caught Covid-19 during their week of intense dust and revelry. In 2023 there were 73,000 attendees. This drop in attendance may be reflected in tech industry layoffs and certainly in the impact of Tropical Storm Hilary. By the end of the week, so much rain had fallen that entry gates were closed, and attendees were forced to shelter in place.

About the fourth day of the festival, my nephew and I track each other down and reveal all of the things we've imbibed and all the amazing revelations we've had. (In the **default world,** we're of different generations, and typically such cross talk would not and could not occur.) Burning Man is different, and the playa becomes a grand venue for culture jumping. In one moment you can be dancing to screechy, loud techno music; in another, being served a slice of berry pie by a cross-dressing waitress with a full beard and a "Betty" name tag; in another, surveying a graveyard filled with dead Barbie dolls or receiving a very full-body massage or writing a wish inside an utterly spectacular soon-to-be-burned temple.

Sex and gender are some of the many things Burning Man plays with. Guards are dropped; what usually seems out of reach suddenly feels around-the-corner accessible. Veteran members of alternative sex and gender practices invite playa newbies to drop by and sample new flavors. While about 4% of Americans practice polyamory, on the playa, it can feel more like the norm than an outlier exception.

Male-to-female cross-dressing becomes another playa norm, with whole camps dedicated to biological males sporting female finery. Accessing the otherwise inaccessible becomes so appealing that Burning Man decompression parties abound in September and October, as burners attempt to reconcile all the things that felt so possible with their more tightly bound default world lives.

While participation at Burning Man can push sex and gender boundaries, typically, it's done with utmost attention to communication and consensuality. A case in point is the Human Carcass Wash sponsored by PolyParadise, a well-respected theme camp for polyamorous burners and their friends. At the wash, participants equipped with spray bottles filled with soapy water take turns washing and scrubbing each other. Before water is squirted or hands are placed on a fellow burner, touch boundaries (e.g., no breasts, no nipples, and/or no orifices) are fully disclosed. In the end carcass-wash participants emerge a bit cleaner and certainly more enlightened about interpersonal communication. The casual nudity afforded by the Human Carcass Wash can lead to chats about body differences and similarities.

During one wash a woman approached me and disclosed, "I once had large breasts like yours; last year I decided to have reduction surgery." I listened with interest as she continued, "Now I'm able to easily run and engage in vigorous sports—I've even lost 40 pounds!" Her body did look lithe and muscular; part of me would love a body like hers. I then examined the scars on her breasts—they didn't interest me at all.

During my first year (1998) at Burning Man, 23,000 people attended the week's festivities. My eyes were forever popping as I'd run through magically lit tunnels and climb through a panoply of erotic, humorous, and sacred spaces. Every couple of years, I'd declare I'd had enough of the dust, the postburn coughing, and feet so torn up it took months for them to no longer feel like sandpaper.

Then something would pull me back. In 2002 I was in the midst of gathering data on polyamory and jealousy toward my doctoral dissertation and decided there would be significant research benefits to camping at PolyParadise. I brought a large stack of questionnaires, pens, and an open mind. I hosted afternoon discussion groups, referred to as Poly High Teas, and chatted up everyone I could. In each tea discussion, I'd raise different questions, ultimately gathering mountains of rich data.

One of the PolyParadise campers was Zhahai Stewart, who coined the term **NRE**, referring to new relationship energy, the attraction phase of romantic love where new lovers have elevated levels of dopamine and norepinephrine. We discussed how polyamorous people learn to process that phase as simply a phase (that will soon end) as opposed to the rest of the world, which considers falling in love a (potentially) life-changing event. After I had spent five days being a dedicated researcher, my lover Chuck flew into Reno.

I spirited myself away from the Black Rock Desert and drove several hours, refreshing myself with extra-cold water and ice cream, before picking him up. After buying fresh fruit for our campmates, we zoomed back into our desert womb. It was my first time to have a lover join me at Burning Man, and everything—I mean everything—changed. Spectatoring other people's sexualities shifted into joining everyone in everything. One of my campmates, "Touch" (many burners give themselves playa names), noted the frequent screeching and moaning coming from our tent and offered up his much larger, better-appointed tent to extend our play. He then volunteered to be our **fluffer**, assisting with the application of copious amounts of lube, a must due to the harsh, super dry desert air. Once I had exhausted Chuck, "Touch" offered to take a turn. We all agreed it would be a great idea ... and during the rest of our time around camp, we functioned as a joyous threesome!

One morning Chuck and I visited Hebegebees Healers camp and requested an erotic massage. While, typically, burners book sessions to heal physical and/or emotional injuries, our request was for erotic enhancement. Our healer was extraordinary, and our session proved to be utterly unforgettable. He placed each of us on the same massage table with our heads on the far edges and our crotches in the middle. He then began to massage the especially sensitive parts of our bodies and eventually placed a glob of lube in each of our palms, instructing us to apply it to our genitals. Then he fit Chuck's cock into my vagina, and we began fucking on top of the massage table. Our bodies were so fired up; we could barely get enough of each other. It was a once-in-a-lifetime massage—not on the menu and only in that moment, for that moment.

One evening PolyParadise hosted a Masturbate-a-thon. In a dome-shaped chill space covered with pillows and foam pads, 30 or so campers washed their hands, helped themselves to lube and a vibrator (if desired), and brought themselves collectively to orgasm. The contagious moans generated a potent yet respectful atmosphere. After a good amount of masturbating, several of us proposed that we culminate all of that solo-orgasm action into some group fucking. While certainly beyond the purview of the workshop, being that it was Burning Man, the organizer nodded a go-ahead, and all of our bodies flew into action.

Another evening Chuck and I competed in the Great Canadian Beaver-Eating Contest-at Gigsville (a popular theme camp). Here exhibitionism, pretzel-style yoga postures, and the feigning of amazing orgasms were far more important than true-blue cunnilingus. While another hot couple got the evening's prize, I wallowed in how much I'd stepped out of my shell.

Our high buzz continued for days following the burn. As we left the playa late Monday afternoon, we faced the fact that we were nowhere near ready to return home. We drove north on Highway 89, not knowing where it would take us. Serendipitously, we arrived at Sierraville Hot Springs and rented a lovely guest room. That night we found our way to the Meadow Pond. Being completely alone in what felt like a huge-yet-shallow, sandy-bottomed lake, we made love for hours. Eventually, we found our way back to our pretty room and engaged in the kind of lovemaking where the brain takes a long nap and bodies completely get each other. In that moment I knew that I'd reached the apex of sex, love, and connection. When I returned home to Los Angeles, my brain (and body) were still overcome by bliss; the serious, cautious researcher was absolutely on hiatus.

Several years later, I decided at the near-11th hour to go to Burning Man as a catharsis for having spent the previous five months fantasizing about a guy who barely existed. (We'd had sex one time, and then the following five months, he kept promising to get together.) I found a ticket on Craigslist and tracked down some friends who were leaving on Tuesday evening. I landed in PolyParadise, and despite the fact that the camp was packed to the gills, I was welcomed with open arms, and within minutes, I felt as if I had arrived *home*. A couple of guys set up my tent and inflated my air mattress; the next afternoon, I was hosting Poly High Teas and making up for all of the touch and hugs I'd been so craving.

While polyamory is about consensual open relationships, camping with over 100 other poly people can bring consensuality to a whole other level. In one moment I'd be making out with one wonderful guy whom I felt an exquisite resonance with, and the next time I'd see him, he'd be embracing someone else with the tenderness I'd thought was exclusively ours. Being that there was a whole playa filled with engaging, wonderful souls, it was absurd to dig my talons into any particular "soulmate." This protocol was celebrated via the services of the Costco Soulmate Trading Camp. There one could bring in a former "soulmate" and happily trade him or her in for a "used" one who might generate that fresh and exciting feeling once again.

At best the culture of Burning Man is about surplus—during the much-awaited week of festivities, just about everything is gifted. Gifts can be handmade, sparkling trinkets; amazing massages; food or drink; or access into the playa's best dance halls and jazz clubs. Over the years I've offered a variety of services. I've worked as a masseuse, delivered heady lectures at Entheon Village (one of the intellectual camps), made cappuccinos as a barista at Center Camp (they fired me because I was too slow), and written stories for one of the playa newspapers. My all-time favorite job was offering sex and relationship counseling at Hebegebees Healers Camp. I'd offer half-hour sessions to gorgeous young women whose boyfriends had become captivated by other gorgeous young women and to near-perfect young men who were worried that their current girlfriend wasn't as perfect as a woman might be. From my sagely perch as a well-traveled sexual anthropologist, I'd dispense reflections and a bit of advice, often to the tune of "You have no idea how good you've got it—dive in and savor every bit!"

Burning Man is also a place for nerdy men to access more female eroticism than the default world ever allows. On Friday afternoon there is the Critical Tits Bike Ride, where swarms of women join in a topless bike ride all over the playa. They are cheered on by even greater swarms of men, who provide post-ride libations.

One year an enterprising and especially nerdy 60-something man set up a Pussy-Washing Camp. He'd dragged in a gynecological exam table replete with stirrups to effectively wash the vulvas of willing females. I questioned several of the women who had partaken of the "service" and ascertained that the washer was well behaved. Still cautious, I watched while a girlfriend received the service. I then slipped off my panties and positioned myself in the stirrups. While the nerdy guy was deferential and well behaved, it was nonetheless a huge mindfuck to allow an odd-looking, dirty-old-man sort of guy view and painstakingly wash my vulva.

If that wasn't enough boundary-pushing weirdness, later that evening, while walking along the edge of the Esplanade, I found the Orgasmatron. Being alone, I cautiously investigated. I stepped inside the booth and found another nerdy man with a contraption quite similar to a **Sybian**. Vibrating Sybian saddles have been around since the 1980s, and I'd been fortunate enough to try them at several swingers' conventions. Perusing the man and the contraption, I figured he and his Orgasmatron looked reasonably safe. I doubted that in the presence of a stranger on the wide-open playa, I'd be able to orgasm. At one moment I noted, "It's not working. Let's give another woman a try." He shook his head, "Give yourself some more time." Out of nowhere, I came. He then offered, "Stay on and come again!"

I did and I did. I'd allowed a strange yet safe man witness my largely clothed body in orgasm. I pondered, "Was it weird? Was it okay?" It did feel good to orgasm; I thanked him and left with a sheepish smile.

My seventh year to attend Burning Man was 2009, and it was the first year I tried drugs. My boyfriend and coconspirator, Jeffrey, opened that door for me. Why did it take me so long? I was really scared to mess up my brain. So much of my identity had been wrapped around my being smart; the thought of compromising my intelligence in any way was quite frightening. For Jeffrey, drugs were treats that he'd used sparingly over the years. His intelligence was intact, and so I decided to trust him. I'd purchased some high-quality **ecstasy** from a friend in Los Angeles, and then while on the playa, Jeffrey picked up some **magic mushrooms**. Under his guidance we fasted for six hours before taking the ecstasy tabs. I watched him swallow his and, for an instant, didn't want to do it. I was still scared, but being in the same altered-state moment as Jeffrey sounded so appealing that I swallowed the tab. During the next hour, our campmates were indulging in deep-fried turkey. It smelled delicious, but the thought of not getting the most out of our ecstasy trip overrode sampling it.

Jeffrey and I biked out to the middle of the playa to distract ourselves from the turkey aromas and gravitated to a crowd of people awaiting the desecration of a grand piece of playa art. Suddenly, the ecstasy began to hit, and my brain began spinning. A light dust storm swirled up, and all I could do was hold Jeffrey tight. In that moment I so needed touch—lots and lots of touch. We looked into each other's eyes and, in the same moment, agreed to bike as fast as we could back to our van. The dust thickened, but our determination to stay close and get to the van quickly overrode all obstacles.

Once in the van, we immediately pulled off our clothes and began kissing and hugging. His touch was absolutely amazing. I lost all self-consciousness about whether my touch was working for him and just touched. Soon we were making love. Every bit of him, me, and us became utterly delicious. The missed turkey dinner dissipated into irrelevance. I swallowed huge amounts of water, ensuring I would not fry my brain over this megadose of serotonin. In that moment life became totally perfect, and ecstasy became my absolute drug of choice.

The next day, I was scheduled to work as a masseuse. Touch was so exquisite to me that every one of my clients remarked on my incredibly sensitive fingers. That evening the man burned, and we tried out the mushrooms. The visual distortion afforded by the mushrooms paled in comparison to wanting to rip off my clothes and slather my body all over Jeffrey. The following year, we did ecstasy again. The fogginess of my brain on ecstasy coupled with the thick, soft playa dust recalled the absolute sweetness of the year before. My trip was once again amazing, while Jeffrey's dose didn't take.

I was in my own delirious space, more alone with myself than together with him. . . . Ironically this portended our breakup; two months later, he met another woman and, within a year, married her. The next three years, I stayed away from Black Rock City. Eventually, I found myself missing the power of Burning Man—of weathering stark desert conditions amongst an ever-expansive community of like-minded souls . . . and collectively getting to the guts of it all by burning the most beautiful things and deepening their essence by witnessing their transformation.

PART VI

Making It Professional

Lecturing on marriage practices.
Photo by Gillian Grebler. Reprinted with permission.

This section describes what led me to pursue a PhD in human sexuality, what my training at the Institute for Advanced Study of Human Sexuality entailed, and the ways I've worked as a professional sexologist following the granting of my degree in 2003. I describe my work as an educator, researcher, and counselor. When I invited students enrolled in my Gender, Sex, and Culture classes to study current attitudes and approaches to negotiating **endogamy** (marrying inside of one's culture/religion) and virginity, a well-regarded study was produced. That process and those findings revealed that many of my Asian, Armenian, and Hispanic students weather a **cultural generation gap** at least as massive as the one I went through with my parents in the 1970s.

CHAPTER 13

Becoming a Sexology Professional

As a young woman, I never thought I would have a career in human sexuality. I was drawn to the research methods and worldview of anthropology—I deeply resonated with **participant observation**. Being a quiet observer who absorbed other ways and gingerly asked questions resonated with my soul. As feminist thought permeated the anthropology that captivated me in graduate school, I delighted in the spinning of "man the hunter" theories into contemplating the skill required by "woman the gatherer."

I recalled that when Polish anthropologist Bronislaw Malinowski conducted field research in the Trobriand Islands of Melanesia, he relied on interviews with men in researching the *Sexual Lives of Savages in North-Western Melanesia*. Considering the paucity of information on women's lived experience, I titled my master's thesis "Towards a Cross-Cultural Understanding of Female Sexuality." As powerful orgasms surged through my own body, I sought evidence for how women in other times and places experienced sex.

Anthropology continued to be an important lens for my interests in marriage patterns, childbearing, parenting, and shifts in gender roles and expression. I loved being a fly-on-the-wall, unobtrusive observer. If a PhD were attached to my name, I feared I would stand out too much, limiting my access to the small stories I so loved. When I was nearly 50, I faced the fact that I had lived small long enough and that I could pursue a doctorate. In that I'd been ensconced in anthropology for over 25 years, I decided that I might gain more by doing a PhD in another field. Sexology intrigued me. It collected professionals from many disciplines: medicine, sociology, psychology, biology, history, and certainly anthropology.

In 2002 I found my way to Dr. Ted McIlvenna's San Francisco-based Institute for Advanced Study of Human Sexuality. It was nearly 30 years after its heyday when Alfred Kinsey's sidekick, Wardell Pomeroy, was on the teaching staff. While some of my staid anthropology colleagues were dismissive of my interests in partnering patterns (e.g., polygamy, polyamory, and swinging), at the Institute, I heaved a big sigh of relief. For once I could unapologetically study sex and sexual behaviors. My fellow students included psychotherapists, medical doctors, erotic massage therapists, porn stars, and fine artists.

The school was like none other. The lecture room was filled with beanbag chairs, and after class, students were invited to soak in the school hot tub. Ted was a warm bear of a man, who dispensed his unique brand of physiotherapy and bore a trove of interests ranging from designing spermicidal lubricants to the social psychologies of sex workers, erotic art, opera, and law. While the Institute's academic foundations were a bit wonky, many sexuality notables have been associated with the Institute, including Marty Klein, Betty Dodson, Carol Queen, and Annie Sprinkle.

Being a student after so many years as a professor was difficult for me. Clark Taylor, a gay anthropologist and my sexual anthropology instructor, witnessed me bursting at the seams with truckloads of commentary. Finally, he invited me to join him on the lecture stage, admitting he knew little about feminist theory, pregnancy, childbirth, and the lived experience of polygyny.

There were moments that were completely extraordinary, like a gay-male erotica seminar filled with hours and hours of male-on-male anal sex films from all over the world. Afterward I nearly believed that penile-vaginal intercourse was a human anomaly! The curriculum also included much experiential fare, which bored me. Having come of age in 1970s Berkeley, I'd been well marinated in encounter groups, social nudity, self-disclosure, and the pushing of boundaries. The school had an extensive pornography collection, which I was required to view. Other than pieces that were truly historical or cross-cultural, I managed to dodge most of it.

Having completed my MA in anthropology 22 years prior, I'd had no academic exposure to Internet search engines, data collection and analysis software, and presentation platforms such as PowerPoint. Being that my anthropological research had largely been self-styled, impossible-to-replicate participant observation, I wanted to learn quantitative research methodologies. I dove into dissertation research, producing "Jealousy and Transformation in Polyamorous Relationships." Being a long-time subscriber to "me-search," where a researcher studies topics that are personally meaningful, I sought to investigate the emotional pain I'd felt four years prior, when my home partner Jon had directed so much attention and passion toward his new lover Violet.

My insider status in the practice of polyamory gave my efforts at quantitative research a big boost. It enabled me to ask important questions in appropriate ways. As a research designer, I accessed an informed outside-in perspective. Certainly, quantitative research that is not informed by ethnographic vagaries can fall flat. As for polyamory, I was fully familiar with the differences between (1) what people say they should do, (2) what people report that they do, and (3) what people actually do.

While self-reporting via an anonymous survey by a research-hungry population veered toward the truth, it was still my task as the data interpreter to make sense of it all. My findings afforded me a perspective on shared polyamorous cultural beliefs and how very anomalous Jon's behavior had been. Amongst the several hundred subjects I surveyed, just 10% saw their nonresidential lovers as often (i.e., every other night) as he was seeing Violet. My female subjects in particular sought equality amongst members of their intimate communities, while about two-thirds of my male subjects sought to visit more often with their favorites (who were typically their newest lovers). To me, this readily explained why Jon was so intent on spending as much time as he could with Violet.

I noted that most of my polyamory-identified respondents very much embraced their subculture and endeavored to process their jealousies as lessons in personal growth and psychoemotional emancipation. Through the lens of anthropology, I assessed that the practice of polyamory had become a unique and recently invented culture with its own language, perspective, and process.

As I thought more about polyamory's unique cultural practices, I noted that couples who sought to open up their relationships were decidedly in the attachment phase of romantic love and were driven to access attraction-phase excitement from new lovers. For some, engaging in polyamory led to dissolving their partnership, and thus, it functioned as slow-motion serial monogamy.

Despite the fact that polyamorous cultural beliefs subscribe to practicing compersion (being accepting and supportive of their partner's other love interests), I noted something that I named *polyarmory*. Here, to avert the pain of jealousy and the possibility of partner loss, new partners had to be part of the poly subculture (they couldn't be fully available singles), and deep entanglements such as overnight sleepovers were forbidden.

Following the completion of my dissertation in 2003, I rode the cusp of a new wave of polyamory researchers. Over the subsequent 16 years, conferences across America booked me to deliver keynote addresses as well as present research papers with titles such as "Negotiating Pair-Bonding, Romantic Love and Jealousy in Polyamorous Relationships." Having become a sexology professional, I was also hired to do contract research; consult as an expert witness on criminal cases; teach college courses such as Gender, Sex, and Culture; and offer counseling to individuals, couples, and, occasionally, triads.

As a professor, I had much fun dissecting differences between polygamy, swinging, polyamory, and cheating, as well as discussing third genders, including the Brazilian *travesti*, Thai ladyboys (*kathoey*), and Samoan *fa'afafine*. My favorite lectures were on the **brain chemistry of romantic love**; I loved showing students the science behind obsessive love and why it's so difficult to restore passion once the dopamine-rich attraction phase is superseded by the oxytocin-laden attachment phase. After 37 years of teaching upwards of 10,000 students, I retired at the end of 2017. I was tired of my stories and so needed to feel fresh and engaged.

Soon after I'd received my PhD in sexology in 2003, I advertised my counseling services in polyamory-friendly publications and in the *LA Weekly*. I mostly attracted men who wanted to have telephone or in-person sessions where they could chat about their fantasies using sexually explicit language. The dynamic made me uncomfortable; after several months, I shut down my practice and focused on teaching and research. It wasn't at all the sexology counseling I'd hoped to do.

Compersion and Polyfidelity Origins

The Kerista commune, which configured an ever-changing group marriage in San Francisco's Haight-Ashbury district between 1971 and 1991, invented the word **compersion** to facilitate their prescribed practice of polyfidelity. One evening several members were engaging a Ouija board: "compassion" and "person" merged, thus describing this jealousy-averting concept. The commune described **polyfidelity** as a multi-adult family structure wherein members related to each other without hierarchy of preference. Group members were restricted from sexual relationships outside of their commune.

In 2016, as I was winding down my teaching career, I decided to revisit counseling. I created a website, secured listings in several online directories that focused on polyamory, and began to attract clients. While some had polyamory issues, many just sought an open-minded counselor who wasn't going to fault their lifestyle as the cause of their problems. I loved being able to think on my feet, listen hard to intimacy and relationship challenges, draw from all of the research I'd done, and

Anthropologists Who Study Gender, Sex, and Partnering Patterns

Beginning with Margaret Mead, who wrote *Coming of Age in Samoa: A Psychological Study of Primitive Youth for Western Civilization* (1928), *Sex and Temperament in Three Primitive Societies* (1935), and *Male and Female: A Study of the Sexes in a Changing World* (1949), anthropologists have used their unique insider-outsider lens to provide perspective on what is possible for humans in the realms of partnering patterns and sexual expression. Contemporary anthropologists study such topics as queer identities; cultural attitudes toward public displays of affection (PDA); cultural challenges faced by gender nonbinaries; reproductive health, including birth control, abortion, and childbirth; cultural practices associated with the HIV-AIDS epidemic; same-sex marriage; and sexual violence.

Swedish anthropologist Don Kulick is known for his groundbreaking book, *Travesti: Sex, Gender and Culture Among Brazilian Transgendered Prostitutes.* Kimber McKay studied Tibetan polyandry in a Himalayan village, reporting on tremendous flexibility regarding choosing and maintaining polyandrous marriages in her TED Talk titled *Are Five Husbands Better Than One?*

Gayle Rubin is the inspired cultural anthropologist who has proposed the sex/gender system to explain how a society transforms biological sexuality into cultural practices, including kinship and marriage exchange. In her chapter "Thinking Sex: Notes for a Radical Theory of the Politics of Sexuality" (Rubin, 1984), she observes that society endorses a *charmed circle* of sexualities, wherein only practices associated with love, marriage, and reproduction are valued. Alternative sexualities would thus be seen as dangerous, destructive, and sadly, sex negative.

Janet Bennion, who grew up in a Mormon polygamous family and became an anthropologist, offers a distinctly balanced view of life in a polygamous household, noting that such marriages can offer women security, social bonds, and satisfaction. She advocates for the legalization of polygamy to "bring it into the light" so that incidents of abuse can be better monitored (Drown, 2012).

Anthropologist William Jankowiak has had a distinguished career studying urban Chinese society, Mormon fundamentalist polygyny, and love around the world. He has edited such volumes as *Romantic Passion: A Universal Experience* (1995) and *Intimacies: Love and Sex Across Cultures* (2008).

Helen Fisher is perhaps the best-known contemporary anthropologist who studies sex, partnering patterns, and love. She has authored several widely read books, including *Anatomy of Love: A Natural History of Mating, Marriage and Why We Stray* (1992/2016), *Why We Love: The Nature and Chemistry of Romantic Love* (2004), and *The Sex Contract: The Evolution of Human Behavior* (1982).

tailor my insights to my clients' particular needs. Conceding that what I was offering was not psychotherapy, the clients I attracted struggled with culture-based topics, including contemporary gender roles and expectations, interpersonal communication, and designing intelligent and flexible relationship paradigms.

It was such a different time than when I had attempted this work 14 years prior. Being that "polyamory" had been bandied around mass media and social media, it had become a thing that anyone could try. Affiliation with a polyamorous community was no longer expected, and clients without access to the language and culture of the organized poly world very much needed counsel. Being that I had made a career of translating cultural ideas to the culturally uninitiated, my information base and how I presented it worked quite well. To keep business expenses down, I created a home office; when the Covid-19 pandemic hit, I opened up a Zoom Pro account to offer sessions remotely.

CHAPTER 14

Learning by Teaching: Insights Into Ethnic Generation Gaps

After I finished my 2003 dissertation research, quantitative research methods began to seep into my Gender, Sex, and Culture class curriculums. **Qualitative research** (participant observation) had been very difficult to teach. Either a student somehow had a collapsible ego (as I did) and was willing to go deep into unfamiliar cultures and be impossibly inquisitive, or they prefaced their projects with morality statements, such as "I believe taking illegal drugs is dangerous, and despite that I studied people who take them, I never would myself."

Quantitative research proved to be quite useful for allowing my morally upright students to unapologetically access the worlds of their peers. In 2005 I invited students enrolled in my classes at California State University, Los Angeles, and at Los Angeles Valley College to collaborate on a survey of the sexual attitudes and partnering preferences of their peers. After agreeing on 27 questions, I provided each of them with 10 copies of the survey to distribute anonymously amongst their friends. They then entered their data on an Excel spreadsheet, analyzed their own findings, and submitted their data for our larger study.

My students were half Hispanic, one-third Armenian, and one-fifth Asian. From class discussions I was well aware of how differently my Hispanic and Armenian students managed their sexualities. The Armenians regarded Hispanic practices of out-of-wedlock pregnancies as foolish, while the Hispanic students regarded the Armenians as fixated upon maintaining their public reputations. (The Armenians were having secret abortions while presenting themselves as virgins to their communities and holding off on marriage until they and their sweethearts could afford homes and businesses.) I hoped that collaborating would enable them to have an expanded perspective.

The survey findings established that the Armenians and Hispanic respondents (average age of 21) were equally sexually active (about 70% engaging in sexual intercourse) but had very different beliefs regarding unplanned pregnancies and endogamy. The Asians were a bit less sexually active (about 50%), with significantly less practice of oral sex (25%) relative to the others, who reported 70%. See Figure 14.1.

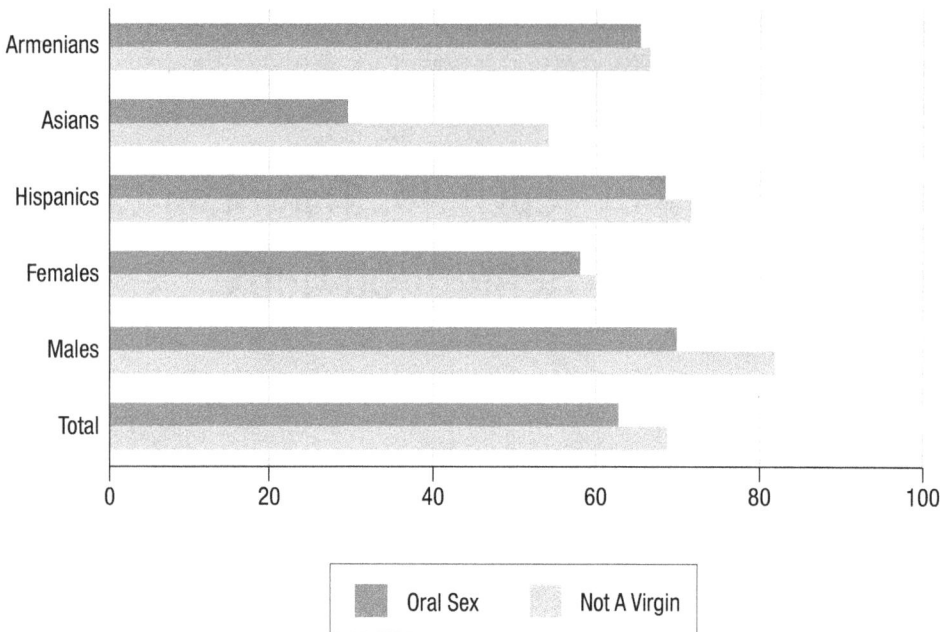

Figure 14.1.   **Incidence of Sexual Behaviors Amongst Study Participants**

The Hispanics, being close to the majority ethnicity in Southern California, were at ease with partnering outside of their ethnicity and religion, while most of the Armenians adamantly sought to marry each other. See Figure 14.2.

About Chinese culture, which fell somewhere between the other two groups in their interest in partnering with one of their own, one student offered the following assessment:

> While earlier generations followed the traditional Chinese cultural norms, the new generation has adopted some Western cultural practices and started to form a new culture. There might be conflicts between older and younger generations, but I believe these will not destroy Chinese American culture. Instead they will help it to evolve into a unique and special ethnicity.

Definitions of Virginity

This study, reflecting the concerns of my students, focused on the sexual experiences of heterosexuals who viewed the loss of virginity as participation in penile-vaginal intercourse; activities that do not break the intervaginal hymen might be practiced to preserve female "virginity." For those who are not heterosexual, there are, nonetheless, virginities to lose. These can include oral sex (both giving and receiving), fingering (as in mutual masturbation), and anal play (including anal intercourse, anilingus, finger penetration, and fisting). Engaging in BDSM in its different roles and various activities could offer new losses of virginities via the engagement of specific roles like top, bottom, and switch and/or the use of scene-specific paraphernalia, such as restraints, whips, and clamps.

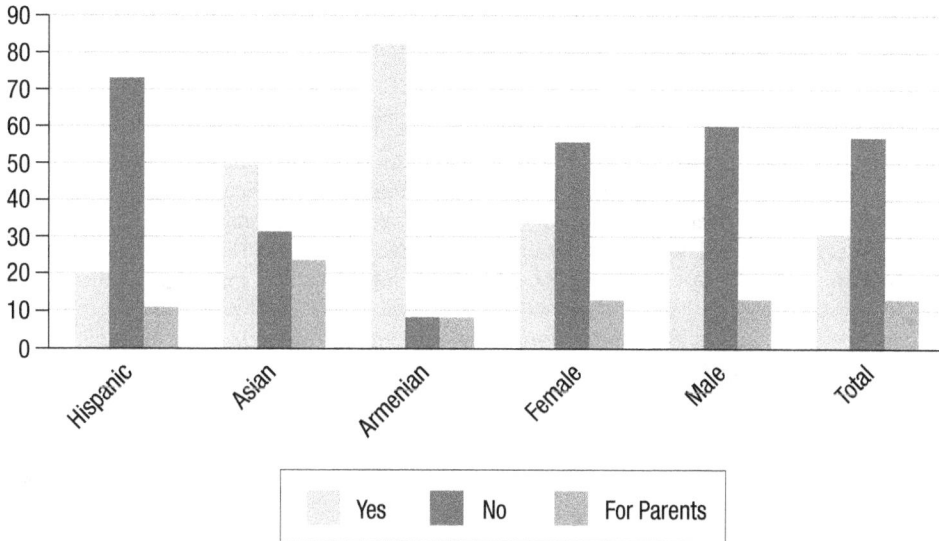

Figure 14.2. Shifting Views on the Importance of Marrying One's Own Ethnicity

As I pored through my data, I saw how cultural beliefs and practices were used to negotiate sexual decision making. Parental expectations were offered as a publicly expressed **cultural excuse** for abstaining. For some young people, this cultural excuse could protect them from engaging in sexual exploration they feared or were uncomfortable with.

I was quite taken by a female Armenian student who had used the cultural excuse as a cover-up for clandestine behaviors:

> No one was ever going to know about it because, being Armenian, having premarital sex is completely unacceptable. Once I decided to do it, I went to a tanning salon and got a Brazilian wax for the big day. I think it's the best thing that has ever happened to me. I had this wonderful secret I would run to whenever I was in need. No one knew. I was seen as this little good girl, yet had sex every week with no strings attached. The sex was amazing.

Some of my subjects were caught in the middle. They saw limited value in agreeing to **arranged marriages** or endogamous marriages, and yet felt thwarted in defying their parents and their communities. Their dilemmas so paralleled the generation gap I'd lived through with the distance my parents maintained from my exploratory practices in the 1970s and their tight-lipped ones of the 1940s. Many of my students were first-generation Americans whose parents, unlike myself, had not themselves come of age in a place like Berkeley at the height of the sexual revolution.

The survey data showed that nearly all of the Armenian mothers had told their children that they were virgins when they married, while about half of the Hispanic mothers had told their children this as well. One of the Hispanic young mothers very personally discussed the changes in her own culture:

> Being a single parent is now something that is common. I already have two children, but I would have preferred to be single until I was 25 so I could be free like a bird. Most Hispanics are not following their parents' traditions. We have seen that being a virgin is not something that is valued. Now we get to decide who we want to be.

The Armenian females were in the biggest quandary. Their survey data established that their male cohorts wanted their future brides to be Armenian virgins, while they themselves were witness to a culture that was very much in transition. According to one young Armenian woman,

> The generation gap between Armenian men of this generation and their fathers' generation is almost nonexistent. Armenian men are holding on to the same views and traditions that their parents (mostly fathers) have had in terms of female virginity, endogamy, and gender roles. Their views about women have not changed much either. They are not treating women equally and have different standards and expectations for and of women. However, there is a change between the women of this generation and their mothers' generation. Armenian women of this generation are not afraid to explore outside of their culture and ethnicity.

In the end my goal had been to cause my students to see their behavior in a larger context. I smiled big when one of my Armenian students assessed, "I learned a lot doing this project—mostly that I wasn't the only nonvirgin and that there were others who were a little rebellious like me."

One male Hispanic student offered some forward-thinking comments relative to how his culture had incorporated less restrictive paradigms:

> I think that there is definitely a shift for the better in the Latino culture. Thanks to changes in female sexual behavior, we now have more independent women who do not need a man to survive. With more women in control and secure enough to express their sexuality without being afraid or embarrassed, the whole family dynamic can benefit.

Ironically, when I shared the study's findings with the next semester's students, several of the Armenians challenged the findings, contending that they don't know anyone who engages in such behaviors. I stood quietly, assessing that issues of privacy and nondisclosure still remained important to Armenian identity.

During 2006/2007, I presented the study "Today's Cultural Generation Gap: Coming of Age Armenian, Asian and Hispanic in 21st Century America" at professional anthropology and sexology conferences. My data was seen as fresh and exciting, and my findings regarding the cultural excuse were well received when I explained that, ultimately, culture functions both as an excuse for maintaining distance from mainstream practices and values as well as a protection for those whose behaviors and activities belie family and community expectations.

PART VII

Exploring Worlds of the USA

Image © CSA-Printstock/DigitalVision Vectors/Getty Images.

The culture of the United States, with its celebration of heteronormative monogamy and the nuclear family, has spawned unique practices. Being that polygamy is illegal and polyamory is practiced by little more than 4% of the population, cheating remains the activity for the sexually (and emotionally) restless. Considering the many distractions young women face prior to deciding to have a family, the infertility business has become a hallmark of family building in the United States. This section explores both of these cultural particularities.

4

CHAPTER 15

Studying Cheating From a Multitude of Perspectives

Sexual cheating is deeply embedded in the human condition. Considering that humans are, by nature, a nonmonogamous species that readily becomes fascinated with new (dopamine-generating) opportunities, cultures everywhere grapple with it.

Followers of every version of the Jewish and Christian bibles have been admonished to "not covet thy neighbor's wife (or house or ox)," and, more explicitly, in the seventh commandment, to "not commit adultery."

In biblical times adultery was more narrowly defined than it is today. Biblical patriarchs were allowed to have multiple wives and concubines and were free to have sex with consenting single women. They were forbidden, however, from erotically engaging women who were married to other men. These concerns were largely about property rights; a married woman (as well as a neighbor's house and ox) were private property and were not to be unwittingly occupied, used, or sexed by anyone but their rightful owner.

My father was the first person to tell me about cheating. His telling was in the form of a story of his friend Harry, who had maintained a long-standing, absolutely hidden affair during his entire marriage. One evening at the opera, he saw Harry with the other woman in tow; the two men acknowledged each other with a

Biological Evidence for Human Nonmonogamy

Evidence for the nonmonogamous mating proclivities of humans includes **sexual dimorphism**, size of the male testes, and intrauterine sperm wars. Sexually dimorphic species (where the male is physically larger than the female) is an indicator of nonmonogamy, as is seen in ourselves as well as our primate kin: gorillas, chimpanzees, bonobos, and orangutans. Species with relatively large testes, such as humans, chimpanzees, and bonobos, are able to produce large amounts of sperm, which facilitates **intrauterine sperm competition**. Researchers have observed that depending on the context of mating (e.g., a home partner vs. an interloper), the ejaculate varies with differing amounts of kamikaze (fighter), blocker, and egg-penetrating sperm (Baker, 1996).

Jesus and a woman who committed adultery.
Image © clu/DigitalVision Vectors/Getty Images.

wink, and introductions were not made. My father's telling of the story did not even whisper of the emotional thunderstorms and strategic challenges that contemporary cheating can imbue. Ultimately, Harry's wife never found out, and Harry passed away as a respected, loving husband and father.

I don't believe my father ever cheated on my mother. His reasons were tied to his marrying at the seasoned age of 45. I was told he'd had many years to "sow wild oats" and thus had not suffered from an absence of sexual variety. As for my mother, her first lover was a married man who initially lied to her about his already-taken status. She respected the rules of the day regarding the comportment of secret lovers and enjoyed the sweetness of the connection until she found other men to date. Eventually, she met my father, who was fully available for marriage.

The first time I dabbled in the world of being a secret lover was when I met Guillermo, the *National Geographic* photographer in Mexico. I was so focused on being mentored in my anthropological studies that it barely dawned on me that Guillermo was married. While I was frustrated by Guillermo's unwillingness to be in touch, I realized that retaining the integrity of his marriage was no doubt more important to him than assisting me with my professional aspirations.

In that my college boyfriend Jerry and I had an open relationship, our dalliances with other lovers rarely ignited the intense emotions associated with contemporary adultery. Six months after we met, I took a four-month solo trip through Western Europe. Being curious, cute, and 20, I had many invitations and a couple of sexual adventures. One was with a Dane I'd met on a train in Copenhagen. He'd invited me to stay with him during my visit. Following the visit, my period disappeared, but sensing no other bodily changes, I rightly assessed that he had not gotten me pregnant.

Back home, Jerry was using my wall calendar to mark off his various dates with a girl named Janie. Upon my return Jerry downplayed Janie, and Jerry made me feel like I was his "one" until I'd had too many cups of morning coffee with his roommate Rick. After a couple of weeks of whirlwind romancing, Rick migrated to becoming a casual lover and a dear friend. I kept the calendar that recorded each of Jerry's dates with Janie, assessing that our breakup had more to do with our mutual desires to engage the mid-1970s sexual revolution than any of our casual dalliances.

When Sean and I became partners in late-1970s New York City, I had my next opportunity to wince at being cheated on. He'd just unfurled himself from living with a top-notch public interest attorney to move in with me, a wide-eyed anthropology graduate student. Considering the stultifying possessiveness he'd weathered trying to do monogamy in the midst of the sexual revolution, we endeavored to have an open relationship. One night he returned very late (there were not yet cell phones for sending one's GPS whereabouts) and explained that in the course of selling poetry on the streets of Manhattan, he'd met a cool couple and joined them back at their flat. While he failed to disclose any details of what had transpired, I felt jealous that I had missed out on what I imagined was an amazing encounter.

In our Manhattan world of the early 1980s, once there were marriage and babies, the permissive rules of engagement that living-together couples allowed each other were swiftly supplanted with strict monogamy. Thus, the darkness of contemporary cheating reared its head. The first emotional thunderstorm I listened in on was that of Gary, a young professor, and Anna, his expectant wife. During Anna's pregnancy Gary took up with Kim, a pretty teaching assistant, and then soon after his new baby was born, he pronounced his love for Kim, and Anna filed for divorce. To me, Gary sounded like the extreme of *cads*; the whole incident heightened my wariness of marital expectations. I doubted that I'd ever be able to ferret out a true dad amongst all the cads in 1980s New York City (Meston & Buss, 2009).

Every time I'd soak in the Jacuzzi following a workout at my Greenwich Village health club, another married man (often with a pregnant wife) would proposition me. In deference to my stirred-up emotions over Gary and Anna, I'd flatly refuse. Then some ten years later, exhausted by my efforts to meet and marry "the one," I took refuge in becoming a secret lover. Every time I'd walk into a party, I'd find myself gravitating to the married men. I enjoyed the rush I'd feel when they'd remark, "You are smarter, prettier and so much more fun than my wife!"

Being single, I had little to lose (other than my time). Altogether I had affairs with three married men. One, Ben, ensured that the whole affair remained a secret, generating an identity for me as a family friend. There were moments I felt tempted to tell his wife, but then I faced that I had absolutely no interest in disrupting or destroying her marriage.

The second, Brad, was much more of a risk-taker and did little to cover his tracks. Soon into our affair, a righteous woman in our community informed his wife. After all was exposed, I was one of several women he was courting. While the others quickly disengaged, I attempted to negotiate a compromise wherein I would become a polyamorous second wife or a live-in concubine. Brad's wife flat-out refused; 14 years later, when they eventually divorced, she blamed me. My feelings were hurt in that all I had requested was for all of us to become "family."

My third married man was Chuck, who, during the several years we navigated our polyamorous love affair, made me feel exquisitely matched and very loved. While our home partners knew when we would be seeing each other, we generated many never-to-be-disclosed secrets. While orthodox polyamorists advocate full disclosure; the world we created together was tender. Our home partners could not fathom practicing *compersion,* the polyamorous term for having loving empathy for pleasure accessed with other lovers.

Perhaps the bliss Chuck and I accessed with each other was too potent. As much as she could, his wife invited me to become a personal and family friend. There were moments in which it worked, but mostly, the precariousness of their connection had filled their home with land mines that I couldn't help but stumble on. While my stepdaughter was well aware that my relationship with her dad was polyamorous, Chuck's children somewhat didn't know. They'd already weathered an attempt by a single woman to spirit their dad away, and the family had buckled in tight to assure that would never happen again. Back home, my partner Jon relished making fun of Chuck and telling me I looked way too smitten every time I'd return from a date or visit. When the passionate cling Chuck and I shared subsided, I felt a sigh of relief.

Being a secret lover with little interest in destroying a lover's marriage is emotionally calm relative to the two other positions in the cheating triangle: cheating and being cheated upon. Having a penchant for disclosure and despising living a socially and emotionally partitioned life, I've only cheated once, and that once was in the context of polyamory. See Figure 15.2.

I was dating a guy named Michel, who had a best friend who was also named Michel. Several months into dating Michel#1, he announced that his best friend (Michel#2) was immigrating to Los Angeles (they'd both grown up in Montreal). I asked if they had ever shared a woman; he told me they had done it many times and that he would be happy to introduce me to Michel#2. As it turned out, I really liked Michel#2 and happily dated them both together as well as separately. I was in such

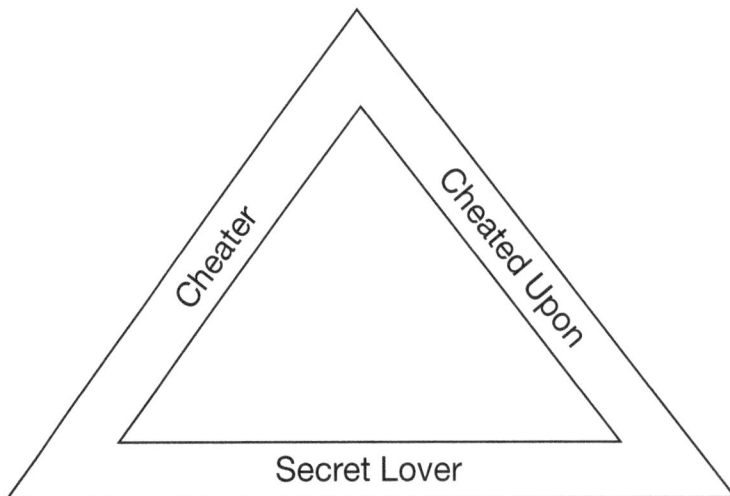

Figure 15.2. The Cheating Triangle

bliss I could barely contain my pleasure when we'd go to parties as a threesome, rent hotel rooms all together (leaving the desk clerk to giggle in wonderment), and have the most fun I could ever imagine.

At the time, I was living with Jon, who only knew I was dating Michel#1. I began to feel guilty that I'd told him so little. We'd endeavored to be honest with each other, and I'd been harboring a secret. The day I told Jon about Michel#2, he had a meltdown, especially on hearing that I'd invited both of them over to share our bed while he was off with his lover Violet. The thought of me making love with two hot guys in our bedroom so boiled his blood that I sought safe harbor at a friend's house. After a couple of days, Jon calmed down, and I promised I'd never again host a threesome in our bedroom if he wasn't included!

Being cheated on is the third position of the cheating triangle and is no doubt a painful one. In that I kept my partners on long leashes with quick-release collars, I'd largely averted any desire on their part to cheat. I detest possessiveness and consider flirting, light kissing, and playful teasing to all be acceptable behaviors. To my knowledge, I've been cheated on just once.

Many of my friends witnessed Jon's interest in Violet, but none of them told me. After several months of him coming home smelling like her cologne, his guarding my access to his email (initially, we'd known each other's passwords), and his suffering "cartastrophes" (like having his car battery die and not being able to get home until 4:00 a.m.), Violet decided to tell me. Hearing what I might have suspected ended the sanctity of my relationship with Jon.

Being witness to the intensity of their private connection was very difficult. The two of them were steeped in the dopamine of new-relationship passion, while Jon and I, at best, accessed the oxytocin-rich attachment phase of longtime, trusting partners. With the trust broken, the oxytocin in my brain crashed, and initially all I could do was to scream and shiver.

Beginning in the spring of 2008, I shifted gears from doing informal "experiential" research on cheating to conducting Internet surveys to collect quantitative data. Because I had a track record for doing survey research on polyamory and swinging, Dr. Ava Cadell invited me to be the director of research for her online enterprise, Loveology University. She was a mix of formal and friendly . . . and a delight to work with.

A Bit on Intimate Partner Violence

While Jon's higher self knew better than to foment violence and he was ultimately a gentle, loving, and supportive partner, I feared he could become violent. Some men engage in violence over the slightest suspicion that a partner could be cheating, even when they are not.

There are four main types of intimate partner violence: physical (beating), sexual (rape), stalking, and psychological aggression, with the latter being the most common. Considering the consequences of a real or imagined transgression and the power of a jealousy response, women through the ages have been primed to either surrender, lie, flee, or retaliate.

I designed a quick 12-question survey that we linked to each of our websites. Responses trickled in; 11 months later, we had 1055 surveys with a 98% completion rate. This dramatically contrasted the enthusiastic networking I'd received from my surveys on the behaviors of people who practice polyamory. During a short survey window of two-and-a-half weeks in March of 2008, 716 polyamorous respondents took my 50-question multiple-partner survey with an impressive 99.6% completion rate.

These respondents were hardly representative of the distribution of cheaters in contemporary America: a recent national survey clocked just 20% of men and 13% of women cheating. At the other end of the spectrum, there are studies that have reported that upwards of 75% of men and 68% of women have in some way cheated in a relationship. Such variances require a deep dive into research methods, including the framing of questions, whether the survey was administered in person or anonymously, the age of respondents, and differences in definition of what constitutes cheating. Certainly, older respondents have had longer sexual careers and thus more opportunities to cheat. While people in polyamorous relationships are open to extra-pair sexual contact, they might consider undisclosed erotic activity to be cheating. Gender can figure strongly as well in that cheated-on females are likely to consider many more activities to be cheating than males who cheat.

Those responding to my Loveology University cheating survey were a completely different cohort. They were not an enthusiastic, data-hungry community like the polyamorists; rather, they were disparate individuals who have enjoyed accessing sexual topics on the Internet. Being that it was called a cheating survey, about 60% of the respondents had participated in one or more sides of the cheating triangle. They had an interest in and involvement with cheating, with 67% of the males in committed relationships reporting having cheated and 62% of the females reporting being cheated on.

I created the category "combo cheaters" to describe the 72% of my cheating respondents who had also been cheated on. I noted that males in this category had the highest appetite for more, better, and different kinds of sex as a cheating motivator. These males robustly justified cheating, with nearly two-thirds citing a sexless marriage and almost half contending that their wives' medical problems prevented them from having the kinds of sex they enjoy. Meanwhile, over half of the combo-cheating females reported that there was "no justification" for their own cheating.

For women who had been cheated on, two-thirds claimed activities like cybersex, sharing emotional intimacy, light kissing, phone sex, and cuddling were absolutely "cheating." See Figure 15.3.

My research concluded that females largely cheat for "attention," while males cheat for "excitement" and to "live out their sexual fantasies." Males consider cheating to be harmless if they are able to get away with it, while females, even if they have cheated, still regard it as an immoral activity.

The following year, Avid Media, the parent company of Ashley Madison, a notorious website that enables married people to connect for discreet encounters, contacted me. They were impressed by the work I had done on the cheating study and wondered if I would like to partner with them for a new study. My mouth watered, thinking of the easy access I might have to a large database of active cheaters, and I readily gulped, "Yes, it would be pleasure!"

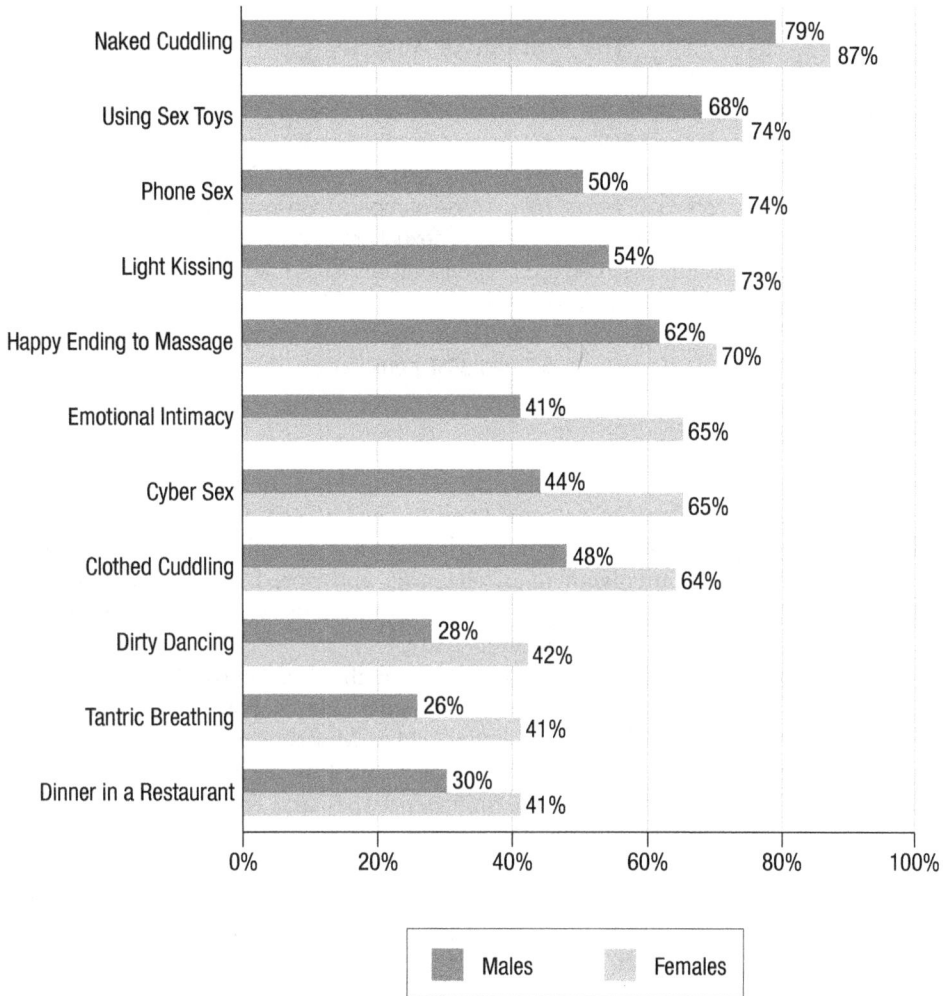

Figure 15.3. Activities That Those Who Have Been Cheated On Consider Cheating

Avid Media's Toronto office immediately began to draft numerous legal documents that assigned rights, explained duties, and promised payments. Due to frequent staffing changes, other than (now-former) CEO Noel Biderman, the rest of the company was forever in transition. They'd noticed that many of their members were clicking anal play on their profiles and wanted to investigate whether couples who were getting enough of this at home would be less inclined to cheat. My inclination as a sexologist was that the absence of anal play in a heterosexual couple's home erotic repertoire was probably not a big factor in cheating. While their observation was right—that a growing number of heterosexuals were experimenting with anal activities—altogether, such stuff was more of an *add-on* rather than a *must-have*.

Nonetheless, I kept my lips zipped tight and quickly educated myself on the requisite paraphernalia by attending anal sex educator Tristan Taormino's workshop at The Pleasure Chest, West Hollywood's premier adult education and toy store. Brimming with information on butt plugs and strap-ons, I drafted a survey. I called it

The Practice of Anal Sex

While male–male penetrative anal sex was practiced by Greeks and Romans 2,500 years ago, according to a 1914 study informed by the clinical work of German sexologist Magnus Hirschfeld, only 8% of gay men participated. By the 1950s participation had nearly doubled to 15%. These numbers then increased exponentially, shown when Edward Lauman's 1994 study of sexual practices in the United States reported that 80% of gay men engaged in penetrative anal sex. My 2011 research for Avid Media assessed anal sex practices of heterosexuals. Participation rates hovered around 50% for Whites and Hispanics and were decidedly lower for Blacks (40%) and Asians (30%). Transgendered folks claimed 84% participation, the highest rate of any cohort.

"The Sex and Relationship Happiness Survey" to make it sound innocuous enough to attract many respondents so to satisfy the quotas laid out in my contract. To not offend the non-anally inclined, I began with basic demographic questions, queried about the respondents' involvement in cheating, and posed a series of questions about oral sex. Then I created **toggles** so that respondents who had no connection to anal activities would be quickly steered away.

The survey was launched in March 2011 through a link on the Ashley Madison site. Over a nine-week period, nearly 5,000 Ashley Madison members completed the survey. To generate perspective on the Ashley Madison cohort, I also invited participation from people on polyamory lists as well as people more specifically involved with anal play via Tristan Taormino's network and Fetlife, an online social networking site for kink aficionados. Altogether we attracted close to 7,000 respondents. I was in survey-researcher heaven!

As I began to crunch the data, my suspicions about anal play not being a big factor in why people seek to have affairs were readily confirmed. While I ultimately presented "Anal Play: Who is Doing It and Why?" to the spring 2012 meeting of the Society for the Scientific Study of Sexuality in Los Angeles, Noel Biderman had sought a report that would normalize cheating in America.

We pored through the data and found what he referred to as a smoking gun regarding oral sex patterns and preferences of the Ashley cohort men. Nearly 60% of these men and a nearly half of the control group men believed that "other couples were having more oral sex with their home partners than they were." The women in both groups were somewhat evenly distributed amongst the three choices "more," "about the same," and "less." See Figure 15.4.

To me, these findings underscored the significance men place on *receiving* oral pleasure. While women tend to regard oral sex as foreplay, the visual and psychoemotional sensation for men is significant. The act of having a beloved place his very private part in her mouth can be both humbling and exquisite.

Our "most-smoking-gun" finding then appeared when we evaluated strategies for dealing with a home partner who refuses to provide oral sex. While two-thirds of our respondents reported that they'd "let it go and focus on what their partner likes," more than a third of the Ashley male cohort claimed they would "have a secret affair," and less than 8% stated they would "seek the services of a prostitute." This interested me. See Figure 15.5.

AshleyMadison.com Cohort

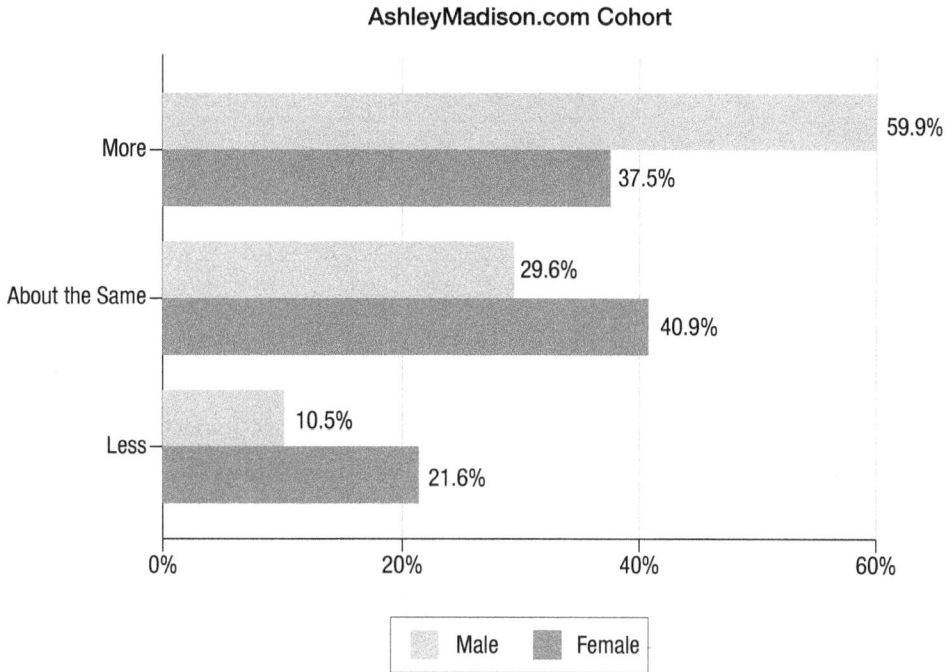

	Male	Female
More	59.9%	37.5%
About the Same	29.6%	40.9%
Less	10.5%	21.6%

Control Group

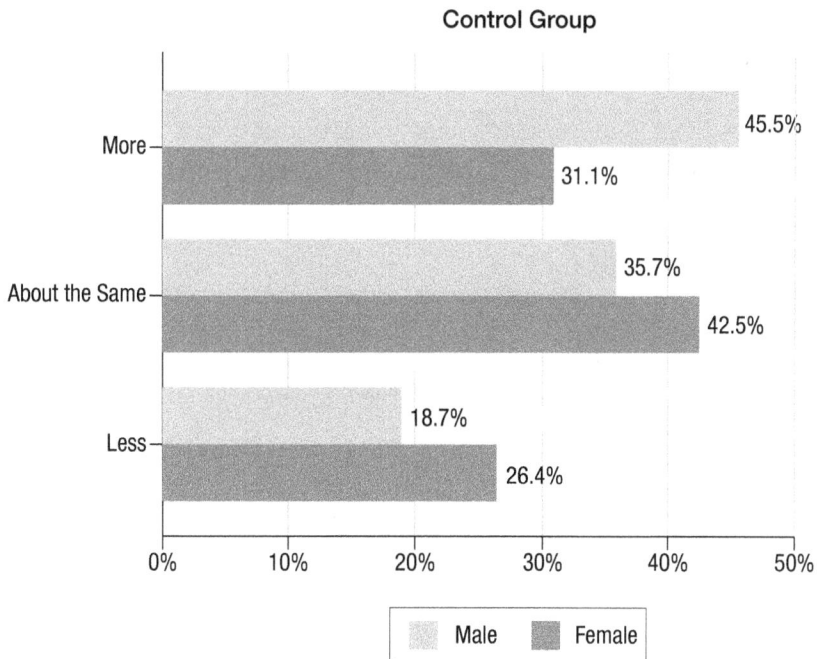

	Male	Female
More	45.5%	31.1%
About the Same	35.7%	42.5%
Less	18.7%	26.4%

Figure 15.4. The Belief That Others Are Having More Oral Sex

Note. The majority of Ashley males (59.9%) believe that other couples are having more oral sex than they are. Females were more evenly distributed among the three choices—they were most likely to select "about the same," not experiencing the sort of oral sex void that the males are.

AshleyMadison.com Cohort

I'd let it go and focus on what my partner likes — 65.6% (Male), 60.9% (Female)

I'd have a secret affair — 35.6% (Male), 35.0% (Female)

I'd find a lover (open/polyamorous) — 14.9% (Male), 14.8% (Female)

I'd consider filing for divorce — 5.3% (Male), 6.2% (Female)

I'd go to a sex worker/prostitute — 7.7% (Male), 0.4% (Female)

x-axis: 0% 20% 40% 60% 80%

Legend: Male, Female

Control Group

I'd let it go and focus on what my partner likes — 69.3% (Male), 68.4% (Female)

I'd have a secret affair — 26.5% (Male), 22.2% (Female)

I'd find a lover (open/polyamorous) — 17.0% (Male), 15.2% (Female)

I'd consider filing for divorce — 6.7% (Male), 9.1% (Female)

I'd go to a sex worker/prostitute — 5.6% (Male), 0.9% (Female)

x-axis: 0% 20% 40% 60% 80%

Legend: Male, Female

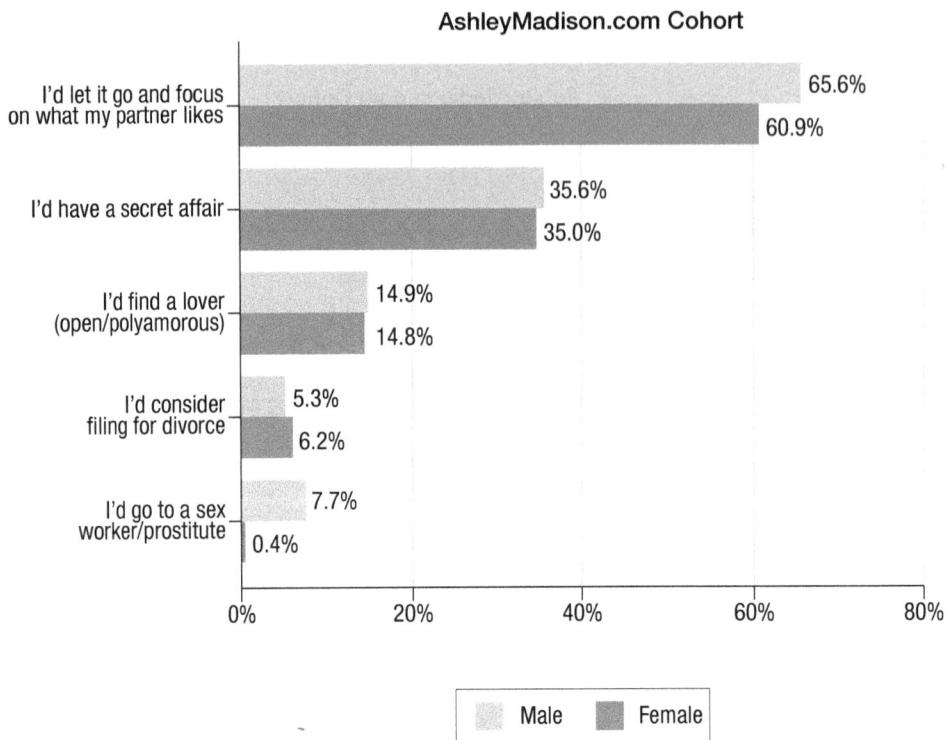

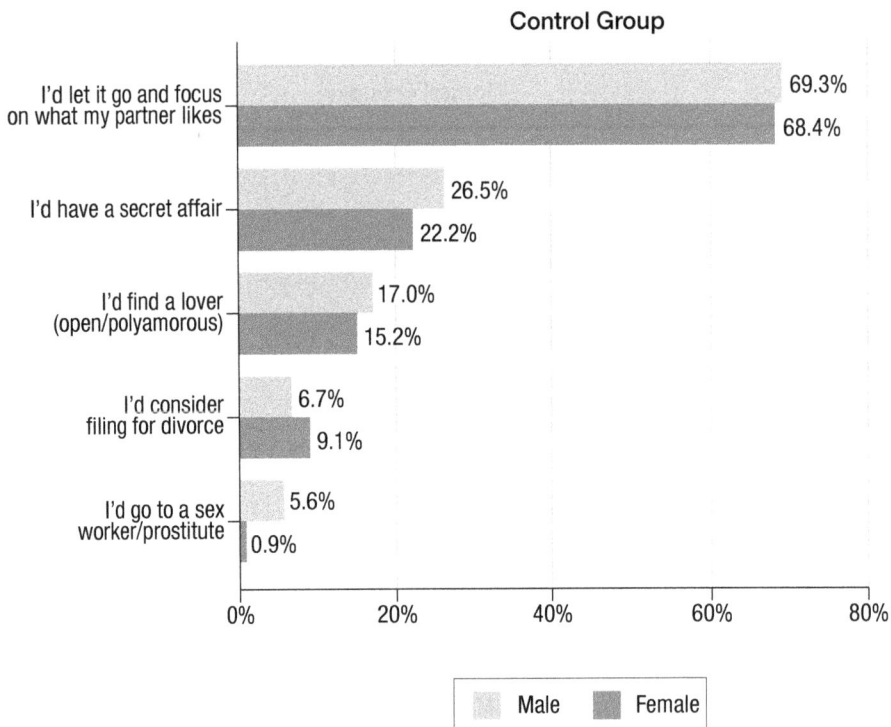

Figure 15.5. Strategies for Dealing With a Home Partner Who Refuses Oral Sex

Note. While both groups were most likely to "let it go and focus on what their partner likes," there was much interest in addressing this void with a secret affair with 35.6% of the Ashley males and 35% of the Ashley females. Finding an open/polyamorous lover was a relatively popular choice for the control group (26.5% of males and 22.2% of females). The traditional practice of going to a sex worker or prostitute was a dramatically low choice for both Ashley males (just 7.7%) and control group males (5.6%).

While my control group males were more likely to seek an open polyamorous lover than a secret lover, they, too, registered low (less than 6%) for seeking the services of a prostitute. This group of largely heterosexual, middle-class, married American men in their 40s and 50s sought (if at all possible) to *receive oral pleasuring from women who love them*. Unlike other ethnic and class cohorts such as Orthodox Jews and working-class Hispanics, who routinely frequent prostitutes for oral pleasuring, these men sought it differently.

I presented my findings at the November 2011 meeting of the Society for the Scientific Study of Human Sexuality in Houston, Texas, and then in December 2011 in my paper "The Oral Sex Void: When There's Not Enough at Home," which was published in the *Electronic Journal of Human Sexuality*. Avid Media had plans to do a press campaign, but their new public relations department was looking for something more sensational. In perusing my findings, they noted that nearly two-thirds of the women on the Ashley Madison site were actively cheating on their spouses and sought to sensationalize this in tandem with the oral sex data. To me, these two findings were unrelated.

Women who've posted profiles on the site tended to have cheating experience and seek more of the same. The men on the site differed little from the control group men regarding cheating experience. Regarding marital happiness, they registered as far happier than the women on the site. From what I could surmise, many men sign onto the site to check out what *is possible* in case they *might* want to have an affair. When I separated the active cheaters from all of the noncheating visitors, the Ashley women (as I suspected) were not driven to cheat for oral sex. Refusing to be part of a public relations campaign that skewed my well-analyzed data, I allowed my relationship with Avid Media to lapse and did not bill for the balance on my contract. Being a pawn for advancing Avid Media's agenda felt ethically disgusting in that my data did not support the conclusion they had hoped for.

In 2015, four years after my study was published, the Ashley Madison site was hacked. Over 70,000 fake female-profile bots were uncovered, establishing that just 15% of the site's members were human females. The site was sued for luring men to spend more money to communicate with the allegedly eager and plentiful women. Being that the respondents to my questionnaire were not bots, my data was not impacted by Avid Media's unscrupulous business strategy.

I began to play with the dataset and saw several fascinating contrasts between the views and practices of cheaters and polyamorous people. From 2012 to 2014, I offered these findings to nearly a dozen conferences around the country in my presentation "Are Polyamory and Cheating All That Different?" See Figure 15.6.

I noted how polyamorous people (relative to cheaters) were more likely to be bisexual, be happy in their home relationships, and engage in more frequent sex with their home partners as well as in more alternative sexual practices, like BDSM and anal play. As for where they'd go for the oral sex they're not having at home, as expected, the poly people would seek it with their poly lovers, and the cheaters would seek it with their secret lovers. See Figure 15.7.

In my work as a sexological statistician, I was not privy to the airtight strategies cheaters use to keep their marriages safe. For this data I'm indebted to several men who I've managed to cajole into sharing their stories. One was a man who sat next to me on a flight between New York and Los Angeles. When I mentioned I do

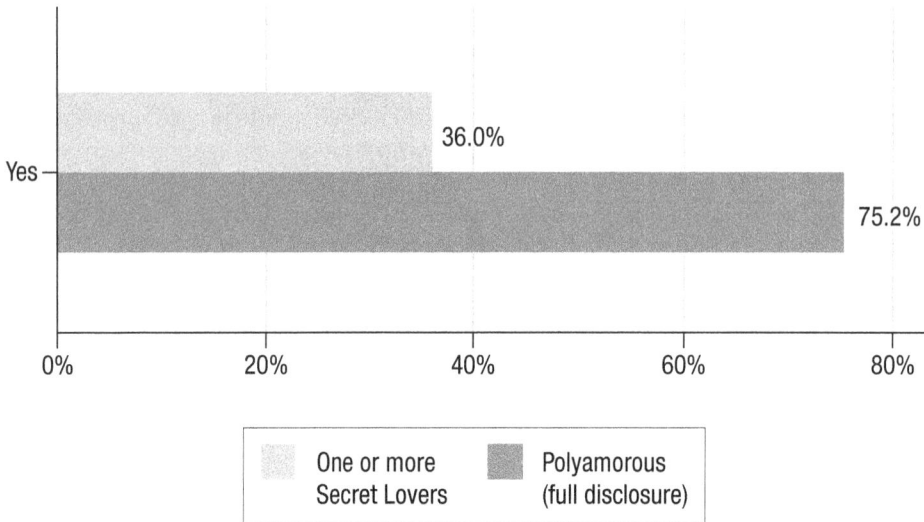

Figure 15.6. **Differences in Relationship Happiness Between Cheaters and Polyamorists**

sexological research on people with multiple partners, he agreed to tell all as long as I agreed to never be in touch with him again. Being that he chose to remain anonymous, I have not given him a pseudonym. During the course of our six-hour flight, he described how he hid his longtime lover from his unsuspecting wife. He used disposable cell phones and calling cards for making dates with his lover, ensuring that there would be neither digital nor paper evidence. When he bought gifts for his lover, he would always buy an identical gift for his wife so that no unexplained purchases would appear on his credit cards.

His dates with the lover were always paid for in cash; one morning, following a lovely night together, he took her out for breakfast. He was out of cash and had to put the meal on a credit card. To cover himself, he took his wife out to eat at the same place that evening and quietly paid cash for that meal so that she'd never suspect a thing. When we discussed the details of sexual performance, he revealed that while he uses Viagra with his wife, he never needs a pharmaceutical boost with his lover. When asked if he ever had thoughts of leaving his wife for his lover, he responded, "Absolutely not! She is emotionally unstable—marrying her would ultimately be a disaster!"

I met Moshe, a Jewish Iranian teacher, at a local café. He'd responded to one of my personals ads, neglecting to mention that he was married. It took over an hour of chatting about this and that before he revealed his already-taken status. Despite the fact that he considers his wife cruel and combative, ending their long-standing marriage would be culturally inappropriate. He'd be exiled from his ethnic community, and his wife and children would regard him as a pariah. For him, the only acceptable thing to do was to find women available for trysting with him in the late afternoons and to "golf" with him on Saturday mornings. As I listened to the tight boundaries he imposed on his consorts, I gained an appreciation for the energy cheaters expend to keep their secrets.

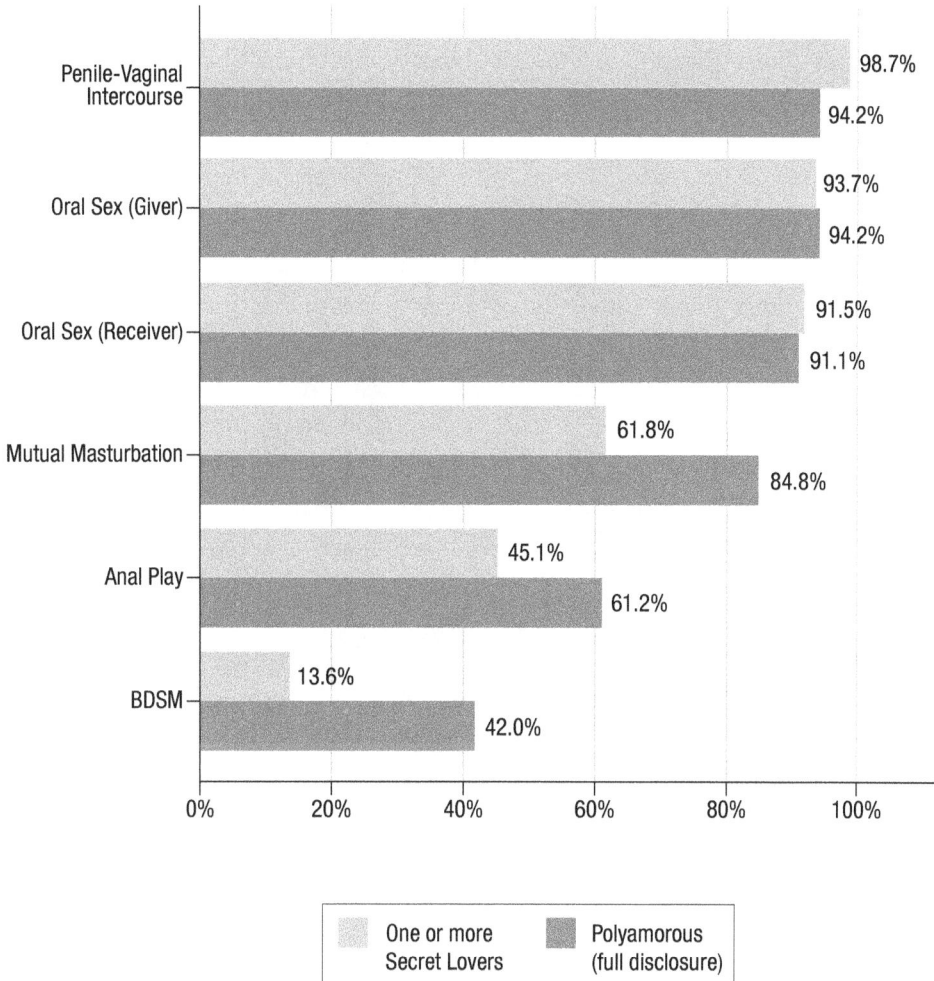

Figure 15.7. Differences in Sexual Activities Between Cheaters and Polyamorists

My final cheating enigma came in the form of Lawrence, a respected artist who lives in my community. We'd met at a party and soon started dating. As we grew closer, he began to tell me about his lover of 20 years who lived several hours away and was married to a much older man. I asked, If he and I were to become lovers, would he then be cheating on her, and would I then become a supersecret lover?

We laughed about how my terminologies made this all sound so complicated. He contended that there were no conditions under which he would either leave her or tell her about me. As I released Lawrence, I assured myself that I had absolutely gone full circle in my exploration of cheating!

CHAPTER 16

In Search of Baby Batter

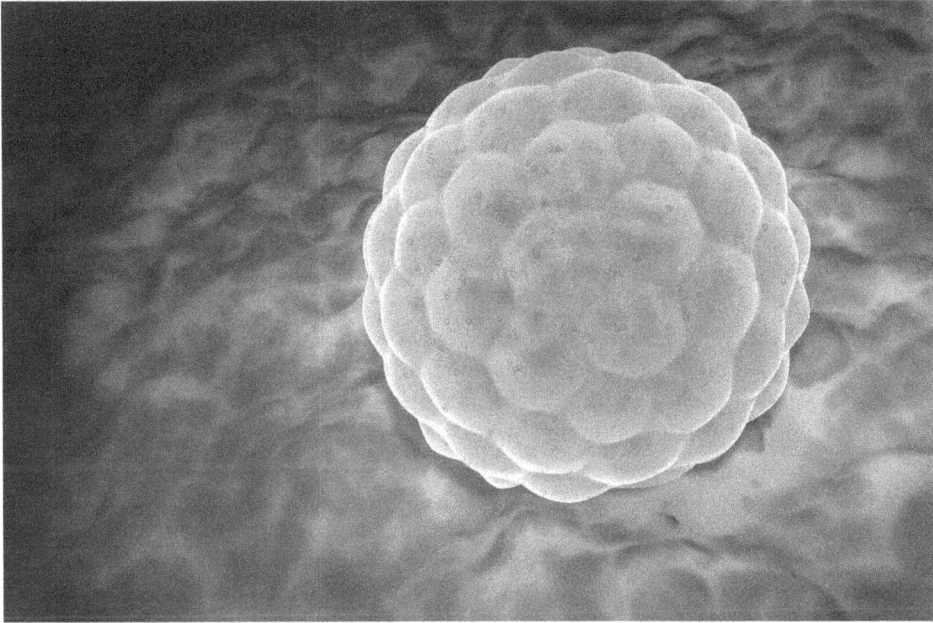

An embryo ready for implantation.

Image © MedicalRF.com/MedicalRF.com/Getty Images

When I was 51, I invited four of my closest girlfriends to be my support family to witness the insertion of three in vitro–fertilized embryos into my hormonally prepped uterus. It was my last-ditch effort to become a mother.

Rather than marrying my college boyfriend Jerry and starting a family in my 20s (when I was very likely fertile), I was on a quest for professional achievement and to be my own unique person. Being that I was born at the peak of the post–World War II baby boom, demographics were in place for there to be stiff competition to find a husband who was several years older. Fewer babies were born in prior years. (Males born toward the early-1960s end of the baby boom also suffered from a demographic imbalance, with there being fewer babies born in Generation X and thus a paucity of younger females.)

These demographics along with effective birth control, the legalization of abortion in 1973 (the year I started having sex), and the feminist agenda of career and self-actualization all contributed to my not even trying to have children in my 20s.

Ironically, Betty Friedan and other early founders of second-wave American feminism were already mothers. To them, "the problem that has no name" was living a sequestered domestic life in service of others (Friedan, 1963).

In 1980, when I was 27 (which was perhaps an ideal age to start a family), I produced a well-regarded booklet, *Giving Birth in New York City: A Guide to Childbirth Options,* for families who sought the services of a midwives and doulas. My efforts to foment the overuse of fetal heart monitors and the rising C-section rate then led to my award-winning documentary film, *Changes in Childbirth.*

Sean, my boyfriend, inspired the publication of the booklet and was a total cheerleader in the production of the film. We were activists who lived on the financial edge and were scrupulous about birth control. Many years later (after he had married and fathered a son), he reflected on my still childless state, "If you had gotten pregnant, we would have certainly gotten married." I was a bit taken by surprise: "Wow! I had no idea how close I was to a kind of normal life with marriage and a baby!"

If that had happened, our child would have been about 44 years old today. No doubt they would have been a savvy activist with a good heart and good looks. Instead, I made more documentary films that reflected the rumbling of our world, including a monumental one on the Rainbow Coalition and Jesse Jackson's 1984 presidential campaign. In my early 30s, Sean decided to enhance himself professionally by enrolling in a midcareer public administration graduate program at Harvard's Kennedy School, while I relocated to Los Angeles to work on more documentary films. Living a continent apart, we found our lives took different twists and turns. We dated others, and eventually, we let each other go. I hoped I could do better. In some ways I never did.

I began to spread my wings. Without a husband or children, my 30s in Los Angeles were a free-spirited second adolescence. While I gave lip service to looking for a partner who wanted children, somehow, I was drawn to men who already had children, and I was curious about LA's sexual underground. I explored sadomasochistic dungeons, tantric sex practices, and the slightly unruly world of swinging. No doubt there was a part of me that was quite scared of settling down or settling at all.

In my late 30s, I fell hard for Brad, a gorgeous married man with two young daughters. I very much wanted him! We were perfect in bed, and our minds danced beautifully. He was well traveled, brilliant, and very much an out-of-the-box thinker. If one of those well-placed condoms had slipped, our love child would have been 34 today. No doubt they would have been drop-dead gorgeous, with a compelling vision for engaging everyone and everything.

In my early 40s, Jon became my home partner. He had the talent for fixing anything and everything, cooked delicious comfort food, had a beautiful nine-year-old daughter named Xiomara, and was as smart as a whip and equally funny. I was happy. And then the rumbling started. His daughter wasn't my daughter. I wanted my own child.

He complied by not using birth control. Xiomara and his older daughter, Josey, who was already grown when we met, were both unplanned. Trying to bring on a pregnancy was an anathema to him. I used a fertility test kit to measure my hormone levels to better time when to have sexual intercourse. "Yup, it was sexual intercourse; not at all lovemaking. And it was so not my fantasy!"

Frustrated, he got involved with Violet, a woman who appreciated him just for who he was, not for his baby batter. I began to date other men. I didn't want to use birth control. I didn't care who the father was. I just wanted to finally get pregnant. All those years of being careful in my 20s and 30s led to my very reckless 40s.

At 50 I completed a midcareer PhD, and then the only piece of unfinished business remaining was that child. Jon and I lived in a pretty house on a hill, and my career as a professor of anthropology was in place. I'd published a well-regarded book and had conducted field research in East Africa, Papua New Guinea, and Mexico. I felt very much self-actualized, other than conceiving that baby.

Altogether I threw $30,000 at fixing this. Everything else I had ever pursued, I'd achieved. I hoped if I tried hard enough, I could achieve this, too. I doubted any of the straitlaced adoption agencies would accept us because of our ages (I was 51 and Jon was 62) and lifestyle (we had an open relationship).

Moreover, I very much wanted the visceral experience of pregnancy, childbirth, and breastfeeding, and thus I chose in vitro fertilization (IVF), designing my own embryos with donor eggs and sperm. After a treadmill test, blood panels, and a meeting with a psychologist, I was deemed healthy and sane enough to carry a midlife pregnancy.

Jon proved to be a reluctant sperm donor, so I accepted a donation from Douglas, an attractive guy I'd met over the summer. Being that my eggs were deemed too old, I enlisted a donation from Miranda, a beautiful former student. For what my child might lack in intelligence, it would certainly make up for in looks!

Miranda was injected with hormones to increase her egg production. Despite my anxiety over needles, every night, I injected a complementary batch of hormones so that our menstrual cycles would be in sync. On donor day, 29 of Miranda's eggs were retrieved and inseminated with Douglas's potent sperm.

My fertility doctor showed me a magnified picture of the three embryos he would be inserting in my well-prepped uterus. My girlfriends held hands and looked on supportively. This baby would be so very wanted!

Sadly, none of the embryos embedded into my very ready uterus. Once my cycle normalized, several of the remaining embryos, which had patiently waited in the deep freeze, were revived. They were then inserted at the perfect moment for implantation. Nothing happened.

I cried. I could no longer fault myself for not super trying. If that beautiful baby had happened, they would be 21 years old today, and I might not have adopted so many puppies and kittens and mentored so many of my tenants and anthropology students.

When it came time to offer a presentation for the annual American Anthropological Association meetings, I faced that I had spent the entire previous year deeply researching fertility technologies. Drawing from the infertility conferences I'd attended, the online and in-person support groups I'd joined, a survey I'd designed, and certainly my own experience, I created "How the Bough Bends: The Creation of Family, Kinship and Community Amongst Users of Donated Gametes" (2006–2009). Ultimately, the project was the most expensive (and emotionally draining) self-funded research I'd ever undertaken.

Anthropologists Who Study Human Reproduction

Anthropologists have focused their cross-cultural lens on reproduction in its many forms, beginning with Margaret Mead's 1949 work on gender role socialization in the South Pacific and then Brigitte Jordan's landmark book, *Birth in Four Cultures: A Crosscultural Investigation of Childbirth in Yucatan, Holland, Sweden and the United States* (1978). Robbie Davis-Floyd studied the anthropology of reproduction and published *Birth as an America Rite of Passage* (1992), *Cyborg Babies: From Techno-Sex to Techno-Tots* (1998; edited collection with Joseph Dumit), and *Birth in Eight Cultures* (2019; edited collection with Melissa Cheyney). Evolving out of her own lived experience, Rayna Rapp authored *Testing Women, Testing the Fetus: The Social Impact of Amniocentesis in America* (1999), pulling together the views and practices of bioethicists, medical professionals, genetic counselors, and cultural critics to address the impact of genetic testing on contemporary families. She and Faye Ginsburg edited the wide-ranging collection *Conceiving the New World Order: The Global Politics of Reproduction* (1995), which examines topics ranging from midwifery to lesbian motherhood, international adoption, the politics of contraceptive research, and postmodern procreation. Conception technology continues to stimulate contemporary anthropological research with such topics as reproductive dreams and disappointments, race and value in human egg donation, and fertility tourism.

PART VIII

Engaging the Cybersex World

A woman absorbed in sexting.
Image © Frank Herholdt/Stone/Getty Images

As the world migrated from in-person socializing to texting, being a sexual anthropologist, I began to pay attention. I became an astute participant observer in the culture of sexting, incorporated cyber research into my teaching curriculum, and testified as an expert witness for defendants snared in cybersex stings.

CHAPTER 17

The Viral Nipple

It all began rather innocently. In 2013 I'd placed an Internet personals ad, tagging myself as a "Slightly wild deep thinker in search of a hug." One of my respondents was Derek, an attractive guy who introduced himself as having a good career, an athletic body, and an interest in both indoor and outdoor activities. I offered him my cell phone number and proposed we find a time to chat. The next morning, a text arrived on my new smartphone that read, "Hi this is Derek. Have a great day!" Later that day, while attending a dull conference, Derek texted again, bantering that with my being so brainy, it would take a lot to keep me entertained. I loved the all-knowing tease sound of his commentary.

The photo I used for my personals ad.

While my teen daughter required a texting plan to function socially back in the year 2000, it wasn't yet an adult practice. Around the time Anthony Weiner mistakenly tweeted (rather than privately texted) a crotch shot, I'd acquired a smartphone. I was horrified when Bob, a guy whom I'd met for dinner and wet kissed in the parking lot, attempted to cajole me into sending him a photo of my nipples. While I might not have designs on running for elected office, the very last thing I believed I would ever do would be to satisfy that request.

Derek was different. He didn't request inappropriate photos; he presented himself as a caring friend. One night he sent me a picture of himself in bed, bathed in the golden light of a reading lamp, wishing me "Sweet dreams." I became intoxicated . . . he looked so delectable. Eventually, Derek agreed to meet for lunch. When I first saw him, a weight of relief lifted as I noted that he was even cuter than his photos. We snuggled our seats close to each other and engaged in a shy game of footsie. On the way home, his text twinkled in, "It was such a delight to meet you!"

I began to feel brave enough to sext. I asked how he liked to kiss. He offered, "Open mouth, gazing, full and exploratory." Wriggles spurted up my spine. Thus began a grand conversation of what each of us like . . . a slow seduction . . . a bit of butt slapping . . . loud moans . . . sleeping close. I fantasized about consummating that kiss.

The following week, he invited me to his house. I felt a bit like a tarty call girl when I gave my name to the attendant at the guard shack, wondering how often Derek hosts late-night visitors. Nervous, I stepped into his house. We made tea. Derek lit candles, put on a romantic soundtrack, and delivered that much-awaited kiss. It was absolutely perfect!

We never got around to drinking the tea.

He eased off my panties, and his fingers reached into my deepest pleasure zones. Many orgasms later, I curled into a ball while he snored quietly and held me tight. The next day, he texted, "My dear, your visit pasted a big smile on my face!"

No further invitations arrived; thus, my sexting addiction began. Whenever the beguiling message square appeared on my phone, dopamine would ping through my body. I began to harangue myself with negative judgments: "Don't I want a full-on boyfriend to share concerts, art openings, and nice dinners?"

Social Scientists' Assessments of Sexting Culture

Social scientists studying the culture of internet sexting have noted such characteristics as the **online disinhibition effect**, **asynchronous chat**, **fantasy role play**, and **de-masking**. Alternative realities are engaged when players know that they are not representing their true selves. They may present as having a different age, gender, and appetites for sexual acts that are far from their lived experience. Being that online chat is often asynchronous, a sensation of heightened interest can occur when looking over an extended period of chat in real time. Part of the game of chat is to try to engage who is really behind the screen by requesting photos or a video chat or scheduling an in-person meeting. When just fantasy engagement is desired, blocking offers or complete ghosting will likely follow.

Desperate, I decided the *healthy* thing to do was to end the relationship. He agreed to stop sending suggestive texts that he could not deliver on. In fact, he agreed to stop texting altogether. For a moment I felt convinced I was on the path to relationship mental health, and then I found myself screaming and crying in utter pain. The attention I'd been receiving from those tease-filled texts had apparently mattered to me. I rescinded the texting ban, telling Derek, "I needed to receive your 'Good morning, Sexy' texts!"

At a loss for hot topics to discuss, I began to send photos of myself. This, too, started rather innocently . . . I texted that I was skinny-dipping at a lake, and he responded, "I would love to *see* you!" I handed my phone to a girlfriend and directed her to capture no more than a slight glimmer of my floating breasts. Derek sent a smile emoji; my mood soared into totally on fire.

Next, I asked a friend to photograph my breasts just slightly peering out of a half-buttoned bodice. As the shutter clicked, I thought about Derek nibbling on my nipples. The photos were exquisite. I was no longer a strident feminist professor; my inner babe had ignited. Seeing Derek in person became incidental to photographing myself for his consumption.

When a girlfriend offered me some bits and images from a sexting website, I was aghast. They were so impersonal; moreover, they had typos and misspellings! I was on a personal journey to uncover and discover my hidden erotic self . . . nothing canned or premade would do.

Meanwhile, Derek was matching me by sending grinning selfies in underwear or low-cut jeans. I began to understand the allure of sexting: we were the directors and the stars of our own personal pornography.

One afternoon I noticed how one of my pretty nipples peered through my turquoise-print sarong. My body was no longer just something I inhabited; it had become hot in its own right. I trained my camera on just that nipple. The image was perfect, and Derek immediately devoured it: "Babe, you are so delicious!" I gasped . . . I had in fact crossed the Anthony Weiner line by sexting a private body part!

My sexting research was then complete: I'd generated a dopamine addiction for receiving commentary on my aging-though-apparently-still-hot body, my nipple was perhaps at risk for going viral, and I very much understood the pleasures of cocreating a personal pornography.

CHAPTER 18

The Petrified Sex Goddess

In 2018 my home partner Doug and I faced that we were not a match. Fearing there might be no one else out there, we persisted in a late-life, sexless relationship. One day I spoke up and proclaimed, "I want to have sex again!" He agreed. And we both agreed that it would not be with each other!

At the not-so-tender age of 69, he opened a Tinder account . . . reducing his stated age to a much lower one. Suddenly, this odd and incompatible ex-partner became megapopular. He had coffee dates, happy hour dates, cook at her home dates . . . and barely spent a night at home. His flurry of activity propelled me to research my own possibilities.

I reopened the OkCupid (Internet dating) account I had used ten years prior, and suddenly, my inbox was filled with erotic proposals. I would text along, claiming all kinds of appetites I could barely remember ever doing: "I *love* to be spanked . . . and **nipple clamps** sound *so* sexy. Squirting . . . OMG, it's my favorite thing! Just finger my G-spot in that special way (I'll show you), and I'll completely drench your bed!"

Eventually, I agreed to meet one of my sexting consorts for lunch. He picked at his food; I devoured half of mine and then took the rest home for future meals. The conversation was fun and full of energy. In the parking lot, we engaged in one of those very long kisses where I dug my fingers into his back and allowed our tongues to tickle and dance. He then asked, "Can we make out in your car?"

I was aghast: "Fully exposed in a public parking lot in the middle of a hot afternoon?" I reached for my mother's timeworn words and said, "No."

Once I arrived home, I texted him, "Thank you for the lunch and the delicious kiss!"

What might have been a simple thank-you exchange suddenly unfurled into a mad stream of accusations. He claimed, "You shut me out!"

I had apparently imposed the "dating rules" of no more than a kiss on the first date. I tried to appease him, describing what we could do one day in my backyard hot tub. "I'd slither my body all over yours, mount you, and kiss you all over!" He then pushed, "Then invite me over right now!"

Overwhelmed, I took a break and queried Doug about the parking-lot make-out offer that I had turned down. "Was I wrong to do that?" He reflected, "No you weren't."

I then returned to my phone and found seven unanswered texts from my date. He accused me of leaving him out in the cold by taking an unannounced texting break. I retorted, "In *texting culture* it's acceptable to not answer back immediately." He blared back, "During that half-hour break I lost interest—*you* are way too much trouble!"

I tried to pull all the texting stops by texting, "In the heat of the moment, I love being spanked!" He gleefully responded, "I'd love to meet your needs!"

For a moment I thought I'd reeled him back in; I then got petrified that I wouldn't be able to deliver the hot encounter I'd been promising. I was scared I'd tear and bleed if he penetrated me with all of the force he promised. Trembling in a mix of fear and excitement, I damped it down, proclaiming, "I like to take it slow." He queried, "Are you damaged in some way?" I text-mumbled, "Probably not."

His mind surmised the chaotic person I was presenting, and he emphatically texted, "Not for me. You need a sensitive gentleman, and I am a devouring animal. We are not a match!!" He then proclaimed, "You are a confused, dried-out, post-menopausal woman. Buying you lunch was way more than I should have done!"

While licking my texting wounds, I received another OkCupid offer. This guy, too, was seeking exotic sex. He claimed that his busty **sub** was interested in having a threesome with me. Quickly the banter began: "She loves your pictures! We think you're very hot."

My confidence surged . . . I then claimed, "I would *love* to help you spank your sub!" He then asked, "Would you come over this evening and join us for drinks?"

Quickly, the protective *mother* in the back of my head pulled the reins in, and I cleverly texted, "My **dom** says I have to meet you for coffee in a public place." The guy and the sub readily responded, "We understand." And then they disappeared.

When I told Doug about this second erotically exuberant offer, he commented, "There must be something in your profile that's bringing you this kind of attention." I discovered my profile photos included bikini shots from 10 years ago, with my busty top, flat stomach, dark brown hair, and winning smile.

Photo by Irene Newman, 2014. Reprinted with permission.

I recalled the moment. I had just viewed Amy Webb's TED Talk, "How I Hacked Online Dating" (2013), where she had done an analysis of online dating dynamics that concluded that women who show some skin receive more attention than smart, accomplished ones who just post shots in business attire. I figured I'd play all my cards and slip in the bikini shots.

The moment I removed them, my inbox driveled down to near-empty. I stripped in the privacy of my bedroom and looked at all of myself in the mirror. I noted I was ten pounds heavier but certainly as busty (and imaginative) as ever. As for those bikini shots, I faced that they still are me. . . . I could repost them, referencing that TED Talk that concluded that hot, brainy girls ought to play with a full deck.

Unlike my own travails with dating, Amy Webb had generated an algorithm to find an excellent match for herself. She conducted her assessment from the comfort of her home computer screen: she met up with her one ideal match, and they became a couple and were soon married. I faced that as an exploratory anthropologist, my dating goals were very different. Over the years, I had dated as a means to access as many cultures, people, and scenes as I could. I'd gone on hundreds of coffee dates just to find out how others negotiate the world of sex, mating, and matching. The theater of this offered so much intrigue that the thought of finding "the one" and becoming monogamous kind of horrified me!

As for that "Petrified Sex Goddess," she ultimately accepted the consequences of playing with a full deck. She needed to own her braininess, her love of playful kink, and embrace her skeptical third eye.

CHAPTER 19

Working as a Cyber Sexpert

As my screen of choice became my smartphone, I began to savor texts written just for my consumption. For my students, their preference for personal texts just for the receiver was even more so. They would be so buried in Snapchat and Instagram that they'd forget they were seated at a classroom lecture! I sympathized.

I devised projects that might provide an anthropological lens to this compelling new culture. While previous generations of students happily ventured into gay bars, ethnic beauty salons, Sex and Love Addicts Anonymous meetings, and swing clubs to access nearby subcultures, my 21st-century students were trepidatious. I created a cyber research project where students (with permission) would observe a subject's cell phone or computer behavior. During or after the observation, they would discuss app usage, texting behaviors, Internet searches, and the extent (if any) that cell phones were used to make phone calls. Several of my very shy students adapted the project into something that was more archaeological. Rather than observing direct behavior, they would unlock their phones and swap them with a fellow student to access use of social media apps, email, and texting. Their papers would then assess differences in cell phone behavior between themselves and their subjects. My trove of strategies was then shared at anthropology teaching conferences in "Studying and Teaching the Culture of Cyber Chat."

My Gender, Sex, and Culture students were invited to observe a consenting subject's (live) use of dating apps such as Tinder. They would then report on discussions they'd had with their subject for why potential dates were swiped right (interested) or left (not interested). Transcripts of chats with Tinder matches could be discussed (and perhaps analyzed). Students without a willing subject were invited to devise projects that compared the Indian dating website Shaadi.com with decidedly American dating sites like Match.com. To access an interior experience and explore each culture more thoroughly, they could create their own dating profile.

In 2015 one of my colleagues who had a respected practice as a sexology expert witness invited me to consult on some of his cases. With my having been a participant observer of cybersex behavior, he thought I could assist the attorneys of defendants caught up in internet sex stings. These scenarios typically featured an undercover agent presenting themselves as a precocious adolescent to unsuspecting men (with too much time on their hands.) Having an intimate understanding of the fantasy world of texting and sexting with strangers plus being able to explain it as a professional analyst, I had a skill set he considered to be an asset.

I consulted on several cases, pointing out that actual underage adolescents who consensually engage in cyber sexting with adults would never reveal their true ages. I would analyze sexting transcripts, noting how the language used by the undercover agent could not possibly be written by the adolescent being portrayed online. Finally, I'd expose instances where the agents were leading the conversation into more explicit eroticism and directly proposing an in-person meeting.

After consulting on several cases by phone and preparing written analyses and a number of PowerPoints, I accepted a case at a military base that would require an in-person testimony. I purchased several business suits and began to review the case. It involved a married recruit who was caught in a sexting sting with an undercover agent posing as a teen girl. The recruit was arrested by the undercover team when he'd left the cyber sexting world and walked over to meet his supposed chat partner.

The standard fantasy defense was offered, claiming that the recruit could distinguish between the make-believe language of an adult impersonating a teen and an actual, vulnerable teen. Employing such a defense, the defendant would have simply been intrigued by a so-called 14-year-old who texts like a savvy adult. Their fantasy meetup would then extend such role-play (between consenting adults) into a real-time encounter.

The jury didn't buy it. All they could surmise was that the defendant willfully left his barracks to meet an alleged 14-year-old girl. Cases like these are very hard to win. By the time a defendant consults with an attorney who enlists the services of an expert witness offering a fantasy explanation for his misbehavior, he begins to believe that's why he did what he did. The logic of fantasy role-play posits that the defendant has a full understanding of the dynamics of the situation. While such defendants desperately seek exoneration for leaving their computer screens, their decisions to meet in person rarely resonate with the straightforward thinking proposed by prosecuting attorneys.

Ironically, pedophiles are unlikely to get caught in such stings; they typically engage young-looking 18-plus consorts. Getting convicted has serious consequences, including a lifetime listing on the **National Sex Offender Registry** and a long prison sentence. Moreover, these defenses are very expensive, often costing a defendant their life savings.

The scene very much disturbed me. The accused was found guilty, receiving a dishonorable discharge and a prison sentence. His wife and young child would be left penniless. I wanted to give the $20,000 I was being paid for a week of service to the wife. After that stressful week, I faced that I didn't have it in me to do this kind of consulting.

PART IX

The Marriage Question Continues

My moment with the Gerewol Festival dancers of Niger.

Photo by Angels Ferrer, 2018. Reprinted with permission.

Throughout my career my ears perked up for marriage and courtship patterns that deviated from Western cultural practices. This section opens with "Engaging India's Courtship With Love Marriage," which draws from my 2007 field visit, where I compared contemporary matchmaking in India with the generational shifts between my grandparents' arranged marriage, my parents' love marriage, and the relationship conundrums of today's world. The second chapter deconstructs Niger's Wodaabe people's **Gerewol Festival**. Arriving in 2018, I had read that it was an annual "marriage market." By asking questions, observing ritual practice, and drawing comparisons to the relatively prudish Western world, I came to assess that the festival unabashedly celebrates the beauty, eroticism, and reproductive potentials of its adolescent boys.

CHAPTER 20

Engaging India's Courtship With Love Marriage

As a young girl looking over my mother's family photo album, I noted a picture of an upright, stern-looking woman who was the matchmaker who introduced my maternal grandparents. Being that her work had led to the creation of my mother and then, ultimately, me, I gazed intently, acknowledging how her efforts had led to my own existence. My grandparents were an unhappy couple who stayed together for their children. According to my mother, my grandfather was a righteous tyrant, while my grandmother was a dutiful wife and a doting caregiver.

My parents' generation went to dances and socials and were able to freely choose their dates and mates. When my mother was in her early 20s, her father attempted to marry her off to an unattractive rabbi. When the guy arrived, she was so aghast at her father's meddling that she locked herself in her bedroom, declaring she would not come out until he left the family apartment.

Growing up, I was entertained with countless stories of how my parents ruthlessly broke up with less-than-appropriate boyfriends and girlfriends until they found each other. They met at a dance at a Jewish country club in the Catskills. My dad approached my mom, whose long, outstretched legs caused him to first query, "Would you like to dance or am I too short for you?"

My mom looked him over and responded, "I'll accept a dance!"

They ultimately danced all night, and ten weeks later, they got married. They were very attracted to each other and very much in love. Thus, I was raised in a culture that celebrates what many Indians and Middle Easterners refer to as a **love match**.

As a teen, I was shy and completely clueless about how to garner the attention of boys. At high school sock hops, I was largely a wallflower. The boys who asked me to dance were never the ones I considered to be cute; I remember the earnest information-seeking talks I'd have with other girls about how to give the guys we liked "the eye." Eventually, I grew brave enough to more openly flirt with the men who interested me, but being dismissed, rejected, or dumped was always hard. Matching my parents' true-blue storybook romance was a sheer impossibility.

When I visited India in 2007, discussions about the benefits of love marriage were in the air. Nearly every tour guide and train compartment companion had something to say. On a train ride from Rishikesh to Agra, my third-class, air-conditioned women's train compartment was abuzz as every passenger explained her beliefs. One recently married woman who was in a love marriage with a husband whose family was from a lower caste than her own reported, "My new family's meals lack the variety I am accustomed to, but that at the same time, I am happy to have freely chosen my husband!"

Another woman in our train compartment noted, "I am in an arranged marriage, and fortunately, it is a good one. The positive support we receive from our in-laws very much adds to our lives."

Nonetheless, her 12-year-old son, who was defying her strict vegetarian practices by eating eggs, contended, "A love-match would be the only sort of marriage I will accept!"

The following week, while I was seeking assistance at a cell phone store in Allahabad, an attractive female manager asked me to join her for tea in her private office. Suddenly, I was bombarded with questions about love marriage: "Do you think dating for love (and marriage) is a good idea? Would you recommend it for me?"

I offered cautious and conservative answers, pointing out, "You will have no family support if you fall in love with someone your parents do not approve of." I continued, "Do you really feel you can handle the ups and downs of romantic love all on your own?"

With a quizzical and concerned look, she copied down my email address, and we stayed in touch.

Several weeks later, on a 30-hour train ride from Kolkata to Mumbai, I heard the troubling story of Sita, a woman who had become estranged from her despicable arranged-marriage husband. She was returning from the wedding of her daughter, who had married her longtime boyfriend. Her husband had boycotted the wedding because the daughter's fiancé was from a lower caste, while Sita beamed with joy, considering the happiness in store for her daughter.

Prior to visiting India, I'd read anthropologist Serena Nanda's essay "Arranging a Marriage in India" on Indian parents' strategies for negotiating the marriages of their sons and daughters. She reported that parents can devote many years to looking for a good match that reflects caste, astrology, personality, appearance, and earning potential.

According to *Indian Matchmaking*, the 2022 Netflix series that features Sima Taparia, a Mumbai-based matchmaker, standards for a good match have not changed. Her fickle clients, reflecting the vast Indian diaspora, seek counterparts who are tall (if male), family oriented (seeking to have children), and have engaging personalities and thriving careers. Unlike in other times and places, when marriage arrangements were forced, today veto power can be exercised; one young man featured in the series had rejected over 80 of the matches that were presented to him.

While Nanda noted that even the westernized, best-educated Indians continued to prefer arranged marriages, many of the well-educated Indians I met were very much in search of love matches. Several young professionals confided that they were in better positions to find compatible spouses than their old-world parents could possibly be. Two such professionals were secretly living together, enjoying the sweetness of a new relationship that was all their own making. Another woman, a researcher at a Kolkata think tank, reported that her parents had given up on finding her a match in that her professional network was far superior to what they might locate by running ads in newspapers or using Shaadi.com, an Internet matching service for marriage-minded Indians.

As for the well-heeled participants in *Indian Matchmaking*, marriage introductions are not approached with the blind trust of previous generations. While the series celebrated retaining regional dialects and food traditions, there were signs that these Western-enculturated singles had fallen prey to non-Indian cuisine, like Taco Bell, as well as snarky cynicism. Many had dated so extensively that they were wary of matches lacking in chemistry and were no doubt able to live independent Western lives.

Have arranged marriages really been that bad? Not necessarily. Ideally, they function to generate alliances between like-minded families anticipating that the nuptial couple would fall in love following an elaborate weeklong wedding. Despite the low divorce rates associated with arranged marriages, imported TV shows like *Sex in the City* have led a growing number of young Indians to want to go out on Western-style dates and fall deeply in love. Fueling the appetite for a true-blue love match, the current generation of Bollywood stars has begun to engage in off-screen love marriages, generating spine-tingling passion and romance.

Having been raised in a nuclear-family love-match-celebrating culture, I grew up without the safety and security of a supportive extended family. My parents left their family wombs in New York City to settle in far-flung Palo Alto, California. My maternal grandmother visited once for a couple of weeks when I was a little girl; our blood family connections were largely with distant cousins who had also made the San Francisco Bay Area home. While we'd see these cousins for holiday celebrations, largely, we all lived in isolated nuclear-family satellites.

In tandem with the isolation from extended family, love-match seekers learn to weather the ups and downs of romance. Becoming tough-skinned and resilient is key. Women develop a radar accuracy for ferreting out trustworthy romantic possibilities from the vast field of "players." Strategies are honed, such as acting disinterested to generate mystery and intrigue or sprinkling romantic fairy dust to cause a player to convert into a "catch." The Western love-match culture is rife with fallout, including its foreboding 45% divorce rate, as well as unplanned pregnancies, which contribute to 30% of American children growing up in single-parent families.

Meanwhile, Western media paints a torrid picture of the travails of Indian, Pakistani, and Central Asian young couples who defy suffocating traditions and go off on their own to engage in free-will marriages. Young husbands have been accused of abduction, adultery, and kidnapping, while nuptial couples risk being murdered by their own fathers, uncles, and brothers to restore family reputation and prestige. Such a scheme was the subject of *A Girl in the River: The Price of Forgiveness*, the winner of the 2016 Oscar for best documentary short film.

The whole world hungers for a middle ground. The hard-edged independence of romantically skeptical Westerners is hardly a goal for the Indians and Pakistanis who so want to freely choose. On my flight back from India, I sat next to a guy who was returning to his US home after meeting a match his parents had arranged. He reflected, "I really doubt the girl would leave her whole family to join me in America." I then asked, "Would you move back to India to be with her?" He admitted, "No, I'm happy with my life in the states."

From *A Girl in the River: The Price of Forgiveness*, directed by Sharmeen Obaid-Chinoy and produced by Tina Brown, 2015, 1:42. Copyright © 2015 by SOC Films and HBO Documentary Films. Reprinted with permission.

Was another long plane ride in his future? Perhaps. He'd faced that the kind of commitments that traditional Indian spouses make to each other are what he wants. America's testy dating scene had left him wanting.

As growing numbers of East Asians eye Western-style dating, they strategize a grand, romantic jackpot. Attempting to sidestep all of the no-strings-attached hook-ups and friends-with-benefits arrangements, they hope to find the kind of true love Americans portray in their movies and love songs. While Shaadi.com has expanded to provide users with a virtual matchmaker, several other tech-friendly competitors have emerged that allow customers to do their own searching.

Sidestepping savvy matchmakers, trusted parents, and go-betweens, unhappy married men have been known to use Shaadi.com to search for sexual affairs, while adventurous single women have been prone to date more for nice dinners than for love. From the sidelines, I would say that my family's three-generation expedition from unhappy arranged marriage to free-will love marriage to romantic skepticism has been condensed into a single generation's journey in India.

CHAPTER 21

Deconstructing Niger's Marriage Market

I had eyed the Gerewol Festival male beauty contest for many years. In my work as an anthropologist who studies gender, sexuality, and partnering patterns, this unique festival, where young single men dress and dance seductively to attract lovers, held a prominent place on my must-see bucket list. The attendees, Wodaabe pastoralists who inhabit the Sahel desert in Niger, gather in late September, at the end of the grazing season. Due to concerns regarding safety and security, tourists had not been able to visit the festival for several years. There was anxiety about **Boko Haram**–style kidnappings. Anyone who appeared connected to wealth (e.g., white people) was considered to be at risk.

In mid-September 2018, I landed in Niamey, the capital of Niger. Entry into the airport involved finger scans of both hands, a perusal of my previously arranged visa, a passport stamping, and then an examination (by another official) of the just-stamped passport page. Mahaman, my Nigerien tour guide, flashed a piece of paper with my name on it, and I flashed back a thumbs-up.

Niger felt like the other side of the world. It was hot, the streets were largely unpaved, and most of the buildings were made of mud and straw. Everything was a pale coffee brown. Afternoons were so intensely hot that productivity reduced to a sleepy crawl. Air-conditioning was rare in public places and barely functional in hotel rooms.

It felt reminiscent of Mexico in the 1970s, when I first submerged myself into participant-observation field research. There were donkeys hauling huge loads and barely adolescent girls with babies strapped to their backs, and the cost of everything was negotiated. Cash machines were only found in spiffy hotels in the capital city, and no one could make change. Whenever I had cash, it would quickly disappear. I had no idea what things were actually worth and suspect that I made many donations to conniving vendors!

Mahaman wasn't exactly my personal guide; he was responsible for 50 other guests from all over the world. My roommate was a recently retired flight attendant from Barcelona who relishes visiting remote peoples and places. I was the only one who had ever been to Burning Man, an international festival that also occurs in a remote desert, featuring seduction and the possibility of meeting new lovers.

Our 10-car caravan traversed some of the worst roads I had ever seen. The cars were four-wheel-drive SUVs in varying states of repair. Each time there was a flat tire or a dead battery, everyone halted, and our skilled drivers rushed to the scene. The drive took us three days; it featured a wide-open, dusty-brown desert sprinkled with lakes and small villages, each with a mosque and main street marketplace. During the second and third days, we were escorted by an open-bed truck with state soldiers whose guns were trained on all possible disturbances.

It was evening when we arrived at the Gerewol Festival. As a professor of cultural anthropology, I'd given hundreds of lectures on **pastoralism**—the unique mode of production wherein a people are interdependent with herds of animals. It was my first time fully witnessing this world! The festival grounds were filled with grazing herds of camels, goats, sheep, and cows, as well as domesticated donkeys and horses. Mahaman's crew pitched pup tents, set up tables and shade structures, and made dinner. We were encouraged to visit the dancing that had just started.

I walked through a herd of resting camels and a smattering of goats until I could hear a distant, whining chant. As I approached a clearing, my eyes popped. While many of the tourists quietly peered through long camera lenses, I just gazed in wonderment. There they were—the androgynously slender Wodaabe young men—engaging in the timeworn Yaake dance! Their faces were painted with gold-yellow stripes down their thin tan noses, evoking light and play. Black eyeliner and black lipstick set off their shiny white teeth and the whites behind their beautiful, dark irises. They were no longer *National Geographic* photographs—I could smell them and touch them. They were absolutely real! Eventually, I calmed myself down and focused shots through my own camera lens.

It was a process for me to truly make sense of all that I was seeing. First, there was all that I had previously read—that it was a male beauty contest and a marriage market; then, there was what Mahaman had explained about the social needs of otherwise-isolated pastoralists; and then, there was what I saw with my own eyes. Through the lens of anthropology, I began to assess what it meant to the participating dancers, their families, and then larger theoretical meanings. During the hot afternoons while my tour group sat under shade structures, drinking copious amounts of bottled water, I sat alone in the hot sun and made notes: "Perhaps, the festival is a culturally sanctioned means for the expression of adolescent male sexuality?"

Camping with camels at the Gerewol Festival.
Photo courtesy of author.

My hot brain then reflected on the utter contempt that my own Western culture has for young men's intense needs for erotic expression. I thought about what it would be like if guys everywhere were provided a singular prescription for how to effectively attract women. Like the Wodaabe, they'd be provided with makeup, costumes, dance steps, and an arena in which to present themselves. Moreover, the prescription would be unilaterally endorsed by their communities in such a way that everyone would celebrate their beauty and their sexuality. Over the next several days, this was exactly what I witnessed!

The following night, the gold-yellow stripes gave way to full-faced, dark-red makeup for the seduction dance. An elderly woman and several older men inspected the line of dancers, wielding the same sort of sticks that herdsmen use to keep their flocks in order. A timeworn, culturally prescribed standard was being enforced—the dancing men were to roll their eyes and quiver their lips to effectively display their gleaming and healthy attributes. Those who presented the most effectively were moved to the center of the lineup of dancers. By the third night, two young women were appointed to make their personal selections. The crowd of onlookers swelled in anticipation. These were a people who very much value beauty—and the winning men might possibly find lifelong mates!

As I photographed the anxious men and scrutinizing girls, I was suddenly caught up in a stampede and rushed to the edges for personal safety. Adjacent to the festival rituals, there was a large encampment of attendees who, due to herding responsibilities, only see each other once a year. Each night a big fire was built, and the young men lined up to dance, flashing seductive gazes to gain approval of both the elder judges and, ultimately, their female age-mates.

The seduction dances could net good results. After the ritual choice dance, many less monitored seductions occur. Apart from the theater of "winning" the beauty contest, opportunities abounded for casual hookups. A shared night in a Wodaabe dancer's tent could get serious, and a yearlong trial partnership might ensue. If a baby was produced and the couple enjoyed their time together, the Gerewol Festival would mark the start of a life together. If not, a couple could leave their baby for its grandmother to raise and return the following year to find someone more beautiful!

Nonetheless, there were dribbles of the modern world. Several young men carried boom boxes and took event photos using their personal cell phones. I gratefully patronized a cell phone-charging station equipped with solar panels, a car battery, and a series of power strips. Vendors sold handmade crafts to the tourists; some were recently made, while others appeared to be well-worn. Scatterings of women would show up at our camp, begging for a *cadeau* (gift). I wondered, "Are they being opportunistic, or is Niger's thin infrastructure weighing on them?"

I surmised a conundrum. While the Wodaabe pastoral lifestyle is very much sustainable within the extensive grasslands of Niger, opportunities for higher education and access to life-changing resources barely exist. If a child were to attend school, they would have to live with relatives in a city and leave behind the pastoral way of life. Eventually, all of these unique and sustainable cultural practices might be up for grabs. The people I'd witnessed appeared to be healthy and purposeful. Their robust cultural inventory left them quite impervious to Christian or Muslim conversion as well as to state-controlled marriage.

According to historian Stephanie Coontz's (2005) review of the history of marriage, in many times and places, marriage existed as a business arrangement for postreproductive couples and as a means to generate alliances between families, tribes, and countries. Thus, assessing the Gerewol Festival through a Western cultural lens that focuses on beauty may do little to explain how it in fact functions as a fertility festival that unabashedly celebrates male sexuality with an auxiliary possibility of long-term partnerships.

Ultimately, I was grateful to have been witness to an extraordinary festival with no commemorative T-shirts or Chinese knockoffs and a people who were free to fully access sex, new lovers, and possibly life partners.

PART X

Exploring Other Worlds

With a llama pair along Peru's Inca Trail.
Photo courtesy of author.

Beyond my studies of polygamy in Africa and Papua New Guinea; singles culture, polyamory, and cheating in America; and changes in courtship patterns in India and Niger, my wanderlust has led to me explore sexual topics around the world. I begin by perusing sexual tourism in Jamaica, Thailand, and Peru. Then I report on the gender divide in Morocco, the first Muslim country I'd visited. My 2013 visit to mainland China as part of a delegation of sexologists provided me access to inside information on the state of family, relationship dynamics, and sexuality, which I contrast with my 2003 visit to Cuba, my first communist country.

CHAPTER 22

Scoping Out Sexual Tourism in Thailand, Jamaica, and Peru

Thailand

My foray into sexual tourism in Thailand was largely accidental. Unlike my trip to East Africa, where I came to investigate polygamy, my radar was not set to explore sexual tourism, but once it appeared, I was all ears. The year was 2003, and I had just visited Northern Thailand. My camera was loaded with photos of the ancient Buddhist temples of Ayutthaya, a trek through rice paddies and small villages, and Chiang Mai's fantastic markets.

A Los Angeles friend suggested I look up his old high school buddy Mark, who lives in Pattaya, a coastal town several hours south of Bangkok. It would be my first

Pattaya's downtown Walking Street.
Image © Алексей Облов/Moment/Getty Images.

Anthropology and Tourism

Considering that anthropologists and tourists find their ways to distant lands replete with unique cultural practices, the two can share common goals. In some universities, tourism and anthropology departments are linked in that graduates may prepare for work as cultural experts designing tours and working as guides and museum curators.

Beginning in the 1970s, the critical of eye of anthropology targeted tourism itself as a subject for study. The **commodification of culture** was analyzed, noting how Hawaiian luaus, Native American powwows, and Papua New Guinea sing sings were being redesigned for tourist consumption. Hawaii's Polynesian Cultural Center and Borneo's Sarawak Cultural Village showcase costuming, architecture, and dance representing regional traditions specifically for tourists. A significant way field anthropologists behave differently from tourists are in the photos they take. The anthropologist seeks to document authentic cultural practices and behaviors, while the tourist marks their excursions with photos of themselves in the thick of it all. Selfie sticks certainly facilitate composing such photos!

Sex tourism is decidedly transactional. The tourist pays for sexual access, and local providers negotiate for what they can safely finagle. Sex workers must assess the risks of participating in an unregulated exchange vs. the potential value of such earnings and the possibilities of generating first-world connections. Anthropologist Denise Brennan details the sex-tourist trade in *What's Love Got to Do With It? Transnational Desires and Sex Tourism in the Dominican Republic* (2004). Her field site, the coastal town of *Sosúa,* attracts European tourists and impoverished Haitian women; the men live out racialized fantasies, and the women "perform love," often with the dream of an enduring relationship that can lead to marriage and migration.

Thai beach town; initially, I thought I'd be taking a break from my cultural tour and relax. The moment I stepped into the town's main street, sexual tourism blared out at me, and Mark became a most perfect informant.

Mark married a gorgeous, much-younger Thai wife and hosted a Vietnam War veterans' chapter in his home. Mark, like many of the members of his chapter, was shipped to Thailand for rest and recreation (R&R) during the Vietnam War. He developed an unforgettable penchant for Thai women. After the war he did what was expected by marrying an American woman and raising a family. Once his kids were launched, he found his way back to Thailand. There he was spirited into a well-worn expat sex-for-money subculture. By the time I arrived, he knew all the players and proved to be a superb guide.

One evening Mark took me out and explained every bit of the scene. We saw pretty bar girls, who could be rented for a fee, and even prettier dancers, whose nightly rental fees were a bit higher. When Mark first arrived in Pattaya, he'd rented a series of bar girls until he met his wife. Once married, he became part of a subculture habited by expat Vietnam vets with young Thai wives.

Members dropped by for drinks at his hardly profitable bar, while their wives and children gathered in the kitchen to cook their favorite spicy foods. These women all bore sad stories of being abandoned by Thai men and left penniless (or

Thai cabaret show.

From "File: Thai-Cabaret-show wIMG 5013.jpg," by Per Meistrup, 2013, in Wikimedia Commons (https://commons.wikimedia.org/wiki/File:Thai-Cabaret -show_wIMG_5013.jpg). CC BY-SA 4.0.

baht-less, being Thailand). To resurrect their lives, they hoped to forge connections with foreign men. Such men typically hailed from Australia, Europe, or America and were regarded by the women as ATMs/cash machines.

While Mark lives in an expat community, there are many Western men who come to Pattaya for a sex vacation. He escorted me to some of the after-hours sex clubs, where women with highly trained vaginal muscles entertained the largely male audience with pussy tricks like tossing Ping-Pong balls and puffing at cigarettes. One night he took me to see a stage show featuring singing and dancing *kathoey* (ladyboys). Being that the tickets were pricey, the audience was largely Western tourists who savored the ease in which gender bending occurs in Buddhist Thailand. (The Buddhist worldview is much more accepting of gender and sexual variance than the Western Judeo-Christian world.) No doubt, Westerners desiring relief from cultural straitjacketing found a sex vacation and/or relocation to one of Thailand's expat communities to be the perfect antidote.

Jamaica

While in Thailand, I simply watched, took photographs, and made mental notes; three years later, I found myself in a country to which women go for sex vacations. The year was 2006, and the country was Jamaica. For years several friends had bestowed on me stories of the great times they'd had at Hedonism II, a sex-positive resort on Jamaica's west coast. Hedonism II is primarily a couples' resort that attracts visitors from North America and Europe. I arrived with a couple of girlfriends who knew the scene and absolutely loved the place.

Being scheduled to offer a workshop on polyamory, I was provided with a private room. I absolutely needed that room, with its quadruple-jetted shower, to escape from all of the hyperfun. I struggled to have a good time in that it was clearly not my scene. One evening I slipped away from another super silly contest, searching for a sliver of a more authentic Jamaica. As I walked toward the beach, a Jamaican guy called me over. He worked at the resort, and we talked a bit. I told him I was bored with the contests and that the whole vacation scene felt uncomfortably fabricated. He then asked me, "Have you ever tried *Jamaican wood*?" We both laughed. I then asked, "Where might I sample some?"

He explained that he was strictly prohibited from entering the guest rooms and that "it would have to be out on the beach." We then discussed some of his previous encounters with Hedonism II's sex-hungry tourists. Without indulging, I was able to pretty much imagine what it might be like.

The intrigue of Jamaican "wood" aside, I very much wanted access to something of the country's geographic and psychocultural interior. While at the beach looking over a pile of wooden masks featuring the legendary reggae artist Bob Marley, I found the answer came to me. I would ask the guys selling these masks if they could take me back to their village so I might witness how they are made. I'd hit pay dirt.

The next morning, three very enterprising 20-something Jamaican guys arrived at my hotel with a borrowed car and high spirits. After paying them $100, they drove me all over the back roads of Western Jamaica, stopping frequently for me to take pictures and ask questions. Eventually, we made it to their village, and I

Jamaican guide with a freshly carved Bob Marley mask.
Photo courtesy of author.

diligently photographed the mask-production process as well as bits of the surroundings. My favorite image was an abandoned car completely embedded in thick green ivy.

On the drive back to Negril, each of my guides talked about his hopes and dreams vis-à-vis a tourist economy that was largely controlled by nonislanders. I felt for them. Late in the day, we returned to the nauseatingly cheerful Hedonism II resort; I felt blessed I'd been able to salvage my Jamaican getaway. One of my guides had assisted me in making a call home on his cell phone and retained the number. Periodically, he'd call me in Los Angeles to just check in. I had believed that our transaction was complete in that I'd given him $100, and in exchange, he and his buddies had driven me around for the day. He still wanted something; I doubted it was to have me sample his Jamaican wood. Maybe I'd listened to him in ways few of Jamaica's tourists ever do.

Ivy-covered abandoned car.
Photo courtesy of author.

Peru

In early January 2008, I was inches from my 55th birthday and had just landed in Lima, Peru. Having just a day to visit before heading to Cusco and an Inca Trail trek to Machu Picchu, I accepted a taxi driver's assistance in locating a simple hotel. The next morning, with the hotel's tourist map in hand, I set out to explore Lima. I happened upon a beachside cove decorated with hearts and statues of embracing lovers.

I then hailed a cab. The driver, an attractive 33-year-old guy, asked what my astrological sign was. I told him, "Soy un Capricornio." (I am a Capricorn.) He then exclaimed, "*¡Yo soy también!*" (I am as well!)

Then we exchanged birthdates and were doubly astounded to find out that we were both born on January 15, though certainly not in the same year. To him, it was an omen that we should spend the day together. Suddenly, he converted himself from taxi driver into a personal tour guide. He took me to the top of one of Lima's highest spots, where romantic couples might view the city. We held each other and lightly kissed. Eventually, we shared dinner together . . . and considering his limited finances, I gladly paid. I was booked to fly to Cusco early the next morning. He volunteered to take me to the airport.

To take him up on his offer, we had to get through the night. We arrived back at my hotel, and initially, the management would not let me bring him into my room. Part of me wanted the privacy of a night alone, part of me felt uncomfortable having him wait in his car for six hours, and part of me was curious about him. Ultimately, I requested that he be allowed to stay with me, and the management relented.

Suddenly, I was sharing my bed with a working-class Peruvian guy who was born 22 years after I was. He proposed that our day and night together would be our beginning. I would sponsor him to live with me in California—he would

Delfín, V. (1993). *El beso* (The kiss) [sculpture]. Miraflores district, Lima, Peru (Parque del Amor). Photo courtesy of author.

learn English, and we'd have a family together. His offer felt slightly soothing but ultimately difficult for me to dream into. I was on the edge of perimenopause; the likelihood of me conceiving was next to nil.

After kissing a bit more, I sensed that our erotic realities were really different. Clearly, he knew nothing about tantric breathing or effective ways to engage a woman's G-spot, let alone how to sensitively lick her clitoris. He was a working-class Peruvian ruffian. I couldn't train him in an evening; my little experiment in transcending culture and sexual scripting was portending to leave me badly abraded. I switched on the lights and told him I wasn't yet comfortable with him and that it would be best if we just try to go to sleep.

He did his best to concur, pestering me very little during our brief night together. At 5:00 a.m., we quickly dressed, got my bag into his cab, and drove to the airport. As he sent me on my way, I pressed $50 into his hand, hoping to in some way compensate him for his generosity, especially in that it felt blindingly clear we would not see each other again. I'd sampled a bit of sex tourism and felt very much complete.

The Inca Trail trek was amazing. There were so many archaeological sites along the way as well as some gorgeous llamas. On the last morning, we arrived at Machu Picchu; the trek cooks pulled together a delicious cake to celebrate my 55th birthday. I'd kept a steady though relatively slow pace the whole week . . . covering every inch on my own steam!

CHAPTER 23

Engaging Morocco's Gender Divide

Backsides of veiled Moroccan women.
Photo courtesy of author.

In 2009 I boarded a ferry from Algeciras, Spain's southernmost harbor, to Tangiers, a hardscrabble port city at the northern tip of Morocco. The boat was teeming with Moroccans returning home. It was my first time to travel in an Arab country; suddenly, I was surrounded by adult women who were covered in **hijabs, burkas,** and veils.

While in Morocco, the choice to wear such coverings is individual; the preponderance of flowing bright pink, lavender, and aquamarine generated a most alluring visual shield. This first moment of culture shock made me want to photograph it all—I'd hang over the deck railings, pretending I was focusing on the distant port and then train my lens on the dark eyes peering out of a burka. I feared getting caught, sensing that my moment of utter astonishment was all part of the day-to-day ordinary.

The Culture of the Veil

Veiling can be connected to notions of the self, the body, and the community, as well as with the cultural construction of identity, privacy, and space (Guindi, 1999). It can be characterized as a form of sacred privacy, linking women as the protectors of family life and the realm of the private. Distinctions can be drawn between two kinds of head covers, one that covers the head and hair (*milayah*, *'aba*, or *izar*) and one that specifically covers the face (*burqu*, *qina'*, or *lithma*). Depending on their veiling style, women can be regarded as guardians of family sanctuary as well as the world of the sacred.

In the mid-1980s, anthropologists Elizabeth and Robert Fernea observed that the veil signals honor, protection, wealth, and the sanctity of family. They explained that coverings worn in Muslim societies serve many purposes. There are utilitarian benefits to covering one's head (as I noted while weathering a Sahara Desert dust storm), while in urban settings, the benefits are more social and political. A woman can leave her compound unescorted and incognito, accomplishing personal and business tasks without being subject to harassment. A man might even don a veil to engage in private, not-to-be-questioned activities.

No doubt veiling protects women from unwanted attention from men and the presumed vulgarities of public life. In many cultures female locks are considered highly erotic. When a woman runs her fingers through a tousle of her own hair, it can be regarded as a seduction signal. Orthodox Jewish women shave their heads and wear scarves or wigs in public, generating a separation between the sacred and the profane to disable flirtation. Westerners may feel pity and compassion for women seen wearing headscarves; likely, they are cancer patients whose hair has fallen out following chemotherapy.

After landing in Tangiers, I walked through a dusty field to a customs office, where my passport was stamped; immediately, a taxi appeared and I was taken to the train station. While it would have been a relatively short walk, knowing little about Moroccan society, I figured it was best to accept the ride. I boarded a train to Casablanca (where I would be meeting up with a tour group). The ride allowed me six hours of access to the contemporary Moroccan psyche being that many of my coach companions spoke French (and not solely Arabic and/or Berber).

I sat across from a woman whose olive skin seemed almost green; she kept hiking up her itchy pink burka to scratch herself with a small stick. I watched all of the regions she scratched and how very uncomfortable she looked. There was something exquisitely private in being witness to how she was handling her body and the layers of her bulky burka. I slyly photographed her. I captured a pathos in her face, sensing I had taken an award-winning photograph. Her accompanying husband saw what I had done and proclaimed, "Madam, you cannot take her photo!"

I had no choice and reluctantly erased the photo. I handed him my camera to prove to him it was gone. He was correct. I had no right to steal such an uncomfortable-looking image. It really was private. That interaction portrayed the essence of the Morocco I spent my next several weeks trying to understand:

Was that uncomfortable-looking woman scratching herself because of a condition brought on by living in a veiled society? Had her husband protected her dignity by asking me to erase the photo, or should I, as a Western photographer, be able to expose the indignities Moroccan women suffer from being veiled?

During the next several weeks, I saw many veiled women, and from the fleeting privacy of my tour bus, images were occasionally distilled in my far-reaching camera lens. At a small marketplace, I gazed at a woman wearing a full black burka with only a hole for her eye. She was too close to photograph, and thus, I just looked and wondered: What is life under the veil really about? Is she safe? Is she uncomfortably restricted? Does she yearn to show more skin in public?

I really wanted to know. One afternoon in a Marrakesh Internet shop, I received a bit of an answer. After posting photos to my blog, I began chatting with the 17-year-old attendant, who was not wearing a veil. She explained, "Because I am young and unmarried, it's acceptable for me to be uncovered."

Meanwhile, her slightly older girlfriend described what had led her to start wearing a veil: "Following my marriage, I decided on my own that a veil would offer me protection and privacy."

My provocateur self then asked, "Would you be comfortable removing the veil for me?"

She did, and I gazed on her perfectly healthy, though slightly uncombed, head of hair. She smiled sweetly, and then after I'd had a good look, she re-covered her head. I allowed that moment to be that moment, without attempting to photograph it.

During my two-week visit to Morocco, there was just one instance in which I was permitted to photograph women. It was at an argan oil–processing workshop where I witnessed hardworking (veiled) women painstakingly extract precious oils from tough brown seeds. In that the women were engaged in an activity (and not just being veiled curiosities), I was invited to have at them with my camera. They neither posed, smiled, nor grimaced. They simply cranked out argan butter and argan oil and allowed my shutter to click away.

Veiled Moroccan women extracting argan oil.
Photo courtesy of author.

Hijabs, Burkas, and the Western World

France, beginning in 2004, banned the wearing of face-concealing clothing in schools; in 2010, the ban was extended to public places. This was explained as a security measure, though Islamophobic accusations were hurled. Violators were levied a €150 fine and a citizenship education class. For adults who forced a girl under 18 to wear a facial covering, a €30,000 fine and a yearlong prison term were imposed. While several other European countries (Austria, Belgium, Bulgaria, Denmark, Luxembourg, the Netherlands, and Switzerland) followed suit, France had been especially ethnocentric/ antiburka. In 2014 French law was challenged and taken to the European Court of Human Rights. It was upheld, and the value of living together as one French people was cited. In 2022 conservative French presidential candidate Marine Le Pen viewed the hijab as "Islamist attire," signaling adherence to an extremist, anti-Western interpretation of the Muslim faith (Caulcoutt, 2022).

Ayatollah Khomeini, Iran's former religious and political leader (1979–1989), made the hijab compulsory, contending that his nation would be plunged into corruption and turmoil if women's faces and hair were publicly exposed. In September 2022, 22-year-old Mahsa Amini was arrested in Tehran for allowing her hair to peer out from her hijab. The **religious morality police** violently beat her, which led to her death. Widespread protests ensued. Several demonstrators removed their own hijabs and publicly cut their hair; nearly 200 people were killed. Following months of protest, on December 5, 2022, the morality police responsible for enforcing women's dress codes were abolished. Nonetheless, the law remains that, in public, women are required to cover their hair and wear long, loose clothing.

I attended a regional epidemiology conference and heard an intriguing paper that explored why Moroccan women are generally overweight and unconcerned with physical fitness. Relative to the men who are out and about, the women, being confined to private spaces, have little opportunity for exercise. Moreover, the privacy afforded by a willowy caftan or burka reduces the necessity to appear fit and trim in public spaces. The statistics offered in the presentation confirmed that a lot of fat can be concealed under all of that silky pink and aquamarine fabric! As a Westerner who typically wears shape-revealing clothes, I wondered, "How much more might I weigh if I could completely cover up in public?"

One afternoon I managed to access the world beneath veils, hijabs, and burkas when I visited a women's **hammam** (public bathhouse). I purchased a scrubbing in addition to the standard bath to better understand the scene. I'd never had my skin scrubbed so hard. Many tanned layers were removed, leaving me an abraded rosy pink.

Such bathhouses have been around for upwards of 2,000 years and are typically sex segregated. They were introduced by the Romans to increase public hygiene. Being that water represents purity and cleanliness in Islam, weekly visits, typically with friends or family, are standard. These visits, as I quickly saw, are very much social opportunities. Visitors catch up with each other, share gossip, and make new friends.

My eyes never popped so wide! Suddenly, I was in the world of the veilless. Everyone was naked except for their thin little panties. And these otherwise visually protected women were in a private space, and the energy was amazing. They yelled, screamed, giggled, and trilled their tongues. They poked each other roughly and basked in a kind of naked ease I'd never witnessed amongst Western nudists. At one moment my bathing attendant roughly pounded on me, and I lunged over to attack her back. It led to a high-spirited water fight wherein we hurled buckets of water over each other's heads. I glowed not so much from the layers of skin she'd removed as from being able to access this otherwise very private world.

While I had played hard within this high-spirited private space, when I emerged from the hammam, I put on my relatively tight clothes and weathered all the stares that Western women who bare their skin in public endure. Accessing that afternoon of ecstatic play with women so protected they'd never feigned not hearing a whistle or a sotto voce "Mamacita!" was absolutely amazing.

CHAPTER 24

Sorting Out Sex, Culture, and Business in China and Cuba

Presenting "Orgasm in America" at the Sino-US Conference on Sexology.

Photo by Aleida Heinz, 2013. Reprinted with permission.

In 2013 I joined the Institute for Advanced Study of Human Sexuality's (IASHS's) president Ted McIlvenna and a delegation of students, graduates, and friends for several meetings in mainland China. These included the Sino-US Conference on Sexology with the newly formed Chinese Sexological Association. There I presented findings from my research project "Orgasm in America: Current Beliefs and Practices." It was my second time to visit a communist country, the first having been Cuba in 2003. In Cuba I attended the World Association of Sexology's biannual conference, wherein I offered a presentation titled "Why Women Swing" and absorbed much of the sexual scene.

Cubans have navigated eroticism via an accumulated culture: the secularized Creole; Catholic and Protestant repression; and dance, movement, and sensuality from Africa. Prior to Cuba's 1959 revolution, the island had been an American playground for all manner of debauchery. Prostitution was rampant, and there was an extreme divide between those with access and resources and everyone else. During my visit Cuba was in the midst of growing pains; its mission to feed, house, educate, and provide full healthcare for all of its citizens was forever being compromised by the black market based on U.S. dollars. Dollar-bearing tourists, such as ourselves, were admonished to patronize certain markets, restaurants, and shops.

Dating and partnering patterns of Cuba's youth were heavily impacted by the Big Brother style government. Young people felt little pressure to work things out with their sweethearts in that a pregnant girl could receive all that she needed regarding health care, housing, and education from the state. In that professional salaries were capped at levels barely above those of janitors, there was little incentive to excel at anything. The restaurant fare was largely mediocre; talented musicians and artists schemed about defection to Europe and North America.

Visiting China in 2013 was a whole other story. While capitalistic enterprise was promulgated, the government maintained an ever-present watch over unauthorized childbearing, forcing even near-term mothers to abort. In 2016 China's one-child policy was put to rest; then in July 2021, all limits on family size were lifted.

Meanwhile, product manufacturing had been literally unchecked, with much government support for startup research and innovation. We were taken to a burgeoning industrial park in Hangzhou, which felt a bit like Beverly Hills. People dressed to the nines, sporting fancy cars and cool motorbikes.

As for sexual expression, the country appeared to be buckling at a crossroads. Despite the rich tradition of finely illustrated pillow books offering graphically precise instructions for engaging erotic pleasure, contemporary Chinese carry memories of having had their heads hammered down by antierotic, individualism-quashing ideologies promulgated by the Cultural Revolution. This was unsettling, as I fondly recalled thumbing through Chairman Mao's inimitable Little Red Book as a 1960s high school student in search of righteous answers for how society should be organized and power distributed. It was difficult to consider that Mao had caused such harm.

The Chinese youth I met, while underschooled on sexual pleasure for its own sake, were enthusiastic team players, exuding a cooperative spirit rarely seen in the Western world. In 2013, Chinese marriages existed for social reputation (generating extended family ties), financial security, and to produce a single child. The single-child law was touted as a panacea for China's economy, enabling burgeoning levels of prosperity. Ironically, during the previous 40 years, independent, ruthlessly capitalistic Hong Kong also lowered its birthrate, not by government dictate but simply in response to the rising cost of living.

In that marriages were utilitarian affairs in China, Western romantic dreams of supreme partner communication and sexual satisfaction were rare. The government's heavy-handed meddling in reproductive choice had forced births beyond a single child (until 2016) to either be aborted or heavily fined.

This had led postbirth couples to be wary of marital sex. Thus, a spa complex emerged. Housed in hotels and in freestanding venues, male patrons could rent a room and receive several hours of service from an attentive female for about $100. Spa girls would begin by carefully pampering the man, cleansing each part of his body and soothing it with nurturing touch. Despite it being illegal, for an additional charge, oral sex and intercourse were offered. The experience was ultimately very different from the standard Western male seduction of a female, where he gauges her readiness for intercourse, offering her oral sex and perhaps his saliva when extra lubrication is needed. Here the man simply receives pleasure.

Much of the focus of our delegation's visit was to celebrate the opening of the IASHS's satellite, the Resource Center for Sexuality Studies in Hangzhou, a suburb of Shanghai. This center was the brainchild of businesswoman Yu Na, who hoped to use it as a base for marketing sexual aids to the owners of China's women's spas. Fireworks were released at the building's entrance and then again at the unveiling of plaques citing the IASHS's association. The excitement brought tears to my eyes and goose-bumped my arms as I thought to myself, "The Chinese so know how to celebrate!"

No one explained what might really transpire in the rooms of the center. I sensed something reminiscent of my feminist-inspired 20s. Perhaps my American wave of pleasure-centered sexuality would find its way into the hearts and minds of some very excited Chinese women! I questioned several of the young women associated with the enterprise about Western vs. Chinese sexuality. Beginning with a lot of giggling, they reported they've never been with a Western man but nonetheless believe such men would be better lovers!

From what I could gather, the spa would offer education on pleasure-oriented sex, and clients might access orgasms via mounting a **Sybian** (a saddle-style vibrator). I wondered whether the wealthy women who frequented such spas would prefer an attentive man who personally delivers touch, pleasure, and orgasm or if that would be considered risky in that these pleasure-starved ladies might generate overwhelming emotional attachment.

Such a center seemed reminiscent of the exclusive Korean bars in Los Angeles, where wealthy women can "purchase" expensive bottles of champagne that are served by attentive, attractive men who engage her in flattering conversation. Perhaps the spa would deliver the "second course" by means of personal attention and erotic pleasure.

Later I found out that spas that cater to women have been a mainstay in China. Like the men's spas, they (illegally) provide sexual pleasuring for an additional charge. While sex spas were hardly revolutionary, for several years following the resource center's inauguration, IASHS associates traveled to China to offer sexual health and pleasure workshops.

With my anthropological lens in place, I began to wonder if the Chinese have had it right and that Americans, with their penchant for soul-connected love, romance, and eroticism, are the ones barking up an impossible tree. China, with its centuries of sophistication regarding the human condition, might once again have uncovered the answer to that age-old question of what women really want. Perhaps confidently paying for a surefire delivery of attention, touch, and expertly executed orgasm could be immensely more satisfying than hoping for more from a distracted boyfriend or husband!

PART XI

Three Full Circle Stories

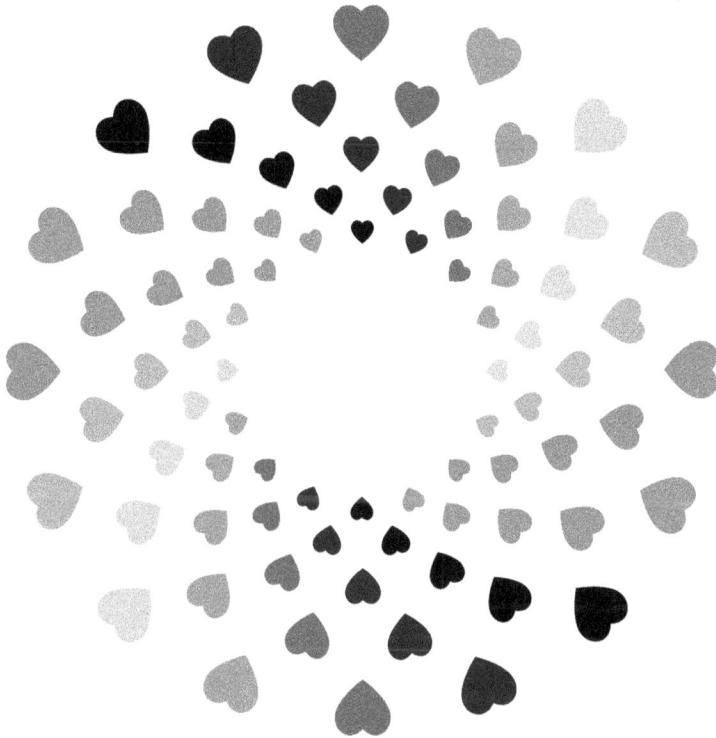

Following the emergence of the #MeToo movement, I reflect upon sexual assault both professionally and personally. I then peruse the whole story of connecting and reconnecting with my lover and friend Brad. In "Full Circle Love," I recount how we finally accessed a love and intimacy that I believed I had always wanted. Finally, I recount my first field visit to Maní, Yucatán, in 1975 and contrast it with my last visit in 2018. I reflect on recent trips to central Mexico, including one in fall 2019 with Brad, where I presented my study "Changing Perspectives on Sexual Assault" to an international sexology conference in Mexico City. Considering the Mexico we then engaged, I assess that it, too, had come full circle.

CHAPTER 25

Reckoning With #MeToo

Women's March, Los Angeles, 2017.
Photo courtesy of author.

In the spring of 2016, my anthropology department chair challenged the syllabus for my signature class, Gender, Sex, and Culture: "You do not have a section on sex and violence."

Rather than applaud my efforts to engage my class with readings on cybersex, the brain chemistry of romantic love and multiple-partner sexualities, she'd found fault via her box-checker, microdetail mentality. I thought about it. Having taught the class for over 20 years, I had left out sex and violence—what had led me to do this?

I had grown tired of describing the details of female circumcision. I hated screening the very graphic video which detailed the removal of a young African girl's clitoral head. And I was tired of the explanations that cultural anthropologists had offered to justify this brutal and mutilating act.

Despite the World Health Organization's 1979 recommendation that governments "work to eliminate the practice," anthropologists continued to explain how it preserved the integrity of patrilineages (male family lines) by ensuring premarital celibacy.

Then I thought about rape: What had led me to leave this out too?

I faced that, for me, this was personal. Very personal. I thought back to 1975, when I was raped on a desolate, rocky promontory in the Acapulco Bay. My decision had been to stuff it and tell almost nobody. I did not want my public identity to be that of a rape victim. I wanted to be an anthropologist, a professor, and a writer. And that's what I became.

That spring the world had begun to shift. Stanford University student Brock Turner was convicted of raping Chanel Miller following a 2015 fraternity party. Turner's father offered the court a statement, calling the act "20 minutes of action," exacerbating the standard narrative that "boys will be boys" (Miller, 2016). Miller's poignant statement went viral; social media exploded over the very short jail sentence he'd received.

Six months later, a 2005 video featuring Donald Trump was spewed across the airwaves with his braggadocio that "When you're a star, they let you do it. You can do anything. . . . Grab 'em by the pussy."

I began to incorporate readings about rape in India, where the law protects husbands who rape their wives, and the story of the 2012 gang rape and subsequent death of a physiotherapy student that fomented massive protests.

I then invited my students to discuss their own experiences with sexual assault. I quietly introduced the topic stating that I, too, had been victimized. The students sensed the intense emotion percolating inside of me, respecting my choice to not disclose details.

In October 2016 I launched an Internet survey, "Changing Perspectives on Sexual Assault," sensing that a major cultural shift was in the making. While we humans

From "File: Agitation to protest violence against women, Gadhinglaj-Kolhapur, Maharashtra, July 2014.jpg," 2014, in *Wikimedia Commons*. (https://commons.wikimedia.org/wiki/File:Agitation_to_protest_violence_against _women,_Gadhinglaj-Kolhapur,_Maharashtra,_July_2014.jpg). CC BY-SA 4.0.

and our primate relatives have been forever assaulting our weak, our young, and especially our females, perspectives regarding what constitutes assault and how consent might be assessed had changed. While in colonial America, children as young as 10 years old were considered mature enough to consent to partner sex, our current culture embraces a hypersensitivity to abusive behavior.

My survey findings established significant variance between males and females regarding the meaning of "No means no": 14% more females believed it means "one is not interested in any sexual contact," while 8% more males believed it means "a partner could still be persuaded into having sex."

Baby boomers also differed from millennials in this regard: 10% more boomers contended "a woman could be persuaded into having sex." See Figure 25.3.

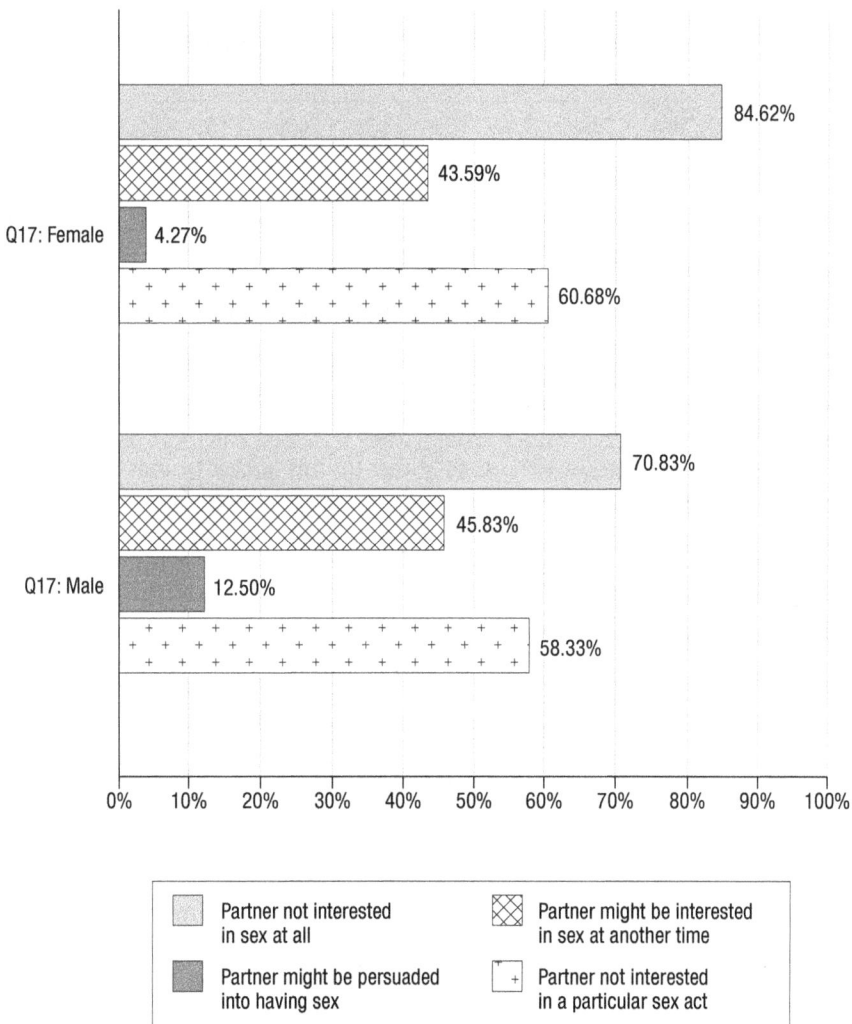

Figure 25.3. Variations in the Meaning of "No Means No"

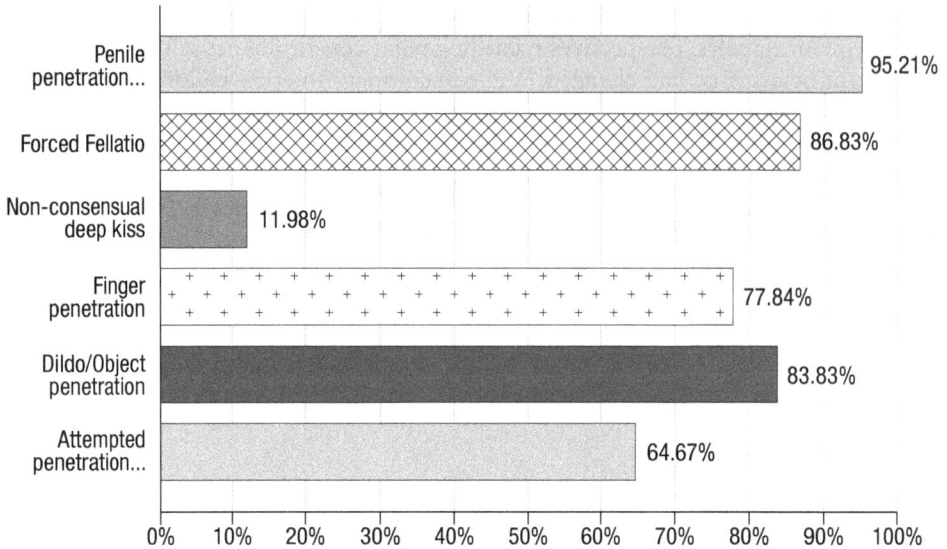

Figure 25.4.   What Counts as Rape?

My survey respondents' definitions for what constitutes rape fell on a contin-uum: While over 95% agreed that penile-vaginal penetration was rape, 35% con-tended that an attempted rape (where penetration did not occur) was not rape, 22% contended that finger penetration was not rape, and 13% viewed forced fellatio (oral sex) as not rape. See Figure 25.4.

As media coverage skyrocketed, a culture shift exploded. Women who had participated in activities where they had subordinated their will to the desires of men engaged the #MeToo lens. Overnight they assessed they had been trafficked, groomed, and unjustly manipulated. High-profile offenders in entertainment and politics were summarily fired, 19 states enacted sexual harassment protections, and over 200 bills were introduced in state legislatures. Like the witchcraft trials of the 15th and 16th centuries, accusations of sexual misbehavior followed a parallel absolutism. Men who were engaging in previously normative patterns of teasing and seduction suffered loss of station, reputation, and employment.

Beginning in 2017, I was invited to present my research to anthropology and sexology conferences in America and internationally. I decided to make my

History of the #MeToo Movement

In 2006 Tarana Burke, the founder of the #MeToo movement, first publicly shared her status as a sexual assault survivor on Myspace. As an activist, her purpose was to empower sexually assaulted people to establish the enormity of the problem. In October 2017, following the *New York Times'* expose of Harvey Weinstein's egregious sexual misconduct, the #MeToo movement exploded. More than 12 million Facebook members posted their stories incorporating the #MeToo hashtag; altogether, 45% of users in the United States had a friend who claimed the term.

presentations personal by coming out as a rape survivor. It was amazing. For 40 years I had feared that I would lose my credibility as a professional woman if I disclosed that I had been raped. Instead, I received respect and admiration.

I thought about my mother, who was nearly 98 when she passed away in 2017. During the last years of her life, dementia had loosened her tight-lipped propriety. Whenever I would visit, she would vividly recall what her eldest brother had done to her as a blossoming girl. I discussed her in my presentation so she, too, could come out. Our family had suffered enough with her pain—how she had stuffed it for so many years and how that stuffing likely contributed to how I managed my body and my sexuality being that I, too, stuffed my pain to guard my reputation. I shrieked, "Halleluiah! I am finally free to be beautiful and sexy and to fully assert when 'No means no' and 'Yes means yes!'"

Reflecting further, I believe we humans are far too complicated to readily engage such a direct negotiation concerning our genitals and our passions. While someone might look good from a distance, in person, they might not smell right, taste right, or touch in an appealing way. Attraction can grow . . . and it can diminish. In one moment a potential partner can look absolutely alluring, and in the next, that same person can transform to uninteresting or even repugnant. Attraction is one of the few interpersonal human dynamics where political correctness is not expected. We can change our minds without explanation.

As **consent training** ramped up on college campuses, it was presumed that young women (always) knew what they wanted and what they didn't want. As a young, attractive woman recently explained to me: "I don't need a seduction dance. If there's someone I am interested in, I will let them know!"

Thus, to her, "No means no" functions as a final statement rather than part of a negotiated conversation.

For the world I came of age in, if a woman said "No," that was regarded as part of the seduction dance, and eventually, she could be coaxed into a "Maybe" and eventually a "Yes." I still question the presumption that women fully know when they are sure they do or don't want to have sex.

Each time I suffered through a date rape or acquaintance rape, there was always someone who tried to show how complicit I'd been: "Why did you accept the boat ride from a stranger?" "Why did you go skinny-dipping with him?" "Why did you accept a kiss?" "Why did you invite him into your bed?" "Why were you wearing such skimpy clothes?"

These are all rape myths. But, when feeling shaky and vulnerable, I thought these did sound like good questions. It was only when #MeToo emerged that I faced

Consent Training

Consent training workshops became required curricula in business settings and on college campuses. They discussed distinctions between regulation-based consent and implied consent and the dynamics of force/coercion. Some evaluated negotiation strategies and the emotions of feeling pressured to say yes while wanting to say no. The particularities of consent in kink interactions were included in some curricula.

Johnny Depp and Amber Heard's Defamation Lawsuit

In the spring of 2022, the culture sobered over the wrongness of men and the rightness of women as actor Johnny Depp sued his former wife, actress Amber Heard, for defamation following her 2018 *Washington Post* op-ed, where she presented herself as a public figure representing domestic abuse. When Heard countersued Depp, a captivating trial followed where Heard emerged through an onslaught of social media reels and memes as an exaggerator and altogether as more the abuser and instigator than Depp. While Depp owned his misbehaviors, Heard presented herself as innocent and mistreated. Beyond suffering in the court of public opinion, the jury found Heard at greater fault for defamation than Depp, assessing her misconduct at $15 million, while Depp was assessed at just $2 million. Heard regarded the verdict as a setback to times when women's voices were routinely squelched and those who spoke out could be publicly shamed; the infallibility of #MeToo may have suffered a beating as well.

that, despite my apparently compliant behavior, I had the right to change my mind and have that be respected.

For someone who had been raised to take full responsibility for the consequences of her behavior, this get-out-of-jail "ticket" was quite unbelievable: I truly didn't have to feel at all guilty for bringing on painful cases of **blue balls**. I could just say "No" and leave!

Still, there were the messy date rapes where I'd agreed to sex that only afterward felt like a violation. Guys would think I knew what I wanted because I am a smart, professional woman. But then there was this shy, submissive part of me with a bumpy self-confidence. I would feel so embarrassed about having changed

With my sexually assertive kitten, Lola.
Photo courtesy of author.

my mind that I would grit my teeth and go through with it. While there were clear moments when I wanted the sex to stop, silent compliance was often easier than disclosure of my tender feelings.

While women have a long tradition of exchanging sex for goods and status, it's quite another thing for a woman to truly own her inner animal and blurt out a full "Yes."

Culture separates me from my kitten Lola, who hit her first heat at four-and-a-half months. She became incorrigible: yowling, screeching, rubbing, and presenting.

I thought about myself. I could fantasize about sex in the context of a man who matched a romantic fantasy of being a perfect life partner. Even then, I carried this self-image of only wanting an appropriate amount of sex—a nice go-around at bedtime and then a bit more in the morning. When my lover suggested a second bedtime go-around, a little voice in me thought I should say, "I've had enough. Let's go to sleep."

Instead, I allowed my brain to flip. I agreed to as much sex as our animal bodies wanted. And that night we did it nine times. This then led me to consider that outside of cultural overlays and expectations, desire and the resolution of desire can be very simple.

CHAPTER 26

Full Circle Love

When I was 37, I lived in a simple one-bedroom apartment in the Hollywood Hills with Poppy, my timid Russian blue cat. I was in the midst of exploring multiple-partner sexualities. I noted how boring and emotionally trapped monogamous pairings felt and decided the best thing would be to have my own house, my own social identity, and financial independence. And I would bear and raise children on my own. While I found group sex distasteful, I admitted that I very much enjoy having intense connections with multiple lovers . . . my favorite configuration was being the exciting *other woman* to married men who seek relief from the confines of bedroom sex with their wives.

The two married men in my life were Ben and Brad.

Ben, an MIT-trained scientist who I met at a polyamory support group, was the father of two young daughters and married to Catherine, a woman he'd met in grad school. For the first several months of our getting to know each other, we'd have lunch at a French café in Sherman Oaks. He would tell me about his studies in fulfillment technologies.

Eventually, we began to conduct "research" (with information he had gleaned from More University workshops) on a bedspread laid across my living room floor. He'd stroke my clitoris in a repetitive and prescribed fashion for extended periods of time, telling me to fully experience receiving. This was unusual for me. It felt geeky and decidedly unromantic. To me, interacting by touching back generated an erotic conversation.

Nonetheless, I played along and eventually surrendered into just feeling and then found myself moaning and shrieking in delight! Several weeks into this research, he began to insert a finger . . . and then additional ones as I begged for more. I would drip and shudder from the deep, full-body orgasms that followed. Eventually, we would make love to help my body integrate the overwhelming intensity.

Ben invited me to become a family friend, including playing with his children and helping his wife plan his birthday celebration. Family time was delightful. He would tell me that when the time was right, he would propose to his wife that I be fully added as a second wife.

I noted that he struggled with depression and that we had connected during one of his socially extroverted periods. In the end all I could do was be grateful for the brief window of erotic ecstasy and feel relieved that his wife Catherine did not find out about our "research."

Tandem to my visits with Ben, I met Brad. He was an inventor and an entrepreneur who also had two young daughters and an unsuspecting wife. We met at a business support group he was hosting in the living room of his West Hollywood home. I was filled with ambition to have my own radio show on sex and gender, launch a storytelling business, and write my first book. He was drawn to my starry-eyed ambition, and I was in awe of his world. His home was forever brimming with interesting people and fun gadgets.

I was flattered when he asked me to join him for a series of philosophy lectures at UCLA as well as at many events and gatherings. One evening, after one of our outings, he came up to my apartment to continue our conversation. Suddenly, I was pinned against the wall as he placed his lips on my lips. I was quizzical for about 20 seconds and then consented. We landed on my bed . . . and became lovers. His touch was exquisite. I was smitten with everything about him—his looks, his brain, his beautiful body, and his fantastic sense of humor.

I wanted to be with him much more than he was available. He was running a demanding business, was a devoted father, and had a high-spirited wife named Sofia. There really wasn't room for me. But somehow, we saw a lot of each other. He'd call me from his car phone (there weren't yet cell phones), I would send him personal faxes (email didn't yet exist), and we would meet up with each other everywhere we could.

One day he told me he needed to focus more on things at home and wouldn't be so available. I soon found out he had begun to spend time with a single woman named Sasha. Sasha began to feel duplicitous about dating a married man and reached out to Sofia. Together, Sasha and Sofia confronted Brad. My relationship with Brad was exposed.

I then sat with Brad and Sofia at their kitchen table and attempted to defend Brad and myself. I explained with the authority of a cultural anthropologist and multiple-partner researcher (with a heavy personal agenda) that Brad was not a candidate for marital monogamy. I proposed to Sofia, "If you want to save the marriage, I should be incorporated in as a family member/lover. I love him, love your family, and it would be my dream to have a child with him."

Sofia was aghast and muttered, "You have been conned by Brad." I proposed, "What about the cottages in your backyard? I could live in one and help out with your kids!" Sofia shrieked, "No way! That's absolutely absurd!"

I pointed out, "In other world cultures, polygamy is the norm for successful men. Considering that Brad is now the CEO of a successful company, he should be able to live like the man he is."

Brad appeared cowed and stayed quiet. He faced that he had young daughters whom he very much loved and a reputation to uphold. Despite his appetite for an iconoclastic life, Brad promised Sofia, "I will be with you and only you. It was a mistake."

The affair part of our friendship ended, and I was relegated to being a family friend. I declared to myself, "I will never ever again get involved with a married man who does not explicitly have an open relationship!"

I never ever strayed or relented from that agreement with myself.

Several months later, I got a book deal for *Women Who May Never Marry*, and the following year, I met Jon. Soon he and I shared a home together, and I became a stepmother to his nine-year-old daughter.

One evening Jon devised a sharing game where we placed secrets in one box and wishes in another box. We read the wishes out loud, placed them in an incense burner, and then set them on fire. As for the secrets, we unfolded them and read them. I read Jon my most potent secret, "I still think about being with Brad."

Jon muttered, "I knew it."

Knowing there was no place for me in Brad's life, to keep peace with Jon, I agreed to cease all personal contact. For several years the only times Brad and I could see each other were for big events, like his 50th-birthday celebration.

Four years into my relationship with Jon, what I believed I'd so wanted with Brad and Sofia arrived. Jon had become lovers with a woman named Violet. Suddenly, a multiple-partner relationship was at my doorstep. After a year of emotional thunderstorms, Violet and I faced that we were just not that into each other.

Jon continued to see Violet separately. As much as I could, I lived an emotionally and erotically independent life. Six years later, Jon met an accomplished writer named Jacey, and declared he would be visiting her every other night. I asked Jon, "When do you plan to see me?"

He mumbled, "I suppose in the afternoons."

At that moment, I felt I had lost everything. Other than our dogs and cats, there was nothing left for me at home. Having heard that Brad had divorced Sofia and had his own place, I asked Jon, "Do you mind if I see Brad again?"

Jon stammered, "I can't stop you."

Brad and I met at a West Hollywood café and then drove up to the top of the West Hollywood Hills, the site of his new home. We gazed at the beautiful swimming pool, removed our clothes, and dove in. We reached for each other and began to make love. In that unfettered moment, freedom rang up and down our wet bodies.

We dated for a several months. He gifted me useful things, including my first laptop computer, my first digital camera, and a roller bag for air travel. One weekend we flew to Seattle, where I gave a keynote address at an alternative lifestyles conference. Afterward we spent several days visiting friends and family. Ultimately, he was restless and needed space to explore.

Eventually, he generated his own approach to relationships, which he described as "satellites" that "orbit" around and through his life. Some are casual, others more intense. Whenever he landed in a near-monogamous relationship, any mention of marriage would put an abrupt end to it all.

Thirteen years later, our largely dormant relationship began to orbit into front and center. The previous summer, I had invited him to join me for the Gerewol Festival in West Africa. Unavailable, he proposed we go to Ireland in the spring. Recalling how impulsive he can be, I was dubious he would make himself available. When I called the following February, he surprised me. He invited me to HowTheLightGetsIn, a philosophy festival in Hay-on-Wye, Wales. I agreed to develop an itinerary for visiting more of Wales and then Ireland.

He told me to book rooms with one queen bed for the two of us. I hadn't spent time with him in years. I began to wonder what he would be like in bed.

As the departure date neared, we began to spend drizzles of time together. We met for coffee. I dropped by. He dropped by. We soaked together in his hot tub and took stock of each other's much older bodies.

Then there was a more planned date at his Venice beach home. The rumble of misty waves filled the late-night air. The touch between us was electric—tinged with the old exuberance and marinated in years of knowing each other, familiar and yet compelling.

I was not sure I should mention the postmenopausal state of my vagina. I gazed into his eyes as it woke up. Suddenly, I was wet and absolutely craving him. My extremities tingled all over, and orgasms tumbled through my body. We wriggled into extended moments where memories of our high-spirited past melded with the intensity of the now. We were visited by angels as our bodies tumbled and shook. He declared, "This is the best sex ever."

I was a bit astounded by the declaration, considering all of our many lovers and everywhere each of us had been. But with the momentousness of our reconnection, I decided to agree and proclaimed a full-on "Yes!"

We finalized our plans to meet in Hay-on-Wye for the HowTheLightGetsIn Festival and then travel by car through Wales and Ireland. The festival proved to be tidy and proper relative to Burning Man . . . when I mentioned Burning Man to anyone, they gazed with jaw-dropping envy.

Arriving ahead of Brad, I attended a live Donovan performance. Aged with scraggily gray hair and lots of pithy commentary, Donovan belted out his classics like "Catch the Wind" and "Colors." I was in utter heaven. These were the songs I came of age with as a teen in California. Eight time zones away, a packed audience of British age-mates joined me in mouthing every lyric.

Meanwhile, Brad, who'd flown to London Gatwick 10 hours prior, was still on the road. What I'd believed would be a simple four-hour drive wasn't. He'd been struggling with where to position the car from a right-side-of-the-road perspective in a left-side-of-the-road country and was stopped by the police for appearing to be drunk. After passing a breathalyzer test, he found his way to a pub to celebrate with a pint of Guinness. As the concert ended, he called. He had just arrived in Hay; I offered coordinates for his GPS. In a breathtaking five minutes, his engine roared as I stepped out into the street and waved.

We nestled into our well-appointed glamping tent. It was freezing, and there was a crack between the two mattresses of our camping bed. We held each other tight in search of warmth and connection. We kept landing in the crack. The next morning, we shoved extra blankets into the sides of the bed to reduce the crack. Not being able to sleep soundly, we had lots of sex. The sex was noisy and crazy and much fun. We started out at night, woke each other up at 3:00 a.m., and then jumped each other again at sunrise.

The festival talks addressed everything from Brexit to the impact of digital culture on human social behavior. At night I danced wildly with the young, sweaty kids, and then we settled into watching amazing documentaries about gender, exotic cultural practices, and climate change. We ate whatever we could find: corn chowder, crunchy salads, chocolate chai, flat white coffees, and pastries. Our favorite condiment became clotted cream. We would order anything that might be combined with that cool, buttery whiteness. We dove into the same bowls and plates until the finale, when he then mixed everything altogether with dollops of mayonnaise. Preferring to savor tastes and textures separately, I refused to sample the final concoction, declaring, "I've had enough!"

The festival world was quite manageable. We would wander off separately to talks and debates. My solo wanders led me into a deep conversation about sex, gender, and the future with a fascinating British writer. The last day, we attended the prestigious Hay Book Festival. I tracked down tickets for primatologist Franz de Waal's extraordinary presentation on animal emotions, a talk on music and brain waves, and then one on the impact of gender on cognition. It was all quite glorious.

I was trepidatious about postfestival travel. How would my appetite for engaging cultures and people on their own terms fare with his for cracking jokes and disrupting boredom? We would soon find out.

Our first stop was a bed-and-breakfast in Cardiff, the capital of Wales. I stepped in gingerly, waiting for cues from our hosts. Brad hobbled in on a cane that functioned as one of his many props. The first thing to roll out of his mouth was a crazy joke. I was initially horrified and contemplated, "Should I laugh to assure the hosts he is joking?"

I held back. They laughed along with him as he peppered in the local vernacular "wee" for "little." Soon he was their favorite guest, and I just sat back in awe.

The joking never stopped. Sometimes, it seemed that it was orchestrated just for me. When we landed in the vibrant town of Galway, I teased Brad that to fully experience travel in its many dimensions, we ought to check out the youth hostel. I figured he would take a quick tour, note that the sleeping arrangements were all bunk beds in funky dormitories, and then book a double room at the Victoria Hotel. Before I could blink twice, he'd paid for beds in a mixed-gender dorm with other sleepers! I could not contain my hysterics.

Clearly, he had done this for an emotional moment that can only be accessed by *doing* (and not just considering.) Our dorm mates included a young guy from Nebraska, who was looking for restaurant work, and an old Irish man, who bundled himself up tight and snored. In the middle of the night, Brad found his way into my bunk, and we cuddled very quietly. Over breakfast, the guy from Nebraska remarked, "You two have really great chemistry for an old married couple!"

I briefly explained, "We actually met 28 years ago, but this trip is the first time we've been able to spend real time together."

On our drive to Belfast, I asked Brad to share one of his podcasts. When he removed his headset and connected his phone through the car speakers, I discovered that he was listening at one-and-a-half speed (so that his mind wouldn't wander off). I wanted to hear the actual voice tone and begged that he slow it down to normal.

Instead, he brought it down to half speed and began to speak in half speed. Upon arrival at our hotel, he slowed his whole body to half speed and painstakingly hobbled to the front desk. I led the bell hop to the car to pick up our bags in that Brad was doing half speed and was quite useless. My body was completely overcome with laughter; what had started as a small spurt of pee suddenly gushed out uncontrollably. By the time we settled into our room, my jeans were soaked. I looked at him squarely: "Why do you do this to me?"

"Darling," he said, "I want you to live every moment fully!"

And we did. I calmed myself down long enough to wash the jeans with the hotel hand soap and then slung them over the towel warmer to dry.

It was Saturday night. We hired a local guide to take us on a tour of the glorious street art and show us the pub scene. After dancing up a storm, taking in a postmodern play, and sharing a couple of Irish coffees, the guide faced that his main function was to keep us from getting impossibly lost!

With Ireland as a backdrop, Brad and I finally got to know each other. We told each other many more of our life stories. We had both picked grapes in Southern France in the 1970s . . . We wondered, What might have happened if we had met then?

The sex kept on being amazing. In our small Airbnb bedroom in East Wales, a guest pounded on our wall for making so much noise! In our lovely hotel room in Dublin, Brad brought out thick towels from the bathroom so I could fully receive the gushiest G-spot massage ever. Then there was the full morning of lovemaking at our Cliffs of Moher hotel, which caused us to completely miss breakfast.

I told him that I very much love him. And he told me the same. With neither Jon nor Sofia having a say over our connection, he proclaimed,

> I still get to love you. It's my love and my business! And we had the most amazing time! And you get to have your love too. It's yours! Just own it and love it and feel how lucky you are to have all of these feelings, as opposed to people who play it too safe and have no feelings!

Eventually, the bubble of ecstasy that Brad and I shared got pricked. While our 2019 travel adventure in Ireland and Wales kicked up much dopamine and deepened our longtime friendship, our differences proved to be an insurmountable challenge. In 2022 we teamed up for a road trip exploring much of Croatia. While we savored the fascinating history, the gorgeous Dalmatian Coast, and the cheese and cherry strudels, I wasn't as quick to laugh at his jokes.

Smiling at the Cliffs of Moher, Ireland's west coast.
Photo by Boyd Willat, 2019. Reprinted with permission.

Little Donegall Street scene, Belfast, Northern Ireland, June 2019.
Photo courtesy of author.

Dubrovnik Harbor, Croatia.
Photo courtesy of author.

We both blew up at each other when he woke from a nap and screamed at me for driving in the wrong direction when, in fact, I wasn't. He claimed that I should follow his lead even when I knew full well that he was wrong because that's how women should behave toward men. I was aghast. While women of yesteryear might have engaged such a dynamic to help their men "discover" the right way, I was too much of a 21st-century feminist to play such a game. Eventually, he apologized.

The short-fused bitch in me came to view his appetite for disruption as rude in comparison to my patient style of absorbing culture by being an observer who quietly asks pointed questions. I hated his know-it-all sub personality, which had no capacity for playing by the local rules. One Sunday morning, we walked down the narrow road that hugs the coast of Hvar Milna Beach and found our way to a cliff-side espresso café. I offered to counsel several of his subpersonalities who were causing a lot of trouble. Each time a different personality needed to be heard from, we placed another chair around our table. Nearby coffee drinkers rolled their eyes at our crazy circle of chairs. Suddenly, Brad shifted gears and began to counsel my short-fused bitch. We faced that it was she who could not tolerate his know-it-all persona! We then declared that we still care about each other, but these two had much to work out!

Slowly, the tension subsided. A couple of days later, while picking up eggs at a market near our Dubrovnik apartment, he asked the cashier (as if he was visiting another planet), "Are those from chickens?"

A quizzical look crossed her face, and giggles filled my brain and body. I could barely find my way to our apartment in time to avert pee-soaking my jeans!

We faced that, despite our disdain for the parts of each other that do not at all match, our connection remains. Perhaps all of those years of passionate friendship enabled us to engage intense yelling, screaming, and swearing, knowing that, at the end of the day, we'd still laugh hard and find our way to sweet lovemaking.

CHAPTER 27

Return to Mexico

My 1975 six-month journey through Mexico was formative to my identity as a self-styled anthropologist and an untethered sex researcher. I considered my middle-aged male professors at Berkeley to be "armchair anthropologists" who kept a safe distance from their third-world peasant subjects. One maintained a fancy home for his field visits. Another interviewed young men in local cafés while staying in a comfortable hotel. Perhaps it was my limited finances that led me to go deep and cheap. Or perhaps it was my collapsible ego.

Following the suggestion of Guillermo, the *National Geographic* photographer who had invited me to join him in the beachside *palapa* in Zihuatanejo, I decided to go to Maní, Yucatán. Traveling overland, I found it took me a while to get there. Along the way, I visited Guanajuato, San Miguel de Allende, Oaxaca, and San Cristóbal de las Casas. Eventually, I landed in Mérida, the Yucatán capitol, and then caught a bus to Maní.

As a destination, Maní was only in my mind. No one was expecting me. Moreover, it was a remote village that was surrounded by cornfields and jungle vegetation. Perhaps it was the insistence of my arrival that forced a welcome. What stepped down from the bus was a thin 22-year-old Berkeley-hippie/feminist *gringa* with a highly collapsible ego.

Soon I was situated in Marta and Manuel's pink-and-yellow tiled room with a hammock hanging on the side and a small table and chair. Marta spoke with a decided Yucatec twang, dragging out her vowels and landing hard on the consonants. I paid her "*quince pesos diarios*" (fifteen pesos a day, which converted to a mere $1.20) for room and board. She taught me how to pat out tortillas and introduced me to all of her relatives, who gradually became my extended Yucatec family.

Every day I would take walks, write in my journal, and eat Marta's delicious cooking. Soon I met a very compelling young mother whose name was Maria Cruz. Cruz was curious, outgoing, and absolutely unstoppable. At 29 she'd had eight children and proclaimed that she was done birthing babies and was ready to get birth control shots (**Depo-Provera**). We would discuss the finer points of the romantic situations portrayed in her favorite graphic novellas, and then I would tell her about the world beyond Maní. Cruz had a fabulous sense of humor and loved to draw me into all the family joking.

Several weeks into my stay in Maní, I moved in with her family. There, everyone slept in the living room with hammocks strung across the walls. My hammock was simply incorporated into the mix; one evening, her youngest son crawled into my hammock, believing he was sleeping with his father! We all laughed about it the next morning and forever after.

I was perhaps the first anthropologist to engage in an extended stay in the village of Maní. I was unique to them, with my light, rosy skin; my above-average height; and my contact lenses. Every time I inserted them, a curious crowd of onlookers would emerge, wondering how these tiny plastic disks allowed me to see as if I was wearing glasses! My status as a single young woman who had arrived without her parents was an ongoing mystery, as was my practice of Judaism. They would marvel when I would declare, "*No creo en Jesus ni los Santos!*" (I don't believe in Jesus Christ nor the Catholic Saints!)

Largely, what bonded me to Maria Cruz, her family, and the people of Maní was my extreme loneliness. When I arrived in Maní, I'd already been on the road for four months and sorely missed my friends and family in California. I'd been straddling two worlds—one of the nascent sexual anthropologist who had been experiencing the lovemaking styles of a variety of Mexican men, and the other, a marriageable young woman who, at 22 (by Yucatec standards), was nearly an old maid. I attempted to rectify this disconnect by frequently discussing my passionate interest in an American photographer I'd met during my travels.

Eventually, I left Maní. It was too small to sustain my wild drive to become a writer and a professor of anthropology. I kept returning to check in on my friends. Every time I'd return, there would be *cambios* (changes). When I returned in my late 20s, the town cenote (well) had been replaced with potable water spigots. Several years later, the two black-and-white TVs the village men would huddle close to watch every night had given way to many privately owned color TVs.

Maria Cruz and her husband Salvador fomented many of the changes. When I first met them in 1975, travelers who passed through Maní would be offered home-cooked meals at a simple table in their kitchen. This then led to their opening an actual restaurant, El Principe Tutul Xiu. During one of my visits, I helped translate the menu into English so American tourists could order such Yucatec delicacies as *pavo negro* and *poc chuc*.

Between 2015 and 2019, I made several trips to central Mexico. It was time to make peace with the country that I so loved and so hated. I loved the vibrancy, the food, and the emotional warmth. And I hated how I'd been deceived, robbed, and sexually violated. During these trips I was traveling with a male partner, which generated a very different dynamic.

A memorable moment of my December 2015 trip was making love with my boyfriend Doug in a beautiful Huatulco condo that overlooked the Oaxaca coast. We were 300 miles south of Acapulco, overlooking the same Pacific Ocean where I'd been raped 40 years before. This time I was in a king-sized bed with a partner who I very much enjoyed. I cried for joy, wallowing in being safe, happy, and respected.

In January 2018 Doug suggested we explore several of Mexico's expatriate retirement communities. He thought, with my fluency in Spanish and ultimate love of Mexican culture, that I might want to retire there. We visited Lake Chapala, San Miguel de Allende, and then returned to Maní. During our week in Chapala, we stayed in Ajijic, and I befriended several delightful American women. The place was barely Mexican. Many of the expats did not speak Spanish and ultimately "engaged" Mexico from their own cultural bubble. San Miguel was wonderfully vibrant, filled with artists and writers, and had a substantial Mexican community. I was quite taken.

We then flew to the Yucatán and visited Maní. I wasn't sure who would still be around. It had been 15 years since my last visit and 42 years since I'd celebrated my 23rd birthday with the Manileños. Doug and I arrived late in the evening. We drove in on the new *carretera* (highway) that connects Maní with the Yucatán interior. Nothing looked familiar. Neighborhood cantinas were blaring ranchero tunes; compared to the old Maní, it looked like a carnival. We found the plaza, and I asked for Cruz: "*Sí, vive en su misma casa.*" (Yes, she still lives in her same house.)

The hammocks had given way to beds and bedrooms, but her infectious spirit was absolutely intact. I stepped in the living room and announced, "Es Leanna!"

Immediately, we were embracing, and tears were running down our cheeks. It was as if I'd been there all along. Each of her children had married, and there were grandchildren galore.

My eyes popped at the changes. Maní was now in line to be a designated Pueblo Mágico (magical village), and Cruz hosted us in her just-opened hotel. As for the family restaurant, there were now four branches in nearby towns as well as in Mérida. Maní was crowded with craft boutiques, cafes, and cantinas; the central plaza had a basketball court and a designated disabled parking space. Cruz's youngest daughter, Erika, took us on a real estate tour. We marveled at her older sister Maria's architectural innovations of employing traditional thatch with skylights

Embracing Maria Cruz upon my return to Maní.
Photo by David Lloyd, 2018. Reprinted with permission.

and 15-foot-high walls. I was so taken by the new Maní that I considered buying a plot and hiring Maria to design my retirement home!

In October 2019 the World Association for Sexual Health (WAS) held its biennial meeting in Mexico City. Brad agreed to join me. I had been invited to present my research on "The Three Waves of Polyamory" and on "Changing Perspectives on Sexual Assault." The last time I'd attended a WAS meeting was in 2003 in Havana, Cuba, where I'd presented, "Why Women Swing." A sexologist from Colombia who heard that talk recalled it so fondly that he made a point to attend this one! I connected polyamory's contemporary practices to its rich history beginning with the patriarchal 19th-century Oneida community. I contrasted the feminist-inspired second wave I had chronicled in my doctoral dissertation and then recent millennial practices, including **relationship anarchy**, where no one expects or imposes priority over anyone else.

By bringing my sexual assault research to a professional audience in Mexico City, I truly went full circle. I was amongst sexual scientists who could follow the cultural history I had tracked as well as the survey data I had crunched. There were no more lame excuses for sexual misconduct—not in America, not in Mexico . . . not anywhere!

Presenting my sexual assault study in Mexico City.
Photo by Boyd Willat, 2019. Reprinted with permission.

Afterward Brad joined me at the conference party, where we danced, sang, enjoyed amazing food, and drank too much tequila. The following week, we traveled to Guanajuato for the Cervantine International Arts Festival. Topping off our week of theater, dance, music, and film, we danced in the streets with the locals and ate some of the best *chile rellenos* ever. Afterward we revisited San Miguel de Allende to connect with friends and absorb the vibrant art scene.

Our final destination, Oaxaca, was exploding with craft and food markets, wonderful chocolate mole tamales, and fantastic festivals celebrating the Day of the Dead. We engaged Oaxaca to the fullest—joining a bike tour of the town's iconic murals, diving into Day of the Dead street parades, and joining a family to celebrate the memory of their beloved grandparents at the town cemetery. The Mexico we visited bore a prosperity and savvy I had never before seen. Coupled with the warmth and absolutely delectable food, it, too, had gone full circle.

San Miguel de Allende evening laughter.
Photo by Carolyn Studer, 2019. Reprinted with permission.

PART XII

Conclusion

Relaxing in a tatami room in Magome, Japan.
Photo by Paula Achter, 2023. Reprinted with permission.

CHAPTER 28

Healing Through Culture, History, and Context

Brad and I returned home from Mexico in November 2019 with no idea that Covid-19 was lurking. We had planned a round-the-world, culture-jumping trip for the spring of 2020, with plans to meet in the Seychelles, followed by a week in Qatar and then a month in Japan. Every detail had to be canceled as we hunkered down into global quarantine.

Existential concerns emerged. Without physical community, did the rest of life matter? In my prepandemic life, I was constantly in motion. I would drive across town just to hear a lecture, followed by a treat at an exotic café. My calendar was packed with distractions. I barely assessed how much I wanted to do anything; I just kept doing.

The forced isolation led me to access an inner resilience. I didn't need to be in motion to be alive or even fulfilled. Being that there was so little happening in the physical world, all vestiges of fear of missing out (FOMO) faded. I lived quietly, binge-watching one Netflix series after another. Every week or so, I would visit Brad, and we would cook simple things and soak in his hot tub. Largely, the pandemic taught me to sit with myself.

When *Good Luck to You, Leo Grande* began to stream on Hulu in June 2022, Emma Thompson's character, Nancy Stokes, hit a chord for women of a certain age who yearn for sexual attention from a man who is easy on the eye and comfortable in his own skin. While Nancy's lack of exposure was far from my story, I very much fantasized about accessing no-strings sex visits. Then one day, I swiped right on a dating-app profile of a good-looking younger guy. Soon my own Leo Grande arrived!

He'd presented himself as married, polyamorous, and as a freeway-flying adjunct professor of design. An overextended father of twins, his visits were largely about sex. When he'd arrive, I'd hand him a fresh bath towel, and after showering, he'd land butt naked in my bed. Being a generation younger than Brad, he was up for the kind of sex my body craved. His erections lasted, ejaculate spurt everywhere, and any position I dreamed in was absolutely possible. And unlike Nancy, who'd provided payments to her sex worker, Leo Grande, mine would visit for free in that one of his kinks was being with an older woman. I sensed it would be a win-win until one of us had had enough.

Reflecting upon my research journey, I saw how it very much gave me license to ask nosy and compelling questions and to do my best to make sense of the world I was born into, as well as to fully engage the many worlds I'd found along the way. Being a participant observer became my identity as well as my excuse for asking hard questions and soothing myself by contextualizing the cultural worlds I'd encountered.

Participant observation is certainly not for everyone! Most of my students felt fraudulent going into places where they didn't belong. Playing along to access another culture's worldview could feel obtrusive, if not just downright rude. Befriending others for cultural data could feel insincere and manipulative. My curiosity somehow gave me license to get sticky, wet, and altogether dirty in my quest for the biggest picture possible of why we humans seek erotic connection and generate deep partnership.

When I reflect on my journey of experimentation and adventure, with several mean prickles along the way, I am both relieved and troubled by changes in our sexual and social worlds. I was privileged to come of age just as abortion rights were granted without exception, thus honoring a women's right to choose. Now, state by state, those rights are being rescinded. It's ironic that, in medieval times, having sex outside of marriage was a sin that abortion (without much regard for the fetus itself) was used to cover up; now the "rights of the unborn" have been imposed as an ideology to contest the sexual rights of women.

As a young woman, I suffered from the absence of a #MeToo movement and the preponderance of rape myths that viewed victims as provocateurs and had "Boys will be boys" attitudes. Nonetheless, I find myself uncomfortable with contemporary rigidities regarding consent. In the world I came of age in, seduction mattered. Declaring a hard "No" that cannot be persuaded into a "Maybe" and eventually a "Yes" is an anathema to the courtship that makes my juices flow. Within today's consent culture, I am often tongue-tied in being able to assert a "Hell yes!"

The dynamics of dominance and submission exist amongst both animals and humans. The submissive cowers as the dominant strikes. In sexual play, roles are negotiated and can be switched. As #MeToo impacted the cultural climate, those of us who had once (or many times) been slapped, fondled, and/or seduced in manipulative ways sought to upend these wrongs. A grand disconnect emerged as we revisited these dramas of disempowerment. In our fervor we failed to acknowledge our compliance in (and appetite for) these timeless human/animal dynamics. We now live in a climate of such anxiety that erotic adventure is distrusted. Men are fearful of the consequences of acting on their desires, while women sit upon their self-made righteous thrones, alone and lonely.

Finally, while I opened this book relating how I was raped and my mother was abused, I consider our stories to be human stories. Those amongst us who are larger, older, and more skilled at manipulation have forever imposed their will on those who are smaller, younger, more innocent, and (often) female. Ultimately, we humans are a resilient species. While my mother largely stuffed her pain, I have had the privilege of training in anthropology and sexology to employ considerations of time, place, and cultural context to heal mine.

Glossary

adultery—Sexual intercourse between a married person and someone who is not their spouse.

aftercare—What comforting care partners offer each other following sex. This concept originates from the BDSM culture, where submissive partners are provided warmth and connection following a flogging or other power exchange.

anal play—Refers to sexual activities involving the anus that include anilingus (licking the anus), fingering, penile intercourse, and fisting (inserting a hand into the anal sphincter).

arranged marriage—A marital union where the parties are selected by individuals other than the couple themselves. It is distinguished from a love marriage, where the decision to marry is driven solely by the couple.

asynchronous chat—A form of online messaging where participants communicate intermittently rather than in a real-time, back-and-forth exchange.

autoethnography—A style of memoir where a researcher employs an ethnographic lens to connect personal experiences to wider cultural, political, and social contexts.

BDSM—Consensual erotic practices or role-playing involving bondage, discipline, dominance and submission, and sadomasochism. Participants may or may not consider themselves to be part of the BDSM community or subculture.

bicurious—A heterosexual who is interested in exploring bisexuality. This can be a lifelong status that does not transition into identifying as bisexual.

bigamy—Entering into a concurrent marriage while already married to another person. In the United States, bigamy is illegal in that it would by definition involve deception in that only one legally licensed marriage is allowed at a time.

bisexuality—Being sexually or romantically attracted to both men and women or to more than one sex or gender.

blue balls—An erection that lasts for an extended period of time that does not result in orgasm. It is medically known as epididymal hypertension. While rarely a serious condition, it can cause testicular pain.

Boko Haram—A Nigerian-based group that seeks to overthrow the Nigerian government and replace it with a regime based on Islamic law. The U.S. State Department considers them a Foreign Terrorist Organization; in April 2014, they gained notoriety when they kidnapped 276 schoolgirls.

brain chemistry of romantic love—Three categories of romantic love (lust, attraction, and attachment) that can be categorized by their own unique set of hormones. Testosterone and estrogen drive lust; dopamine, norepinephrine, and serotonin create attraction; and oxytocin and vasopressin generate attachment.

bride price—Money or property that is paid by the groom or his family to the bride's family. When a family does not have such wealth, a prospective groom may engage in bride service, where he performs work for the bride's family to validate the marriage.

Burning Man—The weeklong end-of-summer festival that gathers at the Black Rock Desert in Northern Nevada. It collects celebrants from all over the world, who create a community based on art, self-expression, self-reliance, and gifting. The peak event is the burning of an effigy of a man; the final event is the burning of the festival temple. Those who return each year often refer to it as home.

cad vs. dad—These reflect two distinct appetites that women have in men. Cads are dominant and physically attractive, and they satisfy short-term interests. Dads, though often less handsome, are stable, warm, and are drawn to invest in family life. According to evolutionary psychologists, when a woman is ovulating, she is most drawn to cads for their good genes; otherwise, she will find dads to be better matches.

celestial marriage—The Mormon doctrine that marriage can last forever in heaven. Spouses (including plural wives) and their children can all be sealed and thus eternally be together.

cenote—Deep natural well or sinkhole embedded in the limestone crust of Yucatán, Mexico. The ancient Maya relied on *cenotes* primarily for water; on occasion, they functioned as sites for ritual sacrifice.

cheating—Sexual infidelity. It is seen in couples (or polyfidelitous groupings) who break their agreements to limit erotic expression (however they define it).

coitus reservatus—A sexual practice of the 19th-century Oneida community wherein a man suppresses the ejaculation of semen to prevent conception. It is also practiced in Taoism as well as in Indian tantra and Hatha yoga.

commodification of culture—The conversion of human, social, or cultural value into market value; it occurs in the context of cultural tourism.

co-mothering—When a woman serves as a second mother to a child who isn't her biological child.

compersion—Embraced by practitioners of polyamory as a positive emotion when witnessing (or hearing about) their partner engaging in intimate behavior with another person. Regarded as the opposite of jealousy, as in feeling happy that one's partner is happy.

concubine—A mistress; a concubine lives with a man and his wife but holds a lower status than the wife. Concubines might be incorporated into a household for sexual pleasure, and depending on the cultural context, they may produce additional offspring, particularly male heirs.

consensual—When all parties are in agreement. An intimate relationship is consensual when participants take full responsibility for themselves to prevent abuse and violation of each other's well-being.

consent training—A program to educate on the specifics of interpersonal communication in intimate relationships. Consent is regarded as an ongoing conversation, verbal or nonverbal, between all people engaged in a sexual interaction.

co-wives—Women who share a husband, as in the practice of polygyny.

cultural excuse—When a culture's norms and values authorize behavior different from mainstream cultural practice.

cultural generality—A cultural practice that occurs in many but not all cultures. The nuclear family is considered a cultural generality in that it is widespread but not universal.

cultural generation gap—The generation gap most referenced in the United States is the ideological one between baby boomers and their parents in the 1960s and early 1970s. Values and mores were dramatically upended with the emergence of second-wave feminism and the sexual revolution. A cultural generation gap, following the immigration of large waves of Hispanic and Asian families, followed this trend of values disparities between youth and their parents in the 2000s and 2010s.

cultural imperialism—When the values, practices, and meanings imbued in powerful foreign cultures are imposed upon more native cultures. Negative consequences include loss of culture and language, as well as generating preference for Western brands and perspectives.

cultural particularity—A cultural practice that is unique to few cultures. The large sums of money that many Americans spend on their weddings are referenced as a cultural particularity.

cultural relativism—The effort to understand cultural practices of other groups in their own cultural context. Cultural relativism endeavors to counter ethnocentricism by contending that the norms and values of one culture should not be evaluated by those of another.

cultural universal—A universal feature of all cultures. Examples include symbols, language, gift giving, marriage (with much variation), body adornment, the incest taboo (also with much variation), and rules of hygiene.

culture of poverty—The theory that people in poverty develop certain habits that cause their families to remain in poverty over generations. Noted by Oscar Lewis in 1963, its features include marginality, helplessness, dependency, and a present-time orientation.

cunnilingus—Oral sex act wherein the vulva is stimulated using the tongue and lips.

cybersex—A broad term that encompasses the engagement of erotica via an online environment. Sexual messages are exchanged, and sexual activity is performed remotely by means of virtual reality, such as the use of teledildonics.

default world (re: Burning Man)—For participants in the Burning Man Arts and Culture Festival, the default world is the world outside of Burning Man. This distinguishes Burning Man's unique cultural practices including radical inclusion, self-expression, and self-reliance, as well as gifting and decommodification.

de-masking—An online chat strategy whereby participants attempt to uncover who they are in fact chatting with. This can include requesting photographs or a Zoom chat or scheduling an in-person meeting.

Depo-Provera—An injectable contraceptive, containing the hormone progestin, which suppresses ovulation and thickens cervical mucus (which blocks sperm access). For maximum effectiveness, injections are repeated every three months.

Dobbs v. Jackson Women's Health Organization—Legislation which overturned *Roe v. Wade* in 2022. The U.S. Supreme Court reviewed the constitutionality of the Mississippi law that banned most abortions after 15 weeks of gestation.

do-date—An erotic practice of More University where a partner receives hand/finger stimulation of the genitals in a prescribed manner. OneTaste adapted this practice, naming it orgasmic meditation, where women would receive 15 minutes of clitoral stroking from a male partner.

dom—Short for dominant. This is the person who is in the power position in a dominant-submissive relationship.

dominatrix—A woman who plays the dominant role in a dominant-submissive relationship. A pro-dom sells such services, which, unlike prostitution, exclude sexual intercourse.

dopamine—A neurotransmitter that generates pleasure. It generates focus and the capacity to find things interesting. Too much or too little dopamine can figure in mental disorders, as in schizophrenia (excessive amounts) and attention deficit hyperactivity disorder (ADHD), when a shortage occurs.

DSM—*The Diagnostic and Statistical Manual of Mental Disorders* used by health care professionals. It is reviewed (and revised) by the American Psychiatric Association every five to seven years, noting changes in cultural beliefs and practices.

dyad—A twosome, a pair or a couple. In an intimate relationship, it is distinct from a triad, which would be a threesome.

ecstasy—A stimulant and psychedelic drug that can distort time and perception and enhance pleasure, emotional warm and tactile experiences. Derived from the synthetic drug MDMA (3, 4-methylenedioxy-methamphetamine).

endogamy—Marrying within one's cultural, religious, racial, and/or ethnic group.

ethnocentrism—Applying one's own cultural beliefs and practices as the standard for judging other cultural ways. The opposite is cultural relativism, where the norms and values of one culture are not evaluated by those of another.

ethnography—A report on a people's cultural ways and practices based on qualitative research including participant observation and interviews.

expanded orgasm—More University developed techniques that employed focused genital touch, heightened awareness, and breath control to access orgasms that last upwards of 15 minutes and, in the eyes of some beholders, 3 or more hours. These practices have been adapted by authors including Tim Ferriss, Patricia Taylor, and Nicole Daedone.

extended families of choice—A family of choice (consisting of like-minded friends) that functions in place of the traditional multigenerational extended family.

fantasy role play—A cyber chat dynamic where participants may claim fictional identities (re: age, gender, and erotic appetites) toward the engagement of make-believe activities.

fellatio—Oral pleasuring of the penis or scrotum, better known as a blow job. It may either be an act in and of itself or foreplay prior to vaginal or anal intercourse.

female ejaculation—The ejaculation of a fluid from the Skene's gland mixed with watered-down urine that emerges from a woman's urethral opening.

feminism—The antisexist ideology of the women's liberation movement wherein all genders have equal rights and opportunities.

feminist women's consciousness-raising group—1970s women-only spaces where feelings, needs, and desires were discussed. Topics included gender roles, experiences of sex, abortion, and intimate relationships.

finger-fucking—The use of fingers to erotically pleasure the vagina or anus.

fluffer—A pornographic film-set assistant who keeps the male performer's penis erect between scenes.

focus group—A research method used to collect opinions and feedback from a group of 8 to 10 people about a specific concept, idea, or product. Members are invited to share their thoughts, opinions, and feelings in a facilitated discussion.

frottage—Rubbing parts of the body onto another person for sexual stimulation. Does not involve penile insertion and thus can be regarded as "outercourse."

gay—Homosexual. This is sexual or romantic attraction to people of one's same sex.

gender—Socially constructed characteristics of masculinity and femininity. Gender varies between cultures and can change over time.

generation gap—Any gap between two generations is a generation gap, but here, it is specifically referencing the ideological gap between baby boomers and their parents in the 1960s and early 1970s. Values and mores were dramatically upended with the emergence of second-wave feminism and the sexual revolution.

Gerewol Festival—A yearly courtship competition among the Wodaabe Fulani tribes in Niger and Chad featuring elaborate costuming, makeup, and dance.

gringa—A derogatory Spanish word for English-speaking female foreigners.

G-spot—A mass of tissue inside of the vagina, which is, in fact, the back of the clitoris; it can be sensitive to erotic stimulation and can generate female ejaculation.

hammam—A gendered bathhouse found throughout the Muslim world with both hygienic and social functions.

heterocentric—Having a heterosexual bias or basis.

heterosexual—Straight; opposite of homosexual. It is to be sexually or romantically attracted to people of the other sex.

hierarchical polyamory—the form of polyamory (consensual nonmonogamy) where primary partners prioritize their own needs over those of their secondary or other partners.

hijab/burka—A hijab is a head covering worn in public by some Muslim women. A burka is a long, loose garment that covers the whole body from head to toe.

homosexual—Gay (often males) or lesbian (specifically females); it is the opposite to heterosexual, to be sexually or romantically attracted to people of the same sex.

human potential movement—The 1960s countercultural movement that believes that people can experience a life of happiness, creativity, and fulfillment, which then may bring about positive social change.

intersex—When genitals, chromosomes, or reproductive organs are outside of the male/female sex binary. Some people who are intersex choose gender-affirming options (hormones and/or surgery) to match a preferred gender; others have been modified as infants without consent and wish they had not been.

interview schedule—An ethnographic research method where a series of structured questions are used to guide the interview.

intimate network—An interconnection of partners (and friends) in a polyamorous network.

intrauterine sperm competition—Sperm war resulting from multiple-partner insemination during the female monthly cycle. Ejaculate consists of fighter, blocker, and egg-penetrating sperm that generate a competition to fertilize the egg at ovulation.

kathoey (ladyboys)—Trans, intersex, androgynous, or effeminate gay men in Cambodia, Laos, and Thailand.

kitchen table polyamory—A polyamorous arrangement where everyone in a polycule (romantic network) is on such friendly terms that they can share a meal or have a cup of coffee at the kitchen table.

kuru—A rare and fatal brain disease resulting from ritualistic cannibalism, as practiced among the Fore of Papua New Guinea in the 1950s-1960s.

lesbian—A female homosexual.

LGBTQIA—Acronym for lesbian, gay, bisexual, transgender, queer, intersex, asexual. Since the 1990s it has functioned as an umbrella term for marginalized sexualities and gender identities.

love match—A marriage or relationship for love alone; it can be contrasted to an arranged marriage, where factors of wealth and status are considered.

lumpen proletariat—A Marxist term referring to the unemployed and criminal elements of society who are not interested in revolutionary advancement but remain a useful cudgel against the proletariat as a reserve army of labor. In this scheme the proletariat are the employed working class, the petite bourgeoisie are the middle class, and the bourgeoisie are the capitalist class.

machismo—A Spanish term for the strong sense of masculine pride that is deeply embedded in Hispanic culture. It can be regarded as a display of strength and power that is overbearing and demeaning toward women.

magic mushrooms—Psilocybin mushrooms, which may create psychedelic effects including vivid visuals and distortions in reality.

male chauvinism—The belief that men are superior in ability and intelligence relative to women.

man the hunter—A once-paleoanthropological hypothesis that human evolution was primarily activated by the cooperative and toolmaking skills of big-game hunters.

marianismo—The female counterpart to *machismo*. It is a set of female gender-role values and expectations that encourage passivity, self-sacrifice, and chastity.

Marxist anthropology—The view of society that challenges the notion of an integrated whole (as in functionalism) but rather sees it as one characterized by conflict and struggle. Marx contended that religion imposed a cultural system that prevented the spread of revolutionary ideas—specifically, the notion of class consciousness.

Me-search—When a researcher uses their personal experience to tackle academic questions.

metamour—A polyamorous partner's partner—for example, a partner's spouse or other girlfriend or boyfriend.

#MeToo movement—A global and survivor-led movement against sexual violence. The name originated with Tarana Burke's 2006 Myspace posting. The MeToo hashtag went viral following the October 2017 *New York Time*'s exposé of the sexual misconduct of Hollywood producer Harvey Weinstein.

monogamy—Marriage to one partner. It can also describe having a sexual relationship with only one partner. In contrast, folks who are monogamously married may have open arrangements that allow multiple sexual partners.

More University—Founded in 1968 by Victor Baranco in Lafayette, California, as an experiment in pleasurable group living. Courses were offered in communication, gender dynamics, and sensuality. The group became known for its pioneering work emphasizing the importance of clitoral stimulation and the practice of orgasm lasting as long as three hours.

Muria—Tribe in central India in the Chhattisgarh state. Their sex education practices were detailed in *Kingdom of the Young* by Verrier Elwin.

Muria *ghotul*— Mixed-sex dormitory where Muria adolescents are provided guidance in sensual and sexual communication.

mutual masturbation—A masturbation practice where a couple use their hands and/or toys to stimulate each other's genitals.

National Sex Offender Registry—A U.S. Department of Justice registry that tracks the whereabouts of sex offenders. It was named for Dru Sjodin, who was abducted and murdered in 2003 by a sex offender who had been recently released from prison. Depending on the severity of the offense, defendants can petition for removal with terms varying by state.

nipple clamps—A sexual aid that enables intense sensation to the nipples. The hands and mouth are thus free to stimulate other erotic zones.

nonbinary—A gender expression that is neither male nor female. Nonbinaries may identify as a third gender, more than one gender, or no gender, or have a fluctuating gender identity.

norepinephrine—A neurotransmitter in the brain and spinal cord that increases alertness, arousal, and attention. Elevated levels may be produced during the attraction phase of romantic love.

NRE (new relationship energy)—A term used by polyamorists to describe the elevated state associated with the attraction phase of romantic love. Here, intense focus is placed on a newly formed relationship, and in-place relationships may feel put aside. Polyamorous folks consider the disregard for in-place partners to be a phase that will eventually pass.

online disinhibition effect—The lack of restraint one may feel when chatting online contrasted with communicating in person. Due to anonymity, participants may readily disclose personal information and emotional feelings.

oral sex—Stimulation applied to the genitals by the mouth, tongue, lips, or teeth. Cunnilingus is oral sex performed on the vulva, while fellatio is performed on the penis. Anilingus is the oral stimulation of the anus.

orgasm—A powerful feeling of physical pleasure that can follow sexual stimulation. Regarded as the peak of sexual excitement where tension is released, the orgasm is experienced when the perineal muscles and the reproductive organs rhythmically pulse and endorphins are secreted.

orgasmic meditation (OM)—A practice of Nicole Daedone's One Taste where the clitoris is stroked in a prescribed manner for 15 minutes. While pleasure is presumed, an orgasmic climax is neither the goal nor expected.

outlier—A data point that is far outside the statistical average.

parallel polyamory—Polyamorous relationships in which participants are aware of each other's partners but have little or no contact with those partners. It engages a differing approach from kitchen table polyamory, where partners of partners engage each other socially.

partible paternity—A practice of Amazonian tribes, including the Canela and the Bari, where multiple "fathers" contribute semen that accumulate in a pregnant woman and function to create the fetus. While it is counter to cell biology's understanding of reproduction, the net effect is the engagement of multiple supportive fathers following the birth of the child.

participant observation—The primary research method of cultural anthropology wherein the researcher immerses themselves into a community to gather rich and detailed data toward the construction of an ethnography.

pastoralism (and other means of subsistence)—Pastoralists have a symbiotic relationship with their herds, tending them and, in turn, eating a diet rich in dairy and meat. Humanities' basic means of subsistence is *foraging*, which includes: hunting, fishing, gathering, and scavenging. *Horticulture* refers to basic gardening and *intensive agriculture* involves large-scale food production employing many technologies.

patrilineage/matrilineage—A patrilineage traces descent through the paternal (father's) family line, while a matrilineage traces descent from the maternal (mother's) family line.

pavo negro—A typical Yucatec Mayan dish made from turkey prepared with a savory stuffing and a rich sauce.

playa (at Burning Man)—The 7-square mile desert floor of the annual Burning Man Festival, which occurs the last week of August in the Black Rock Desert of Northern Nevada.

poc chuc—A signature Yucatec Mayan dish made from pork soaked in a sour orange marinade and then grilled. It is typically served with rice, refried beans, pickled onions, and avocado.

political economy—The study of how economic systems are governed by political systems, focusing on the relationship between individuals and society and between markets and the state.

polyamory—Consensual nonmonogamy. Polyamory can take many forms ranging from open couples and/or a polycule (intimate network) to solo polyamory and relationship anarchy.

polyandry—A rare form of polygamy (.5%) where a woman has multiple husbands.

polyfidelity—A form of polyamory where all members are committed to each other and do not date or engage in sexual activity outside of their group.

polygamy—A multiple-person marriage where a spouse of either sex has more than one mate at the same time. The two main forms are polygyny and polyandry.

polygyny—The most common form of polygamy (84.5% of cultures), where a husband has multiple wives.

poppers—Amyl nitrite that is inhaled to relax the muscles of the sphincter, anus, and vagina, which raises the heart rate and increases erotic sensation. (The FDA considers this drug to be dangerous.)

postmodernism—An ideology that challenges explanations that purport to be valid for all groups, cultures, and traditions, acknowledging that observers can never be fully objective.

qualitative research—The study of things in their natural settings so as to understand the meanings people bring to them. Participant observation is a qualitative research method.

quantitative research—A research method that focuses on numeric data and unchanging data and detailed convergent reasoning. Surveys and questionnaires are used to collect data from multiple respondents to then analyze trends, patterns, and correlations.

quinceañera—The 15th-birthday celebration of Hispanic Catholic girls, marking their transition into fertility and adulthood.

rape—The nonconsensual penetration (or attempted penetration) of the vagina, anus, or mouth with any body part or object.

relationship anarchy—A consensual romantic relationship structure in which the only standards are those reflecting the needs and desires of each partner.

religious morality police (Iran)—Officers tasked with warning women (and sometimes men) to correct the way they dress in public, such as proper wearing of headscarves/hijabs and the wearing of loose-fitting clothing.

retrofeminism—A revisionist practice wherein feminist goals of female independence and gender equality are subverted to the dichotomy of passive femininity and dominant masculinity.

Roe v. Wade—The landmark 1973 U.S. Supreme Court decision that granted a woman's right to choose an abortion, making such decisions a matter of privacy between doctors and patients.

sadist/masochist—Sadists derive sexual gratification from the infliction of physical pain or verbal humiliation on another person. Masochists access erotic pleasure from experiencing pain and/or humiliation.

señorita—Unmarried Spanish-speaking girl or woman; it is a diminutive of señora. Señorita may also imply sexual virginity.

serial monogamy—The partnering pattern where one goes from one romantic (and monogamous) relationship to another, as contrasted with bigamy, polygamy, and polyamory.

sexual assault—Sexual contact that occurs without explicit consent of the victim; it can include attempted rape, unwanted fondling, or touching and forced oral sex.

sexual dimorphism—Differences in size and structure between males and females of a species. Amongst gorillas and orangutans, there is dramatic sexual dimorphism, with males being twice as large as females. Humans, too, are sexually dimorphic. Amongst species where there are pronounced differences in size, nonmonogamy is routine.

sexual misconduct—Conduct of a sexual nature that is nonconsensual or is threatening, intimidating, or coercing. It includes sexual harassment, sexual assault, domestic and dating violence, and stalking.

sexual revolution—The 1960s–1970s social movement that challenged traditional codes of behavior related to sexuality. There were increases in sex outside of heterosexual monogamous marriages, including homosexuality, premarital sex, masturbation, and alternative sexualities. These were fueled by the normalization of contraception (particularly the birth control pill) and the legalization of abortion.

single mothers by choice—Women who openly become mothers by means of sperm donation, embryo adoption, or adoption of a baby or a child. This is distinct from women who become single mothers due to an accidental pregnancy, death of a spouse, or divorce.

singles culture—The unique culture of single folks who generate community via "family by choice" relationships. Despite societal expectations about being partnered and/or married, nearly half of U.S. adults are unmarried, and half of that population are not interested in dating.

solo polyamory—Practitioners of solo polyamory have multiple intimate relationships but do not seek to nest with (live with) any of their partners. They consider their primary relationship to be with themselves.

stirpiculture breeding program—Designed by the Oneida Community between 1869 and 1880 to produce their next generation. Members were purportedly selected for spiritual, physical, and intellectual characteristics; ultimately, male elders were paired with attractive (and presumably fertile) females, wreaking havoc with the young men of the community.

sub—Short for submissive in a BDSM encounter or relationship.

subculture—A cultural group within a larger culture, carrying beliefs, interests, and behaviors at variance with the larger culture. Religious, ethnic, and gender groups can all be considered subcultures.

submissive—A person who takes the submissive role relative to a dom (dominant) in BDSM relationships. Submissives may "top from the bottom" wherein they in fact control what happens in a scene/encounter.

survey research—A research method where human subjects are offered a list of questions for assessing beliefs and behaviors. Variance in findings depends on how a population was sampled and on the bias in administration and questionnaire design.

survey research toggles—Toggles refer to "if, then" survey switches, causing only those who respond with a particular answer to be able to view the next series of questions.

swinging—A recreational sex subculture where singles and couples engage in casual sexual encounters. Swinging couples frequently engage rules that discourage romantic attachment with play partners.

switch—In the BDSM subculture, a switch engages both dominance and submission.

Sybian—A motorized and remotely controlled mountable, saddle-shaped sexual aid with a protruding dildo.

tantra—A sexual practice that incorporates mindfulness and deep connection. Originating from Buddhist and Hindu meditation where, unlike Western "red Tantra," sexual enhancement and partner bonding was not a goal.

third genders—Genders embraced by many world cultures that are outside of the male-female binary. These include the *fa'afafine* of Samoa, the *travesti* of Brazil, the *kathoey* of Thailand, the *hijra* of India, and the two-spirits of Native North America.

triad—A bonded three-way polyamorous relationship. In a V-triad two of the three people are not emotionally involved with each other, while the person in the middle may be referred to as the hinge.

virgin—Traditionally, someone who has not engaged in sexual intercourse. Considering that many sexual practices do not include penile-vaginal insertion, there are thus many virginities!

woman the gatherer—A theory popularized by feminist anthropologists in the 1970s to counter the "male the hunter" hypothesis. Knowledge about food safety, acquisition, and preparation were regarded as products of cultural evolution.

zocalo—Spanish term for a Mexican central plaza or town square where folks gather and connect.

References

Dr. Leanna Wolfe's Research

"Adding a co-wife," https://www.slideshare.net/drleanna/adding-a-co-wife (August 26, 2009):
- Society for Anthropology in Community Colleges, Santa Fe, New Mexico, April 17, 1998.
- *Loving More Magazine, 15,* Fall 1998.
- *Teaching Anthropology: SACC Notes, 5*(2), Fall–Winter, 1998.
- Southwestern Anthropological Association, Fullerton, CA, April 16, 1999.
- *California Anthropologist, 26*(2), 1999.
- *Annual Editions Anthropology 06/07* (29th ed.), McGraw-Hill/Dushkin, 2006.

"Anal play: Who is doing it and why?" https://www.slideshare.net/drleanna/who-is-doing-anal-play-and-why (2016, February 7), Society for the Scientific Study of Sexuality Western Region Conference, Los Angeles, CA, April 22, 2012.

"Are polyamory and cheating all that different?" https://www.slideshare.net/drleanna/are-polyamory-and-cheating-all-that-different (March 4, 2012):
- Open New York City, New York, NY, June 28, 2012.
- Network for a New Culture, Seattle, WA, November 12, 2012.
- International Academic Polyamory Conference, Berkeley, CA, February 22, 2014.

Changes in childbirth, documentary film (1986):
- Winner, Tucson Video Festival, 1986.
- Finalist, Hometown USA Video Festival, 1986.

"Changing perspectives on sexual assault," https://www.slideshare.net/drleanna/changing-perspectives-on-sexual-assault-89502284 (March 3, 2018):
- CA Community College Anthropology Teachers Conference, Paso Robles, CA, January 14, 2017.
- Southwestern Anthropological Association, San Jose, CA, April 28, 2017.
- Society for the Scientific Study of Sexuality, Atlanta, GA, November 12, 2017.
- Los Angeles Sexology Association, Los Angeles, CA, March 2, 2018.
- World Association for Sexual Health, Mexico City, Mexico, October 12, 2019.

Flatbush from the youth perspective: Histories, research and stories of Afro-American and Caribbean youth, Flatbush Development Corporation with support from City University of New York and Citibank, 1981.

Giving birth in New York City: A guide to childbirth options, New York Public Interest Research Group, 1981.

"How the bough bends: The creation of family, kinship and community amongst users of donated gametes," https://www.slideshare.net/drleanna/how-the-bough-bends-users-of-donaed-gametes (August 26, 2009):
- Southwestern Anthropological Association, Pasadena, CA, April 29, 2006.
- Communal Studies Association, Marshall, CA, September 29, 2006.
- American Anthropological Association, San Jose, CA, November 15, 2006.

"Jealousy and transformation in polyamorous relationships," http://wisewomansexandrelationshipconsulting.com/Jealousy and Transformation in Polyamorous Relationships.pdf (June 24, 2003):
- Society for the Scientific Study of Sexuality, San Jose, CA, April 11, 2003.

- PhD dissertation, Institute for Advanced Study of Human Sexuality, San Francisco, CA, June 2003.
- Loving More Conference, Harbin Hot Springs, Middletown, CA, July 27, 2003.
- Live the Dream, Winnetka, CA, September 6, 2003.
- Institute for 21st Century Relationships, Seattle, WA, October 19, 2003.

"Just below the surface: The erotic power of jealousy" (2002):

- Lifestyles-East Convention, Miami, FL, April 13, 2002.
- Lifestyles Convention, Reno, NV, August 3, 2002.

"Negotiating pair-bonding, romantic love and jealousy in polyamorous relationships," https://www.slideshare.net/drleanna/negotiating-pairbonding-romantic-love-and-jealousy-1, International Conference on Monogamy and Non-Monogamy, Berkeley, CA, February 12, 2016.

"The oral sex void: When there's not enough at home," http://www.ejhs.org/volume14/Oral Sex Void Final.pdf (2011):

- *Electronic Journal of Human Sexuality*, *14*, December 26, 2011.
- Society for the Scientific Study of Sexuality, Houston, TX, November 4, 2011.

"Orgasm in America: Current beliefs and practices," http://wisewomansexandrelationship consulting.com/Orgasm in America.pdf:

- Sex and Culture Lecture Series, May 30, 2012.
- *Women's Health*, June 2012.
- Sino-US Conference on Sexology, Dongguan, China, March 7, 2013.

"Studying and Teaching the Culture of Cyber Chat: How Our Students' Native Access Can Inform Research and Practice," California Community College Anthropology Teachers Conference, Paso Robles, https://www.slideshare.net/drleanna/studying-culture-of-cyber -chatpptx (January 16, 2016).

"The three waves of polyamory, "https://www.slideshare.net/drleanna/polyamorys-three -waves:

- Society for the Scientific Study of Sexuality, Atlanta, GA, November 11, 2017.
- Rocky Mountain Poly Living, Denver, CO, April 14, 2019.
- World Association for Sexual Health, Mexico City, Mexico, October 13, 2019.

"Today's Cultural Generation Gap: Coming of Age Armenian, Asian and Hispanic in 21st Century America," https://www.slideshare.net/drleanna/sex-culture (2006–2007).

"Towards a cross-cultural understanding of female sexuality," Master's thesis, New School for Social Research, New York, NY, 1979.

"Who cheats and why?" Society for the Scientific Study of Sexuality, Palm Springs, CA, April 10, 2010.

"Why women swing":

- Lifestyles Convention, Las Vegas, NV, July 28, 2001.
- Sixteenth World Conference of Sexology, Havana, Cuba, March 13, 2003.

Women who may never marry: The reasons, realities, and opportunities, Longstreet Press, 1993.

Sources Cited

Allen, P., & Harmon, S. (1995). *Getting to "I do": The secret to doing relationships right!* William Morrow.

America's abortion quandary. (2021, May 6). Pew Research Center. https://www.pew research.org/religion/2022/05/06/americas-abortion-quandary/

Baker, P. & Harris, J. (August 18, 1998). Clinton admits to Lewinsky relationship, challenges Starr to end personal "prying." *Washington Post.*

Baker, R. (1996). *Sperm wars: The science of sex.* Basic Books.

Bartell, G. (1971). *Group sex: A scientist's eyewitness report on the American way of swinging.* Peter H. Wyden.

Bennion, J. (1998). *Women of principle: Female networking in contemporary Mormon polygyny.* Oxford University Press.

Bennion, J., & Fishbayn, L. (2016). *The polygamy question.* Utah State University Press.

Boston Women's Health Collective. (1970). *Our bodies, ourselves.* New England Free Press.

Brennan, D. (2004). *What's love got to do with it? Transnational desires and sex tourism in the Dominican Republic.* Duke University Press.

Bretherton, I. (1992). The origins of attachment theory: John Bowlby and Mary Ainsworth. *Developmental Psychology, 28*(5), 759–75.

Caulcutt, C. (2022, April 18). Headscarf ban dogs Le Pen's bid for the French presidency. *Politico.*

Comfort, A. (1972). *The joy of sex.* Crown Publishers.

Coontz, S. (2005). *Marriage, a history: How love conquered marriage.* Viking Penguin.

Crocker, W. H., & Crocker, J. (1994). *The Canela: Bonding through kinship, ritual and sex.* Harcourt Brace College.

———. (2004). *The Canela: Kinship, ritual and sex in an Amazonian tribe.* Wadsworth Publishing.

Daedone, N. (2012). *Slow sex: The art and craft of the female orgasm.* Grand Central Publishing.

Dahlberg, F. (Ed.). (1981). *Woman the gatherer.* Yale University Press.

Davis-Floyd, R. (1992). *Birth as an American rite of passage.* University of California Press.

Davis-Floyd, R., & Cheyney, M. (Eds.). (2019). *Birth in eight cultures.* Waveland Press.

Davis-Floyd, R., & Dumit, J. (Eds.). (1998). *Cyborg babies: From techno-sex to techno-tots.* Routledge.

DeVore, I., & Lee, R. (Eds.). (1968). *Man the hunter.* Transaction Publishers.

Dodson, B. (1974). *Liberating masturbation: A meditation on self love.* Self-published.

Dowd, R. (2021, June 22). *1.2 million LGBTQ adults in the US identify as nonbinary* [press release]. Williams Institute. https://williamsinstitute.law.ucla.edu/press/lgbtq-nonbinary-press-release/

Drouin, M., Tobin, E., & Wygant, K. (2014). Love the way you lie: Sexting deception in romantic relationships. *Computers in Human Behavior, 35,* 542–47. https://doi.org/10.1016/j.chb.2014.02.047

Drown, D. (2012, January 26). Bennion writes to decriminalize polygamy. *The Critic, Lydon State College.*

Duignan, A. J. (1993, November 28). [Newspaper clipping]. *Los Angeles Times,* Westside, section J.

Eighth United Nations survey on crime trends and the operations of criminal justice systems (2001–2002). (2005, March 31). United Nations, Office on Drugs and Crime. https://www.unodc.org/unodc/en/data-and-analysis/Eighth-United-Nations-Survey-on-Crime-Trends-and-the-Operations-of-Criminal-Justice-Systems.html

Elwin, V. (1947). *The Muria and their ghotul.* Oxford University Press.

———. (1968). *The Kingdom of the young.* Oxford University Press.

Farrell, W. (1986). *Why men are the way they are.* Berkley.

Fernea, E., & Fernea, R. (1979). A look behind the veil. *Human Nature, 2*(1), 68–77.

Fisher, F., & Faller, B. (2014). *Yin rising: The Chinese sexual evolution.* Griffin Publishing.

Fisher, H. (1982). *The sex contract: The evolution of human behavior.* William Morrow.

———. (1994). The nature of romantic love. *The Journal of NIH Research, 6,* 59–64.

————. (2004). *Why we love: The nature and chemistry of romantic love.* Macmillan Publishers.

————. (2016). *Anatomy of love: A natural history of mating, marriage and why we stray.* W. W. Norton. (Originally published 1992)

Four people in a bed—stock photo. (n.d.). Getty Images. https://www.gettyimages.com/detail/photo/four-peolpe-in-a-bed-royalty-free-image/171583944

Freeman, D. (1983). *Margaret Mead and Samoa: The making and unmaking of an anthropological myth.* Harvard University Press.

Friedan, B. (1963). *The feminine mystique.* W. W. Norton.

Gilmartin, B. (1978). *The Gilmartin report.* Citadel Press.

Ginsburg, F., & Rapp, R. (Eds.). (1995). *Conceiving the new world order: The global politics of reproduction.* University of California Press.

Good, K., & Chanoff, D. (1997). *Into the heart: One man's pursuit of love and knowledge among the Yanomami.* Simon & Schuster..

Gould, T. (1999). *The lifestyle: A look at the erotic rites of swingers.* Vintage Books.

Guindi, F. E. (1999). *Veil: Modesty, privacy and resistance.* Berg Publishers.

Herdt, G. (1999). *Sambia sexual culture: Essays from the field.* University of Chicago Press.

Hirschfeld, M. (2000). *The homosexuality of men and women* (Michael Lombardi-Nash, Trans.). Prometheus Books. (Original work published in German, 1914)

Hite, S. (1976). *The Hite report: A nationwide study of female sexuality.* Penguin Random House.

Holder, M. (1979). *Give sorrow words.* Grove Press.

Horne, C. (2022, April 20). *How many people cheat? Statistics and figures for infidelity in the US.* Regain.

Hyde, S. (Director). (2022). *Good luck to you, Leo Grande* [Film]. Searchlight Pictures, Hulu.

James, E. L. (2011). *Fifty shades of Grey.* Vintage Books.

————. (2012a). *Fifty shades darker.* Vintage Books.

————. (2012b). *Fifty shades freed.* Vintage Books.

Jankowiak, W. (Ed.). (1995). *Romantic passion: A universal experience.* Columbia University Press.

————. (2008). *Intimacies: Love and sex across cultures.* Columbia University Press.

Jordan, B. (1978). *Birth in four cultures: A crosscultural investigation of childbirth in Yucatan, Holland, Sweden and the United States.* Eden Press Women's Publications.

Kephart, W. (1963). Experimental family organization: An historico-cultural report on the Oneida community. *Marriage and Family Living, 25,* 261–271.

Koedt, A. (1970). *The myth of the vaginal orgasm.* New England Free Press. (Originally published 1968)

Kottak, C. (2011). *Cultural anthropology: Appreciating cultural diversity.* McGraw-Hill.

Kramer, S. (2020, December 7). *Polygamy is rare around the world and mostly confined to a few regions.* Pew Research Center. https://www.pewresearch.org/short-reads/2020/12/07/polygamy-is-rare-around-the-world-and-mostly-confined-to-a-few-regions/

Kulick, D. (1998). *Travesti: Sex, gender and culture among Brazilian transgendered prostitutes.* University of Chicago Press.

Kuta, S. (2018, August 8). The extraordinary history of Burning Man. *Far and Wide.* https://www.farandwide.com/s/burning-man-history-6325fb09d8644613

Lauman, E. O. (1994). *The social organization of sexuality: Sexual practices in the United States.* University of Chicago Press.

Lewis, O. (1959). *Five families: Mexican case studies in the culture of poverty.* New American Library.

————. (1961). *The children of Sanchez: Autobiography of a Mexican family.* Random House.

———. (1966). The culture of poverty. *Scientific American, 215*(4).

———. (1969). *A death in the Sanchez family*. Random House.

Malinowski, B. (1929). *The sexual life of savages in North-Western Melanesia: An ethnographic account of courtship, marriage and family life among the natives of the Trobriand Islands, British New Guinea*. Routledge and Sons.

Marshall, D., & Suggs, R. (Eds.). (1971). *Human sexual behavior: Variations in the ethnographic spectrum*. Basic Books.

McKay, K. (2013, November 4). *Are five husbands better than one? Kimber McKay at TEDxUMontana* [Video]. Youtube. https://www.youtube.com/watch?v=U6bYCi-1wF4

Mead, M. (1928). *Coming of age in Samoa: A psychological study of primitive youth for Western civilization*. Blue Ribbon Books.

———. (1935). *Sex and temperament in three primitive societies*. William Morrow.

———. (1949). *Male and female: A study of the sexes in a changing world*. William Morrow.

Meston, C., & Buss, D. (2009). *Why women have sex: The psychology of sex in women's own voices*. Times Books.

Miller, M. E. (2016, June 6). A steep price to pay for 20 minutes of action: Dad defends Stanford sex offender. *Washington Post*.

Montoya, R., Frazier, L. J., & Hurtig, J. (Eds.). (2002). *Gender's place: Feminist anthropologies of Latin America*. Palgrave Macmillan.

Mundhra, S. (Creator). (2020–2023). *Indian Matchmaking* [TV series]. Netflix.

Mundy, L. (2012). *The richer sex: How the new majority of female breadwinners is transforming sex, love and family*. Simon & Schuster.

Nanda, S. (n.d.). *Arranging a marriage in India*. Scribd. https://www.scribd.com /document /90939469/Arranging-a-Marriage-in-India (original essay published 1992)

Obaid-Chinoy, S. (Director), & Brown, T. (Producer). (2015). *A girl in the river: The price of forgiveness* [Film]. SOC Films & HBO Documentary Films.

O'Connell, H., Sanjeevan, K. V., & Hutson, J. M. (2005). Anatomy of the clitoris. *Journal of Urology, 147*(1), 1189–95. https://doi.org/10.1097/01.ju.0000173639.38898.cd

Olson, G. W., & Brussel-Rogers, T. L. (2022). *Fifty years of polyamory in America: A guided tour of a growing movement*. Rowman & Littlefield.

Rapaille, C. (2006). *The culture code: An ingenious way to understand why people around the world live and buy as they do*. Broadway Books.

Rapp, R. (1999). *Testing women, testing the fetus: The social impact of amniocentesis in America*. Routledge.

Rubin, G., (1984). Thinking sex: Notes for a radical theory of the politics of sexuality. In C. Vance & K. Paul (Eds.), *Pleasure and danger: Exploring female sexuality* (ch. 9). Routledge.

Scheper-Hughes, N. (1992). *Death without weeping: The violence of everyday life*. University of California Press.

Sher, A., Berger, J., Feeley, S., Robbins, C., & Howell, S. [Executive producers]. (2022). *How to build a sex room* [TV series]. Netflix.

Suler, J. (2004). The online disinhibition effect. *Cyber Psychology and Behavior, 7*(3), 321–26. https://doi.org/10.1089/1094931041291295

Vogelstein, R., & Stone, M. (2021). *Awakening #MeToo and the global fight for women's rights*. Public Affairs.

Web, A. (2013, October 2). *How I hacked online dating* [Video]. Youtube. https://www.youtube.com/watch?v=d6wG_sAdP0U

Whipple, B., Ladas, A. K., & Perry, J. (1982). *The G-spot and other recent discoveries about human sexuality*. Holt, Rinehart, and Winston.

World Health Organization. (1979, February 10–15). *Khartoum seminar on traditional practices affecting the health of women and children.* https://apps.who.int/iris/handle/10665/254379

World Population Review. (n.d.). *Rape statistics by country 2022.* https://worldpopulation review.com/country-rankings/rape-statistics-by-country

Yetter, D. (November 9, 2022). Proposed Kentucky constitutional ammendment to end right to an abortion defeated in vote. *Louisville Courier Journal.*

Index

About the Author

Dr. Leanna Wolfe's sex research was spirited by her coming of age in the thick of the 1970s sexual revolution and feminist movement in the San Francisco Bay Area. Her curiosities and academic appetites led her to engage in field research in Mexico, Africa, India, and Papua New Guinea, earning an MA in anthropology from the New School for Social Research and a PhD in sexology from the Institute for Advanced Study of Human Sexuality. From 1980 to 2018, she worked as a university professor teaching and researching topics ranging from orgasm, multiple partner sexualities, and sexual assault. In 2016 she launched Wise Woman Sex and Relationship Consulting, providing counseling through her unique lens of sexual anthropology.

www.ingramcontent.com/pod-product-compliance
Lightning Source LLC
Chambersburg PA
CBHW080132270326
41926CB00021B/4449